HARDPRESS.NET
HOME OF HARD-TO-FIND BOOKS

Truth, Love, Joy, Or, the Garden of Eden and Its Fruits
by E. M. King

Address:
HardPress
8345 NW 66TH ST #2561
MIAMI FL 33166-2626
USA
Email: info@hardpress.net

TRUTH. LOVE. JOY.

TRUTH. LOVE. JOY.

OR,

The Garden of Eden

AND

ITS FRUITS.

BY

E. M. KING.

MELBOURNE:

PUBLISHED BY THE AUTHOR; AND SOLD BY

WILLIAMS AND NORGATE,

14, HENRIETTA STREET, COVENT GARDEN, LONDON

AND

20, SOUTH FREDERICK STREET, EDINBURGH.

1864.

100 u. ...

PREFACE.

I ʜᴀᴠᴇ debated long with myself whether I would own this book to be the work of a woman. I do so now with great reluctance.

Thinking that the writing, if known to proceed from the pen of a woman, would not have its due weight, but would be better received, and have more influence as coming from a man, I at first intended to affix only my surname and initials to the title page, believing it of no consequence to the reader to know to which sex the writer belonged. But, as I do not wish to try to cast a shadow of disguise over my words, and also, as one chapter touches upon the vexed question of woman's right to an equal position in the world, which has hitherto not been granted her, I would not have these views accorded more credit than they deserve, or aided forward in any manner, by endeavoring to make them appear to emanate from one of the other sex, who would be unbiassed on the subject. I desire my words in this particular, as in the whole volume, to either stand or fall, only as they are true or false.

Some witty writer says, " The women now-a-days are screaming for a fair field and no favor." I have no intention of "screaming" about it, for that would be very ridiculous, and also exceedingly futile : for by "screaming" I should only become hoarse, and and lose my voice, so not be able to scream any more. But for the sake of the Truth, I do only ask for " a fair field and no favor."

I am not too proud, however, to ask the reader's indulgence for myself as a writer.

Living in a colony, I am thereby greatly debarred from the opportunities of knowledge I could have had in living near a great centre of civilization. It is no slight disadvantage to have your thoughts appear six months after date, in this hurrying age, when, perhaps, the interest in the subject you are writing about, has nearly died out, or become a bore.

It is no slight disadvantage, also, to live in a place where there are no railroads, no daily post, no daily paper, communication "from foreign parts" only once a month, and periodicals and general news three or four months old.

I have to calculate that before my book can reach England, all I have thought will have been before thought and spoken. I can, then, only hope that the same belief having been arrived at by another mind in another position, and in different circumstances, by its coincidence, may assist in establishing the Truth.

For the subject and matter of the present volume, I can offer no apology; but for the manner and style, I would ask the reader's kind indulgence, feeling most painfully, as I do, my awkwardness and ignorance in the working out or treatment of the subject. The questions on which I have endeavored to think are no easy or light ones, so that even a failure to think them out aright, might not be considered quite disgraceful or contemptible.

By publishing anonymously, I might, perhaps, have spared myself much personal annoyance, but to do so, always seemed to me a piece of cowardice, unless for some special reason. Those who give their inmost thoughts to be scanned by every one who chooses to read them, should be, or try to be, strong enough and good-tempered enough to bear and take either praise or blame or ridicule, knowing that in all probability a share of each may fall to their lot.

A gentleman asked me did I think it was my *duty*, or had I any business to write on religious subjects, making, at the same time, a pointed allusion to St. Paul. To enter upon an argument on the subject, would be foolish and useless. It is a question that must be answered "by its fruits." However, for the benefit of any reader, who may make the same inquiry, I answer, in the words of another, which show that woman's ideas on the subject are desirable and desired :

" We hardly any of us know what is the spontaneous religious sentiment of woman, for, when developed hitherto, it has been nearly always under the distorting influence of some monstrous creed imposed on her uncultivated understanding. We have had enough of man's thoughts of God— of God, first as ' the King,' ' the Man of War,' ' the Demiurge,' ' the Mover of all Things,' and then, at last, since Christian times, as God ' the Father of the World.'

" Not always have men been very competent to teach even this side of the truth alone ; for during more than one thousand years the religious teachers of Christendom were men who knew not a father's feelings, who thought them less holy than their own loveless celibacy.

" But the woman's thought of God as the ' Parent of Good Almighty,' who unites in one the father's care and the mother's tenderness, *that* we have never heard. Even a woman hardly dares to trust her own heart, and believes that as she would have compassion on the son of her womb, ' so the Lord hath pity on us'—[are *pity* and *compassion* the right words for a *mother's* feelings ?]

" Surely, surely, it is time we gain something from woman of her religious nature ! And we want her moral intuition also. We want her sense of the law of love to complete man's sense of the law of justice. We want her influence, inspiring virtue by gentle promptings from within, to complete man's external legislation of morality. And then we want woman's practical service. We want her genius for detail, her tenderness for age and suffering, her comprehension of the wants of childhood, to complete man's gigantic charities and nobly-planned hospitals and orphanages.

" How shall we get at all these things " ?

Reader, will you think me very presumptuous, or conceited, in saying that I feel I can supply *some* of these wants, for to me it seems that my life has been working to that end. I can, at least, offer a woman's free thoughts of God, for, both from natural disposition and outward circumstances, perhaps few women have been so little led by the influence of male relations or teachers. From the influence of books none who read can wholly abstract themselves, but all the books that have assisted me while writing have been named.

The writer to whom I am most indebted is Emerson; not so much in being directed or led by his thoughts, as being encouraged through him to think my own thoughts. Such sentences as these have been golden mottos to me:

"To believe your own thought; to believe that what is true for you in your private heart is true for all men—that is genius."

"He who would gather immortal palms must not be hindered by the name of goodness, but must explore if it be goodness."

"Accept your genius, and say what you think."

"The way to speak and write what shall not go out of fashion, is, to speak and write sincerely."

I have endeavored so to think and write, and those chapters are the best where I have thrown aside all books and all other men's experiences; and written from my own life and my own heart.

The first half of the book I might improve by entirely re-writing, but I think it best to let it remain as it is, as I could not now place my mind exactly in the same position as it then was. By leaving it as it is I may, perhaps, be better enabled to get *en rapport* with minds thinking as I then thought, and be able to lift them along with me as I mount upwards.

I particularly solicit the attention of my own sex, not that they may be led by what I think, but that they may learn to think for themselves.

I fear I have talked about "I" too often; but as I

have drawn from my own life, I found it difficult to avoid doing so, and "we" did not seem natural.

In the rest of the volume I have not written as a woman only, but as one of the race of mankind—one to whom the truth is as dear and as valuable as to the greatest and noblest.

CONTENTS.

---

xiv.

CHAPTER VII.

CHAPTER VIII.

CHAPTER IX.

CHAPTER X.

CHAPTER XI.

CHAPTER XII.

CHAPTER XIII.

CHAPTER XIV.

CHAPTER XV.

TRUTH. LOVE. AND JOY;

OR,

THE GARDEN OF EDEN AND ITS FRUITS.

CHAPTER I.

REASON.

WE have reason given us. For what purpose? Primarily, to discern between good and evil, right and wrong. This is the very first step reason takes.

The first glimmering of reason which enters the mind of a child, relates to what is good or bad for its bodily feelings, and afterwards, gradually, to what is good or evil for the mind.

Without the power to distinguish between good and evil, and freedom to choose either, men could have had nothing beyond the instinct of the animal.

The second step is the knowledge of the law of cause and effect, which contains the germ of all religion, leading us to trace all natural events to natural causes, and all spirit or thought, to the one Great Spirit, the one cause of thought and nature.

The third step is the apprehension of the intimate union of the two previous steps of knowledge—the union of thought and action, as soul and body, both caused by one spirit—and also the inseparable connection between good and evil, and cause and effect, that a good *cause* will produce a good *effect* and an evil *cause* an evil *effect*.

This is the last lesson reason has to learn, and it has yet to be fully understood.

Why all this controversy about the lawfulness of using our reason in matters relating to God and our own souls ?

We can know nothing of either but by, and through, reason.

The most perfect belief or faith in what is called revelation or inspiration is as much a product of reason as disbelief.

On one hand it supposes it is *good* to take the Bible without doubt to be infallibly the Word of God, and *evil* to question the grounds of its infallibility. On the other hand it imagines it is *good* first to find the proofs of its being the Word of God, and *evil* to put faith in it as infallible without sufficient proof.

It is as much an action of our muscles and will to sit down as to walk about. But if a man continues to sit in his easy chair and refuses to walk he loses the full power of his muscles, and finally becomes diseased, while another who properly exercises them not only keeps his body healthy, but increases their power.

So, the man who refuses to make use of his reason loses the strength of his mind, but the other who exercises it increases it two-fold—and what more enlarging and ennobling to the mind than to exercise its powers to attain a further knowledge of its God and cause? But the debate is now not as to the lawfulness or unlawfulness of using our reason to bear upon our belief, but how far it is to be allowed to proceed.

We might ask, What is to stop it?

Nothing but reason can, by coming to the conclusion it is *good* to stop and *evil* to allow our reason to soar too far or too high.

It is said " reason is to be exercised only on matters comprehensible by reason, not on subjects above our reason."

The sentence is a contradiction in itself—if not comprehensible by reason, it is not comprehensible to us at all: anything above or beyond reason, the eye of the mind, is not visible to the mind; we can see no further than our reason will carry us. Therefore *for us* there is nothing beyond our reason.

If it be said Inspiration is as the telescope of the mind, the telescope is only an instrument discovered by science to enable the natural eye to see further; but inspiration is a closing of the natural eye of the mind—Reason—preventing us from looking further into a subject out of our ordinary reach of sight.

It will be said, Is not God above our reason? Undoubtedly, but we see him only as far as our reason will allow.

We can know nothing of God beyond or above our reason.

We cannot understand God—we can understand goodness, justice, mercy, His attributes, having the shadow or image of these godlike attributes in our own souls. So, by the reasoning power of comparison we judge of the nature of God. He may have other attributes beside those we know, but if we have not the clue to them in our own souls we cannot see or understand them, so for us they *are* not.

What alone we can comprehend that alone we have to do with.

What, therefore, our reason pronounces inconsistent with the image of God in our souls we are not bound to receive as the works or word of God, He having given us perception in soul and mind for the very purpose of discerning Him, or distinguishing between good and evil.

Why have some theories or books, Atheistical, Deistical, or what not, died out and been forgotten?

Because not found consistent with reason.

Why have others lived though pronounced heresy at the time?

Because afterwards discovered to be agreeable to reason.

Why have others, though supposed dead and long buried, again now risen to life ?

Because at the time the mass of mankind were not prepared to receive them, so could not see or comprehend their truth. But now reason having advanced is more on a level with the arguments and able to understand them.

Would God give us reason whereby to apprehend Him and then show Himself to us in a manner not discernable by that reason ?

Does God give us digestive organs, and then offer us food, good perhaps for angels, but which we have neither means nor capabilities of assimilating to the nourishment of our bodies ?

What can we know of omnipotence, omnipresence, or any other omni ? As much as we know of eternity. And what know we of that ? Absolutely nothing : nothing but the mere word.

The way we attempt to approach it is by representing it as an extension of Time.

We say if the years of eternity were as numerous as the grains of sand on the sea shore, and we were to live through them, we should be no nearer the end of eternity than before.

It always gives me such a sense of weariness when a thought like this is placed before me, as if the weight of years would be too heavy to be borne. How would it be possible to live through them, even in heaven ?

But in reality, no time, however long, can represent Eternity—it has no relation to it.

Time passes, and as it moves swiftly by, every second as it passes, dies, and another second is born, and then dies. Time is made up of atoms. As inappreciable as a mathematical point is the present, in which only can we be said to live. The atoms of the past are dead, the atoms of the future are to be born.

But this is not Eternity, where no moment dies, and the past and future are ever present; and even now, what more do I see or know ? Nothing. I have no grasp of Eternity, my idea is only a picture of moving time, stagnating and standing still, which to Time or in Time would be death.

I cannot see Eternity, I cannot feel it, I cannot know it till I am in it, and with it, and of it, I can only give my assent to it, but this is not belief; for before I can believe in a thing, my reason must be conversant with it.

But all that relates to God and my own soul in Time, which is the preparation for Eternity, God has given me reason to understand and believe.

Of invisible things, I can know nothing, but only faintly judge of them by analogy from the visible to the invisible, from Time to Eternity.

The Bible, then—teaching us of God and our own souls, and of our conduct in Time, so as to attain happiness in Eternity—is appreciable by our reason; and it is not only able to discern it fully, but it is also our duty to see that it coincides with the image of God in our souls, or truth and love. Now has arrived the time when the Bible must be honestly and fairly examined by this test; is it consistent, entirely and throughout with God's image of truth and love? or is it only part truth and part error? What is truth is the work of God, and what is error and falsehood is the work of man, and needs to be separated from the work of God.

This is an age "in which genius and learning on one side, and orthodoxy and tradition on the other, are engaged in a desperate struggle with one another." It is almost needless to enquire which of the two will ultimately conquer, for year after year the former gains, and the latter loses and recedes. Reason dispels superstition. Having allowed the light of reason to shine in upon our own religious belief, we have also discovered how much truth and goodness have pervaded other religions, which we before considered utterly vile, and the work of the evil one; as if any religion, however degraded, could be his work. Worship, however low the object to which we dedicate it, is the effort of the human soul, however benighted, to reach its maker or first cause.

Truth has been given to all nations, and as much as could be seen by them, embodied in different books of national belief, mixed up with more or less of human errors and mistakes.

No man or nation can see or understand more of the truth than his or their reason will allow.

What beauty can a man with no eye for form or color find in a painting of Raphael, or a statue of Canova? The beauty in them does not exist for him. What delight can a man who has no ear for music, experience in the harmony of Mendelssohn? The beauty of sound does not exist for him. Moreover, however much natural talent a man may have, both the eye and the ear require education, before the hidden beauties of sight and sound can be properly appreciated.

So with truth, no grain of truth can enter the mind but what the reason is educated to understand; and to gain full appreciation of the beauty and excellence of truth requires ages of careful cultivation, or civilization.

As a man strengthens his mental powers so does truth become more apparent. If he thinks seriously at all he will find in the course of a few years his belief has been constantly, though insensibly, changing. That some errors he formerly believed in as truths, he has rejected; while truths he then saw vaguely, have become clear and distinct to his mind.

The advance made will be in proportion to the industry of the mind; how much the mind has worked, so much will be the reward, and, of course it follows, where the reasoning power of the mind has not been suffered to work, there can be no advance. Also, if it has laboured in a wrong direction, or contrary to reason, the reward gained will be error not truth.

Work is sacred, and shall never lose its reward. Guided by reason, it finds truth; discarding reason, it finds error.

This work to discover what is truth in the Bible was commenced by a few isolated thinkers in advance of their age, many years ago. It has reached the minds of all thoughtful laymen; it has been working in the minds of many of the clergy. The bishops alone appear not to have worked or thought; taking it for granted that all truth was seen and known, they saw no occasion for thought, so have not advanced. A few years hence they will find the enlightenment of the age has left them far behind, unknown and un-noticed. We except Bishop Colenso, who (whether his calculations be right or wrong) has thrown open wide a gate that none can shut—has given utterance to thoughts which have been long brooding in the minds of men. The other bishops endeavor to per-secute this brave man, who has, as far as he is able, told the truth; the archbishops and the majority of the clergy are against him, and would also injure him

as far as the laws of the land permit them.   To these
laws Colenso has appealed, and, fortunately, they
protect him from malice, as far as temporal laws can.

What does this show ?   That the laws of the land
are more Christian than the spirit of the church.

Bishop Colenso has appealed to the laity.   It is
to be sincerely hoped he will not fail to meet the support he desires ; and not only he, but also those
clergymen who in " Essays and Reviews," in books,
or in sermons, have not been afraid to examine and
speak the truth.

Most men in the present controversy appear to be
seeking the truth ; but can those who first believe
that one book contains nothing but truth, discover
truth ?

The question of the age is not, Is there a God ?
but, Is the Bible what some men affirm it to be, all
and entirely the word of that God ?   How can those
who first assume the whole question and avow that
it is so, be capable of considering the question whether
it is so or not ?   They have no right to pretend to
be seekers after truth, for they are already fettered
believers in the Bible as the truth.   Lovers not of
truth, for the truth's sake, but of what they believe
to be truth for the sake of the Bible.   Mr. Farrer,
in his " Bampton Lectures," quotes Bishop Butler's
admission, as an incontrovertible truth, " that the
arguments of the Bible are not demonstrative but

only probable, and the evidence of its authenticity not conclusive but only circumstantial." Yet upon this merely probable and circumstantial evidence, we are called upon to base our belief in infallibility.

What have we hitherto rested it on ? Simply this, that when the Bible was first put into our hands, our reason pronounced it *good*. If we say the Bible is true because the Bible says so, or because God says so, we must first have some ground of reason in our own minds to accept the assertion of the Bible as to its own infallibility, and also its assertion (if it contains such an assertion) that God declares it to be so. For God has never spoken to us or to any man living, to tell him so ; we can, then, only believe it as far as it coincides with our reason.

In the infancy of our intellect, finding the Bible to contain more than any other book of what was agreeable to our idea of the truth, we, in our comparative ignorance, accepted it, not as part truth and part error—one divine the other human—but as ALL truth ; we pronounced it good, or God, and worshipped it as a God.

But as the intellect grew and reason advanced, many errors have been discovered in this supposed infallible book ; many now would break the bonds their former ignorance wore around it. Others, though unable to controvert or deny the errors, would still keep around it the bands of infallibility ; one of the principal arguments brought forward in the cause of the infallibility of the Bible is, that all now advanced against it has been said before. It seems to me a most palpable argument for the truth of the objections, that though old they still possess vitality and force.

The opinions to which the majority of mankind, and certainly, nearly all intellectual men, are steadily but surely advancing—have been advanced from age to age by a few solitary thinkers, and truths which, many years ago, they saw dimly and mixed with error, we are now beginning to separate and see clearly.

We may award to the believers in infallibility, inspiration and miracles, the palm of advancing new arguments; they are obliged to find new answers to those old questions, for every successive age throws aside the old answers as useless and fallacious.

As the waves of truth advance, they construct new stops and hindrances, and dams are built up to restrain thought to what they consider its proper and due limits; but in the end it proves a vain endeavor.

I was reminded, as a warning against the supposed audacious and improper use of my mind in these inquiries, that Jesus was asked by Pilate, "What is truth?" and the presumptuous question was left unanswered! So, as Jesus, at the moment when the agony of death was before him, did not enter on this abstract question, and did not give Pilate a short explanation of what was truth, no one after has any right to ask, or endeavour to answer the question. If we inquire, What is truth ?—in the abstract or as a whole—it is God; God is truth. But what we have to find is, what is *the* truth in every thought, word, and deed, which is placed before us ; and if we are capable of judging what is falsehood in these things, we are also capable of judging of the contrary or opposite, which is truth ; but this cannot be spoken in a few sentences, or a few moments—no, nor in an hour, or days, or years. It is the work of the ages of the world.

CHAPTER II.

INSPIRATION.

THE writer of the answers to the "Essays and Reviews" in the *London Review*, says—"But here we are prepared to make two admissions, or rather, to state decidedly two important points connected with the subject [the inspiration of the Bible]. First, some errors may have crept into the sacred text by the frequent process of translation." "To suppose it otherwise would be indeed to suppose the constant existence of a miracle. That a volume such as the Bible, written in different languages, could have been multiplied by human penmanship, in different countries and different ages, without any variation or mistakes being made, would be utterly impossible, even giving the transcribers credit for the exercise of the greatest skill, diligence, and faithfulness. This, then, will account for some errors in names and numbers that may, perhaps, be pointed out. At the same time, we believe we are justified in positively asserting that these errors are so trifling that they are unworthy of notice."

Let us take this, together with another quotation from the same paper:—" But *all* Scripture—

Scripture in all its parts—narrative as well as doctrine, history as well as prophecy—all Scripture is given by inspiration of God." And again, " The Word of God (this is an important expression)—the Bible is not Man's *Word*, but God's *Word ;* and, because it is the *Word* of God it is Holy Scripture. In this we have the true theory of inspiration." I would first remark that the writer before objects to inspiration being called " an idea." He says, " Whatever be the nature of inspiration it is not an idea;" but in the next column he denominated it " a theory."

How can a theory be built up without ideas ? If inspiration be a theory, it is made up of ideas. But the fact is, no natural language can convey the unnatural idea or meaning of inspiration ; no natural or human thoughts or words are applicable to it. If we must have a miraculous communication, we must also have a miraculous faculty to perceive or comprehend it, and a miraculous language to speak or transcribe it into. But see the contradiction involved in the first and second quotation.

The writer affirms that any errors that may possibly be discovered are to be put to the score of the translators. Now, setting aside the injustice to these men, who, whatever their ability or good intentions, are to have all the blame, in order to save the original penman from censure, is there not also implied, injustice on the part of God towards man ?

It is believed that in the Old Testament alone there are about 30,000 various readings; and in the New Testament a number almost surpassing computation. It follows, then, if God granted infallibility and inspiration only to the first original copy, and the writer or writers of that original text, he only gave his pure unadulterated word to the one nation and people who at the time spoke the language in which it was written; to all other nations and times when people became desirous to receive his message, and worship their God, he only vouchsafed an impure and adulterated version; and this original text—this Word of God—which God miraculously gave to the world, we might suppose for the use or benefit of the world, has either been miraculously received up into heaven again or it is still amongst the 30,000 readings: and who is to pick out this from the rest? One would imagine the Word of God would bear a marked difference to the mere human copy or reproduction.

In order to balance, or do away with this palpable piece of injustice, it is asserted that the mistakes are so trivial as not to be worth notice; so some of these *words*, which he declares not to be the *word* of man, but the *Word* of God (the italics are not mine), are in part so trivial as not to be worth notice!

When will reasonable men cease to prop up such nonsense,—open their eyes to the truth, and see the contradictions their errors involve them in ? Jesus said respecting his own words—" I am a man that have told you the truth, which I have heard of my Father, this did not Abraham." Now, if Abraham did not tell the Jews the truth, he told them falsehood.

Immediately, however, a text of this sort is brought forward, the endeavor is to make the least of it, and so to explain away the simple words that in the end they have no meaning at all.

The explanation I can anticipate to such a text may be similar to the following :

I must first premise, that I have never read a single commentary on the Bible. I always had an instinctive dislike to them. I do not mean, that I have never looked into one ; if ever the meaning of a verse was perplexing to me, and I sought the assistance of a commentary, it generally left me more puzzled than before ; so I gave them up. I have often heard others make the same remark, that a commentary only darkened, instead of enlightened the simple text.

I am now exceedingly glad that I kept this resolve, as I am thereby better enabled to approach the Bible without having my mind encumbered with "traditional interpretations."

The objections advanced to the text I have selected would doubtless be, that Abraham, not being a writer, was not inspired. That though Christ said (

c

he did not tell them the truth, it does not follow that he told them absolute falsehood, but only not the whole truth.

It must be allowed that these two explanations would materially alter the obvious or apparent meaning of the text.

But granting that Abraham was not a writer, therefore not inspired, how could the Jews to whom Christ said, Abraham had not told them the truth, have heard or known of him but through Moses, or some other prophet? Then we must imagine Moses or the prophets were inspired to transcribe what was not the truth.

With regard to the second objection, that Abraham could only have been accused of not telling the whole truth—this is a great straining of the text, for if intended to mean only this the word *all* would have been inserted, or Christ must purposely have left it to be implied that Abraham did speak falsely, which by the addition of the word *all* he would have removed, nor is it likely that Christ or those who are supposed to have been inspired to write would have been allowed to cast such an aspersion on the truthfulness of Abraham's words if not intended.

But, in reality, not speaking the whole truth is falsehood. Any witness brought into court has to swear he will speak the truth, the whole truth, and nothing but the truth.

Surely a witness for God, under divine inspiration, can do no less! Keeping back part of the truth may falsify the whole evidence.

If it is affirmed that Christ declared he was the only one who heard truth directly from God his Father, this completely overthrows the theory of inspiration, which asserts that the writers of the Bible DID receive the truth directly from God their Father. To say that Abraham could speak the truth but as far as he knew, is correct.

As far as Abraham or Moses knew the truth they spoke it, and where they did not know the truth they spoke error, for they were human not divine. Had there ever been any direct outward revelation from God there could have been no possibility of error, even the most trifling. There would no more be error, mistakes, imperfections, or want of harmony in the words of His mouth, than we are able to perceive either in the work of His hands.

Both Abraham and Moses spoke some truth, and in as far as they had testified to the truth they had testified to, or were in harmony with, the words of Christ, but they had also obscured the truth by many errors.

When Christ came he removed these, and showed truth by the light of love.

All scripture was and *is* given by inspiration of God, that is every scripture—every godlike word—

every one whoever testifies to the truth and goodness
of God was and is inspired. Yes, I, even I, while I
testify that God is love, I am inspired. Am I bold?
Am I impious?

No. I so acknowledge in the greatest humility,
that the mind of man is not capable of thinking any
godlike thought without the inspiration of God.
That inspiration I receive in my mind, and, accept
through the mind; no man can see or hear God, or
has ever seen or heard Him at any time. If I speak
the truth of God, flesh and blood cannot reveal it to
me, but my Father which is in heaven.

Is God the spirit dead, since Christ came, that it
cannot still speak to my spirit?

When a church discontinues to believe in the mental inspiration of its teachers and prophets, it tacitly
acknowledges that it *is* dead : it has then to go back
and live its life by and through the reflection of another's life. When the Jewish Church was a living
church, their prophets wrote such words as seemed
the truth to them, and one has justly styled this
progressive writing of the prophets somewhat the
same as our liberty of the press; but after the days
of the prophets were over, that is to say, when none
had power to write, these books were collected into
a sacred *canon*, and liberty was gone. Inspiration
then became a term for spiritual bondage, not what
it should be, spiritual liberty. The church was then

virtually dead, no man dare take away one word, that is to say, declare his honest conviction that such a word was not in accordance with truth, or dare he add one word, or advance one original idea to forward the knowledge of truth. The same in the early christian times, when there was vitality in the church, the apostles and teachers wrote each his message, then these writings were afterwards collected into a new *canon*, the seal of inspiration put upon it, the church was in bondage, and real inspiration gone.

But is it not enough to know that God *is*, and is the same for ever, to tell us that he acts towards the hearts of all men alike, and as he did in the beginning, so does he now? And that as he speaks to your soul and mine, so spake he to the souls of Abraham and Moses?

As God *is*, so he speaks, not spoke. But if I speak a word against the truth and love of God, or if Abraham or Moses spoke a word contrary to truth and love, both they and I speak falsely, and that falsehood in the end shall be overthrown.

What mean the words "Lo I am with you alway, even unto the end of the world."?

They were not addressed to the apostles, for they could not live to the end of the world, but to us, and to all who shall come after us to the end of the world; Christ told us in these words, that he would be with *us*, not in person, but in the spirit, the spirit of love, the Holy Spirit, to lead us to the full knowledge of the one God ; and if the teaching of the spirit was to lead us into all truth, and as it has been teaching the world these many years, we must know more of the truth than did the apostles, or the work of the spirit is inefficacious and powerless. I copy the following paragraph from the " People's Dictionary of the Bible," on the subject of inspiration :—

" We deplore and deprecate any unfounded pretensions, which cannot, sooner or later, fail to inflict an injury on religion. Truth is of God, and truth alone can perform God's work. We cite a few words on the doctrine of plenary inspiration, from a letter by the late Dr. Arnold, written to Mr. Justice Coleridge :—' Your uncle's letters on inspiration are well fitted to break ground in the approaches to that *momentous question which involves in it so great a shock to existing notions, the greatest, probably, that has ever been given since the discovery of the falsehood of the doctrine of the Pope's infallibility.* 'Yet it must come, and will end, in spite of the fears and clamors of the weak and bigoted, in the higher exalting and more sure establishing of Christian truth."

CHAPTER III.

MODERN REVELATIONS AND MIRACLES.

LET us cast a glance at America, and see what belief in " the theory " of inspiration and miracles results in, if carried out.

It is asserted by Butler in his Analogy, that the religion of the Bible is the only one not attempted to be supported by miracles.

There cannot be a more false assumption, for the direct contrary is the truth. There is no single religion that does *not* boast of its miracles, and the more barbarous and ignorant the people, the more extraordinary and marvellous they appear.

There are at this time two of the most ridiculous living caricatures of outward inspiration and miracles, —those two pillars on which we rest the Bible—in Mormonism and Spirit-rapping. They hold up before our eyes the absurdity to which either may lead us.

We will look at Mormonism, this very travestie of the Bible.

The Bible was a revelation given by God to Moses and other writers.

The Book of Mormon was a revelation given by God to Mormon, and translated by Joseph Smith.

To Moses, God gave two tables of stone.

To Mormon, God gave two gold plates, and a pair of triangular spectacles enclosed in glass and set in silver, whereby the inspired finder of the plates could decipher the Egyptian characters wherein they were written.

I do not intend, by tracing this resemblance, to mean that the Book of Mormon is as authentic as the books of Moses, far from it; but this I do say, it is only carrying out the idea of an outward or bodily inspiration, on which we choose to rest the Bible.

The Mormons may equally account for the miraculous reception of the gold plates back again into heaven, because after Joseph Smith had translated them, the design of heaven was accomplished; and then God removed them as a trial of their faith, and they affirm themselves to be the most faithful believers on the face of the earth; so indeed they are, if belief in the impossible be faith. We might also ask, what has become of the two tables of stone God gave to Moses ? " And He gave to Moses when He had made an end of communing with him, upon Mount Sinai, two tables of testimony—tables of stone written with the finger of God."—Exodus xxxi, 18. " And the tables were the work of God, and the writing was the writing of God."—Ibid xxxii, 16.

What did Moses with these miraculous tables, the work of the Eternal God ?

He threw them down and broke them to pieces !

It is curious that the work of God should have been so brittle and perishable ; we have not even Moses's reproduction of them. The stones of the Pyramids remain ! where are the tables of stone, written upon by the *finger* of God ?

The Jews believed they were a peculiar people, which belief they say was a revelation from heaven. They were destined to become as the sand of the sea for multitude ; to destroy all the other nations by command of God ; and in time people the whole earth. They believe so still.

The Mormons have a similar faith, that they are a peculiar people, destined by God to conquer the whole of America by overrunning it with countless hosts, and so, by faith, appropriate the goods and property of their neighbors—become, in fact, by permission of God, authorized thieves and murderers.

Let any one look into the Old Testament and see whether such a belief is not inculcated in all the promises given to the Jews.

All the prophesies respecting the Messiah, said to be given by revelation, distinctly led them to expect (if words mean anything) that at some time after they had been sufficiently punished for their disobedience to the laws of Moses—and this correction had led to repentance and obedience—a great conqueror, the mighty king, should come, and restore their temple and worship; make them again a great and mighty nation, and fulfil the promise given to Abraham, which to this time never has been fulfilled. They rejected Christ because he did not perform what their prophetic writings had led them to expect; and they still refuse to believe in him for the same reason.

Why, if it was not intended for them to expect such a deliverance were words given in so disguised and artful a manner that, in fact, the real meaning was impossible to discover until the event predicted had happened.

We may trace the same in the mysterious answers of the oracle of Delphi; no one could tell before the event *what* was to happen; but the event after it *had* occurred explained the sentence which was so cunningly devised that it might be drawn either one way or the other to mean anything. Is it right and desirable we should have an insight or foreknowledge of future events ?

If so, God would have spoken in plain and intelligible language all that was useful or necessary for us to know.

But is it not, on the contrary, both wrong and folly to pry into the future ?

If so,—though we may strain a text here and there to bear a resemblance to an event that has come to pass—if to pry into the future is wrong (and if wrong now it always was wrong), God never gave that text as a prophecy in the sense we would have it : God never spoke those half-hidden sentences to excite men's folly and curiosity to find out from them what should be His future dealings with His children. This is not the intention or province of truth, any more than that the stars above us were meant to become soothsayers and fortune-tellers in the hands of either ancient or modern astrological tellers of falsehood.

Prophecy is only prophetic in the same sense that every event is typical of some other event, and every outward and visible thing bears a shadowy analogy to the invisible things of another world. Every book that is true to our natural feelings and instincts, contains hidden truths, which future generations shall bring to light ; and every thing we look upon shows a parable. Let the seer see—but let him beware that he sees the spirit, and not the letter or the flesh— that with prophetic analogy he soars upwards to the light, not downwards into darkness.

How are the prophecies respecting the Jews ever likely to be literally fulfilled ? The Jews still look forward to their fulfilment, and even we ourselves imagine they will one day come to pass. It has often been remarked that the existence of the Jews to the present day is a standing miracle of the truth of the Bible. We might say the same of the Gipsies, who are equally a distinct race—equally to be found in every country, and, besides, speak their own language, which the Jews do not.

Judging from the past and present to the probabilities of the future, I might venture to predict that in the course of some centuries—whether few or many—the nationality of the Jews will be entirely obliterated; because they are gradually becoming incorporated and amalgamated with the other nations of the world.

When men thought it a degradation to look at or touch a Jew, they kept them a people separate and apart, they could not utterly destroy them, because, from obedience to physical laws, they had gained physical vitality and strength. But from the first day that a Jew and a Christian shook hands together, from that day they commenced to lose their nationality.

Every day that we receive them more into fellowship, no longer keeping them apart from us, but admitting them into our society and parliament, we tend to weaken their nationality.

Immediately a Jew becomes a Christian, he is no longer in faith or nation a Jew, but becomes one of the nation in which he lives. If in England, he and his descendants are lost as Jews, and become Englishmen. What more likely to consummate this than the overwhelming and incontrovertible proofs of the fallacies of their Biblical legends.

The gradual diffusion of light and knowledge must in the end reach them, and convert the most bigoted and ignorant Jew; then they no longer continue Jews, but are incorporated in some one or other branch of the human family.

But to return to the Mormons.

It is worthy of remark that they in Utah hold in reverence the Bible as well as the Book of Mormon; which is a most convincing proof that there are some words and doctrines in the Bible that not only do not contradict their vices, but absolutely uphold them. And so there are.

They take from the Old Testament their excuse for polygamy, or, as they call it, pointing to the source of their belief, " patriarchal marriages." We, as Christians, call it adultery and fornication. They ask, and justly, why, if Abraham, Isaac and Jacob— men whom we suppose received a direct revelation from heaven, who lived in a more close outward connection with God, who, whether literally or figuratively, walked with God—why, if they were allowed several wives, should not we be allowed the same ?

But if polygamy was really wrong, why was it not revealed to these chosen of God ?

Why, if polygamy was not allowed by God, did Nathan the Prophet give this message to David—

"*Thus said the Lord God of Israel:* I gave thee thy master's house, and thy master's wives into thy bosom."

Here is a crime permitted, or given to David as a reward! The parable of the rich man, who had many flocks and herds, and the poor man with his one little ewe lamb, says as much as this to David—"How could you be so ungrateful, after I had allowed you to commit adultery with your master's wives, because they were my and your enemies, to commit the same with the wife of one who is on our side, and he, poor man, had *only* one. If it was only for that you might have had compassion on him."

Are these the words of the Spirit of the same God who said by the mouth of Jesus, that one who casts an impure look on a woman is guilty of adultery; and that God is, "*I am* the same yesterday, to-day, and for ever"?

May we not say, Is it not right to proclaim the truth of God, which is unchangeable, and declare that Nathan spoke a LIE in the name of God? If you cannot say so, you cannot call the polygamy of the Mormons a sin, for, if you say it is a sin, you own it to be as that God not only permitted, but gave as a reward, to the man " after his own heart."

If it be urged that the ancient Jews were allowed many wives in order quickly to become a great people: there are three things to be noted.

The Mormons may urge the same excuse, it is still a crime allowed, and most assuredly it is not possible by such means to produce a great or strong nation. The Mormons, of course, do bring forward this motive, that, by the command of God, they are quickly to become a great and numerous people. In all probability, they will become so in spite of their crimes; for they have within them the two great causes of physical, or outward, strength and prosperity—great perseverance joined to great prudence; but if they continue to keep in their society the greatest cause both of moral and bodily degeneration; if in time they have not the wisdom to cast out this sin from amongst them, it will sooner or later produce its inevitable effects. It is curious, in this day, when in another nation, where this crime has been long allowed, and has made the people who sanction it as weak as reeds before their enemies, that the founders of another nation should take hold of it, and think to become strong by it.

We will now look at the burlesque of Miracles—Spirit Rapping.

These Spiritualists also profess to speak from direct inspiration; they say, What St. Paul did can be done again, and has been done again. It is a most reasonable argument.

If God, by revelation or inspiration, commenced miracles, we might suppose he would also vouchsafe some intimation when they were to end ; but we have had no such intimation.

When can we, for certainty, say they did end ?

They are affirmed by the Romish Church to have been carried on by direct " Apostolic Succession" to the present time. Where shall we Protestants say they stopped ? The only answer I can see given is, When the necessity for them ceased. But if you allow that, every one will declare that in his case there is a most peculiar necessity for a miracle. The coal-porter of Huntingdon " who prayed for leather breeches, which miraculously fitted him," might say there was equal necessity for his having leather breeches, as for the women to have handkerchiefs and aprons from St. Paul's body.*

We might say now, when the church and the Bible are assailed on all sides, and open profligacy is under-mining the moral character of English men and

---

* I am told that the " traditional interpretation" of this miracle is, that " the handkerchief and aprons had some power imparted to them for the alleviation of sickness by St. Paul, but not that those garments were miraculously produced from his body !" My inter-pretation, which is said to be a " new reading," still appears to me the most simple and obvious. Acts xix. 11, 12—" And God wrought special miracles by the hands of Paul : *so that from his body* were brought, unto the sick, handkerchiefs or aprons, and the diseases departed from them, and the evil spirits went out of them. Should it, however, mean that sundry articles, after having been rubbed on St. Paul's body, were worn as a sort of amulet by the sick, the verses only show still greater ignorance and superstition.

English women, that if ever there was occasion for miracles· there is occasion for them now, to stop men, at least, from laying, what churchmen consider, sacrilegious hands on the so called word of God.

Will there be any miracle think you? No, but natural laws will work as they always have worked, and will continue to work. It cannot be said that the power of working miracles was confined to the apostles, because it is said they found a person casting out devils whom they knew not.

Having traced inspiration and miracles down to the disreputable company of mormonists, and spirit rappers, and mediums, would it not be wise to have done with them, see their folly, and go back (or rather forward) to our own simple reason which God has given us, whereby to see Him, as much as, while in the body, we are capable of seeing Him?

Buckle, in his history of civilization says: " Also it is to be observed, that each of these different religions declares itself to be the true one, and all of them are equally based upon supernatural pretensions such as mysteries, miracles, prophets, and the like." What is unnatural is not impossible; it is possible for a man to be born with two heads, or a horse with five legs: there are many such instances of breaking fixed laws, but as these are contrary to a known law, they are called monsters.

We have no difficulty in at once seeing that modern

D

miracles are monsters; why should we not say the same of ancient?

Because they are said to have occurred in remote ages is no proof of their truth; on the contrary, not being able to disprove them by the sight of our eyes and the hearing of our ears, as we can in our own time, our reason ought to be more cautious in receiving them, knowing them also to be recorded by an age more barbarous and ignorant than the present.

If we are assured that the laws that governed the world at that time are the same that rule it now, we may conclude that the unnatural breaking of those laws would be equally monstrous. What have unnatural inspiration and unnatural miracles to do with truth? They are the church props whereby a mixture of truth and error has been bound up together, and called infallible, which has prevented our reason from separating good from evil, as it was commanded to do.

Take away these unholy props, these unholy bands, then shall we see clearly what truth really claims as her own, and falsehood shall crumble to the ground, but not one word of truth will fall, or ever has fallen.

What is true in art, science, philosophy, religion, is all God's truth, shown to us in perfect love and beauty. They shine like the stars of heaven, and no man can hide their light: but religion, the most beautiful, the most glorious, has been robbed of her freedom,—the birthright of the eldest Son.

CHAPTER IV.

MIRACLES.

I will commence this chapter by setting down some very correct premises from "Creation's Testimony to its God," by Rev. Thomas Ragg. The author writes in favor of supernatural revelation.

"However multifarious the forms of error may be, truth is *simple* and *consistent*."

"If there be any revelation from God it must be consistent with all the actual verities of nature, of history, and science."

"I need not now contend for the principle, almost universally allowed, that wisdom is best exhibited in the production of the greatest and most complicated results from the simplest causes. How admirable, as here exhibited, is the economy of nature—using the word 'economy' in its most confined and popular sense."

This book, as well as all books of natural history or philosophy, prove the fact, that from the first monad, or cell, up to the perfect organization of man, the hand of the Master is seen, in that the most minute touch does its work, and that not a single touch is unnecessary or superfluous. There is no waste in nature —neither waste of force nor waste of material—the very crumbs are gathered up that nothing may be lost.*

It is worth observing in this and similar books how correct are the general principles laid down in the beginning as premises, but the end of the volumes would seem to be either completely to subvert these premises, by drawing contradictory conclusions, or the general principles are never fairly allowed to be brought as a test to the particular questions at issue. I have actually been brought more clearly to see the falsity of the theory of inspiration, from the palpable contradictions visible in books written with the express purpose of upholding the theory, than from those written to overthrow it.

Let us bring this test to the truth of miracles. If God produces results from the simplest causes we may take the converse—he never uses mighty causes to produce trifling results. A miracle will, therefore, never be produced unless necessary.

It may be said, that in the former chapter the necessity is only a supposed, not a real one. Granted! Now, if we define what a real necessity is, where will it lead us?

---

* I find I am wrong in this, for in the " struggle for life" there *seems* to be great waste ; but we may yet find that the crumbs are gathered up and nothing is lost. That God works always by the simplest means is undisputed.

We say there is no miracle to be believed in, unless there is proved to be a real necessity for one. This is, in fact, the only firm basis on which to build our belief—to prevent us giving credit to falsehood and imposition, and being led into the utmost confusion. There is only a real necessity for a miracle, when some act, in itself necessary, cannot be performed by natural means. If not necessary in itself, we have no right to call *for* a miracle. If capable of being performed naturally, we have no right to apply *to* a miracle.

Now, no one may shuffle out of the conclusions, which will inevitably be drawn from these premises, by saying a miracle may be performed whenever and however God pleases. We may fully grant this, it has nothing to do with the question, which is : How are men, for whose benefit these miracles were enacted, to judge between true and false miracles—between those which, if true, are for our good, and those which, if false, are intended for our harm ? I think the best, perhaps only, guide to distinguish between the two is the one I have stated. If this is granted, it follows that only those events narrated in the Bible, which are not only necessary in themselves, but also impossible to be enacted by natural laws, are the only real and true miracles. Let us judge two most common and notable miracles by this test, one from the Old and the other from the New Testament.

From the Old Testament, that oft-questioned and doubted one of the sun standing still at the command of Joshua.

It has been called in question, from its impossibility, and answered by the quotation : " All things are possible with God ;" and on this side of the question the answer is good and sufficient. We now question its necessity. Putting aside whether it was a real necessity that Joshua should kill his enemies, or rather, granting it a real necessity, which some men might be inclined to doubt, all that was necessary for that purpose was, that he should have light to continue his work of slaughter. The necessity was not that the sun or the earth should stand still.

I am quite aware that by all scientific, or even commonly educated people, the belief in the sun standing still is thrown aside as absurd ; but I have, even now, met with people so bigoted and ignorant as still to insist upon it, not taking into consideration that the sun standing still would not even have had the desired effect, as the earth turns away from the sun, and not the sun from the earth.

This fact has forced churchmen to own that it must have been the earth and not the sun which stood still ; but, of course, that makes no difference to " the theory" of inspiration. Joshua only made a slight mistake ; he could not be expected to know that the earth moved round the sun, instead of the sun round the earth.   No; but God might have been expected to know, and if God gave his *word* to the writer of the Book of Jóshua to say the sun stood still, he inspired that man to write a falsehood.   I think such a discovery makes a great deal of difference to the theory of inspiration.

I cannot see how *mistakes* and God's *Word* can at all be made *consistent*.

Taking, then, the improved version of the story, that the earth stood still—what mighty means called to effect such a trifling object!

If the half of the world Joshua lived in had two days rolled into one, the other half must have had two nights; but no such phenomena are recorded. By the earth standing still, the centrifugal and centripetal forces must have been suspended. The effect would have been to every one somewhat similar to that caused by jumping out of a railway carriage when at full speed; not to mention the general and utter destruction and confusion to all visible things. To counteract which, an innumerable train of other unnecessary miracles must have been called forth. Suppose God made a supplementary sun for the occasion, or any other miraculous light.

But suppose again, as light was all that was required, instead of stopping the world, or creating a supernatural light to gain it, God made use of natural light—the light of the moon.   The moon's rays reflected upon the ground, which was white with hailstones; the hail storm having just before been mentioned as having taken place—that also magnified into a miracle, and exaggerated into great stones falling from heaven.

Now, do not be offended because there can be found a very simple cause, and a natural effect from our own proper moon, in every way equal to the emergency. Do not insist on keeping your pet miracle, which is quite inconsistent with God's dealings with the world, in using mighty and complicated machinery, when very simple ones, already to hand, would answer every purpose.

I would apply the same test to the alleged miracle of the Immaculate Conception.

If Christ was to assume a human and natural body similar to the rest of mankind, where was the necessity for rejecting the human and natural law of conception, substituting an unnatural and miraculous means, when the natural one was all-sufficient.

The necessity was to make a human *body* to contain the divine *spirit*. It was not to make a divine *body* as well as a divine nature. The conception of the body has no connection with the conception of the soul.

Body proceeds from body, but soul is not generated by soul. *All* the sons of God are born, "not of blood, nor of the will of the flesh, nor of the will of man, but of God."

So is the *spiritual* birth of the Son of God. But as he was also the son of man, he was born as a man.

The spirit is not flesh, neither the flesh spirit. "The Word was made flesh," therefore, not by the spirit but by the flesh.

The spirit and the flesh are separate and distinct; we shall never get rid of the confusion of our ideas and belief till we fully understand and recognize this truth.

The only supposed reason for imagining the necessity of a divine conception is that, thereby, Christ avoided inheriting the sin of Adam. But if the sin of Adam was transmitted by his body through the blood of his descendants, then it was bodily disease, not sin; but, if really sin, it must proceed from the soul, and by avoiding the connection with the human body he did not avoid the sin of the soul.

If Christ was to be born as a man and like a man, why could he not have a human father, or what was the use of tracing the genealogy of Christ from Adam to Abraham, from Abraham to David, from David to Joseph, if Joseph was not his earthly father; and, why was he "subject unto his parents" if Joseph was not his parent as well as Mary?

Are not enlightened men of the nineteenth century ashamed to continue in their religion, to believe as an article of their faith, that old pagan myth of a woman conceiving by one of the gods.

Esculapius was reputed to be so conceived, and was called by his followers, *The Saviour*. Hercules the same, Bacchus the same, and many others.

If theologians *wish* to have the person and life of Jesus eventually thrown aside as a myth and a fable they could not follow a better course than persisting to associate his name with such paltry and contemptible stories from heathen mythology.

I dwell on this point more than I otherwise should, for before all things I desire truth, and it seems to me that this idea of a spiritual cause of a natural birth is the very nucleus from whence we derive the false theory of direct Divine, outward revelation—inspiration, or miracles—each being an unnatural means of teaching truth or causing truth to be born in the mind when the natural means is through our own reason, which is given us for that very purpose.

We have to learn that our reason is the only medium of communion between God and our souls. From God's spirit to our spirit; but if God ever made himself known to us by an outward or external manifestation, or we ever *talked* with God; this was not from spirit to spirit, but from God's spirit to our body, or from our body to his spirit—both impossible, unnecessary, and contradictory.

The assertion of the complete distinction of soul and body does not deny the power of action and reaction of one on the other, but rather affirms it, for two things properly and thoroughly thus to bear on one another must be perfectly distinct and separate, if joined or united they cannot act and react.

Two chemical bodies placed in connection with one another act and react on each till the two have combined in one and a different body, but when that is accomplished action and reaction ceases, and in every step towards union they weaken and gradually lose the power of mutual action on each other.

But the mind and body never cease to act and react, therefore never join ; the power never decreases therefore they never tend to union ; and to maintain the healthy and free play of mutual action, the full force of the healthy and entire bodily powers must act on the healthy and entire mental powers, if not, the entire *man* is not healthy.

Even the test of necessity will still leave a very wide margin of miracles, we may find many which we suppose really necessary in themselves, and also, as far as we now know, not capable of being performed by natural means; but seeing we know little of natural laws, and know the study of them is but in its infancy, and seeing also, by this comparatively superficial knowledge, what wonders have been performed, who can place a limit to what a full and perfect acquaintance with these laws might effect?

Disbelief in supernatural revelation, inspiration, or miracles, does not in any way involve rejection of

Christianity itself, unless we continue foolishly, obstinately, and wrongly to persist in binding them up together. What right has any one to say, as S. Mansell does in "Aids to Faith," that if we disbelieve the supernatural, "all Christianity in short, so far as it has any title to that name, so far as it has any special relation to the person or the teaching of Christ is overthrown at the same time." Such words cannot *make* a man believe in the supernatural, but it may make him an atheist.

What right has any man to declare we shall *not* have Christianity, if we will not have miracles along with it?

And again. "For if he professed to work miracles, and wrought them not, what warrant have we for the trustworthiness of other parts of this teaching?"

Who wrote the life of Jesus? Did he write it himself? or did four Jews called Matthew, Mark, Luke, and John?—and even to find any conclusive evidence that these men wrote the Gospels that bear their names, would be rather a difficult matter.

What right have we to say Christ professed, when it was these men, or some other men, who professed for him?

We have sufficient warrant for his teaching by its truth and good fruits. We can believe in this, without "seeing signs and wonders."

However wonderful the miracles asserted of Jesus,

there are none so wonderful as his own life. G. H. Lewis, in his "History of Philosophy" says: "It is no ordinary man that fable exalts into its poetical region. Whenever you find romantic or miraculous deeds attributed to any man, be certain that that man was great enough to sustain the weight of this crown of fabulous glory."

But because we remove this foolish withered crown, which he wore, do we think less of the man, or the truth he spoke?

Is not the crown a disfigurement, instead of a halo?

The language both of Christ and our own reason lead us to disbelief in the supernatural. But full belief in the power and all-sufficiency of the natural instead of the supernatural, will, in the end, firmly establish Christianity.

It is a glorious thought! how shall I be worthy to speak it?

God is and ever has been true.

True to Himself.

True to man.

True to the earth.

And True to the laws he gave to rule mind and matter, men and things.

CHAPTER V.

FAITH.

We must have the Bible, for in it are great and precious truths, by losing them the world would lose half its light.

But the Bible must be examined and purified by the light, the false separated from the true, that the truth may become glorious.

There is no need of mystery, which is darkness, the truth of God with respect to man shall shine out as clear as the sun at noonday, then shall all men rejoice in its light.

Truth and falsehood being bound up together by the word "inspiration," has caused the Bible to be scorned by many.

Those who are unable to separate truth from error, and who are told also by the church that to endeavor to do so is sin, and would destroy the Bible, seeing unmistakeable errors in it; but assured that belief in the whole is the very life of the Bible, these, men not being able to smother or get rid of their doubts, have at last thrown aside the Bible in disgust—truth and falsehood together.

This is no fault of the doubter, but the fault of the

blindness of those who will not suffer the light of truth to fulfil its right and perfect work.

Faith has been set as a guard over truth.

I visited a friend one evening, to whom some of my supposed atheistical notions were known. The kind soul, with tears in her eyes, said she hoped and trusted and prayed that I "might think differently bye and bye."

As if truth once known could ever be thrust back. She said I was to "pray and have faith."

I asked, what I was to have faith in, more than in God ?

This was a puzzle. Simply faith in God was of little or no use ; and evidently quite a secondary consideration—to save my soul I was to "*have faith*," that was all. But how am I to get hold of this faith ? Shall I say like Macbeth, "come let me clutch thee" ? I cannot grasp it more than the Thane could the dagger ; I must have faith in something, if only in a brass candlestick, or Balaam's ass, and I cannot have real faith in anything, unless I believe it to be true. And I cannot have faith in what is said of Balaam's ass, or in any other nonsense.

How am I to acquire this cabalistic grace, which it appears is the only one that will take me to heaven?

I pointed out one or two most palpable absurdities and contradictions in the Bible, but to no purpose. The answer was "I cannot understand it " "I shall know bye and bye " " I do not want to understand it now," " I shall see bye and bye," " I have faith."

How then is this faith to be acquired? only by voluntarily resigning the mind and soul to utter and complete ignorance. This lady would not look at Colenso, or any other book that questioned the truth of the Bible or Faith, for in the end, belief in the Bible and Faith seemed to be synonymous;* she would not even allow her own unsupported reason to approach her faith. Reason was very good in its way, but it was not to touch or look at faith.

This is what I believe is generally found to be *pure church* religion.

Ignorance supporting faith.

Faith supporting the Bible.

And the intermixed truth and falsehood of the Bible supporting God.

St. Paul saw an altar erected " to the unknown God," he explained to the heathen who was this unknown God whom they ignorantly worshipped.

Suppose these men had preferred keeping this " holy mystery " of an unknown God, and had objected to have that God made clear to them.

Would they have done right or wrong?

Is not this blind faith an ignorant worship of an unknown God?

* Observe, that belief in God and Faith, are not supposed to be synonymous.

It is based on it knows not what, and leads it knows not whither.

True faith is belief in truth and love, based on reason, carried out into daily and hourly life, as its end and aim.

Let us see how this baseless and aimless faith, divorced from reason, is sought to be carried out into the life.

I take a picture from life.

Two ladies were driving together, the one to whom the carriage in which they were seated belonged, was called (perhaps justly) a very religious woman; the other, I suppose, had not the same character. They were approaching at a rapid pace, what the latter considered a very dangerous pass, overlooking a precipice, and she begged to be allowed to alight. "What!" said the former, "have ye no faith? have ye no faith?" "No," said the other, "not a bit! not a bit! let me out!" Now I say the latter had more faith than the former. Her reason told her to have faith in the laws of God, which told her that if she ran into danger, she could not expect to escape injury, and she had no right to suppose faith would protect her. Such a faith would not have been a reasonable faith, but presumption. Even if we cannot avoid facing danger, we may not think that God will set aside the laws of nature in order to preserve our bodies.

E

But if it is necessary for us to run into danger, and we do it then at God's command, we may faithfully resign our souls into his keeping, we cannot reasonably ask or desire more.

Had the lady instead of directing the attention of the timid one to a religious faith for a bodily protection, endeavored to set her foolish and unnecessary fears at rest, by assurance of the perfect training of her horses, and the experience of her coachman, she would have offered a reasonable ground upon which to build faith ; but this meaningless faith seemed so very visionary to the other, that to be allowed to alight on the solid ground appeared decidedly the best assurance of safety.

Let us examine blind faith applied to religion.

When we take up the Bible and attempt to understand it, are we, in everything we do not comprehend, to explain its contradictions to known laws by affirming a miracle ?

Have we, in short, a right to believe a miracle where not positively recorded ?

If we have no right to take away one word from the Bible and no right to insert a single word, why a miracle ?   And if we have a right to affirm a miracle wherever one seems to be wanted, where was the necessity of recording them as anything strange or wonderful ?   Have we a right, for instance, to remove the impossibility of Noah providing food in the Ark for carnivorous as well as herbivorous animals, insectivorous as well as frugivorous birds; in fact, food suitable for the digestive organs of every species of bird and beast, which would have been impossible? are we to say a miraculous sleep passed on all the inmates of the ark? Which supposition is also contradicted by the command to Noah to gather food them; or, are we to suppose God miraculously for helped him to gather it? and after the limited supply the ark would hold was collected, it miraculously lasted (as did the widow's barrel of meal and cruse of oil), and was also miraculously digested by organs not made to digest it? We know from the skeletons of antediluvial animals that their constitution and organization was the same as at present, and then, as now, the life of a dog or a lion could not be sustained on grass or herbs, no more than a cow or giraffe on flesh.

There are innumerable other miracles required: for instance, how fresh air was to be obtained in the ark. Animals requiring a much larger proportion than men, and their breath, whether sleeping or waking, would soon vitiate and poison it for human life.

I ask again, are we to imagine all these innumerable miracles, merely because in no other manner can an incredible story be maintained?

The question is generally slurred over by people

who " have faith," by saying we are not called upon to find out *how* it was done but only to believe that it *was* done.

It is positively marvellous how difficult it is to bring people who " have faith " to anything like reason. But you *must* account for every event, whether you choose to bring it into words or not, as effected either by natural means or unnatural—by the common laws. of cause and effect, or by a miracle—and if an event is positively proved impossible to have been enacted by natural means we must either allow it to be a falsehood or say it is worked by miracles.

This is a fact, however, which most people cannot or will not see ; it is considered so *safe*, pleasant, and easy to dismiss all difficult questions to that wide middle region between, " I believe," and " I do not believe," " I cannot understand "—that twilight of mystery, superstition and *faith*, where we are content to let quietly remain hidden the most momentous questions of life; and we do so from one of three motives, or, more likely, from all three together—from laziness, incapacity, and fear.

Where is the force of miracles, when really asserted, if we place them anywhere and everywhere ?

According to the biblical account, the work of creation was completed on the seventh day, therefore, also, all the laws regulating the creation.

But if we begin at the miraculous garden of Eden to the end of the Old Testament, and patch up everything incredible with miracles, we shall have to conclude that they were the rule, and events produced by natural means, the exception.

How, if this was the case, could Christ say he did the works no other man ever had done? Why, the marvels of the Old Testament far exceed those of the New, in impossibility, not counting the imaginary ones we tack on to them, to make them appear credible.

I mentioned this text relative to Christ's assertion of his wonderful works, to my friend, the answer was, " Christ only affirmed he was the only one who worked miracles in his own name, and by his own power."

This is another proof of explaining away inconvenient texts, so that they mean nothing in the end.

But Christ said of his works that he did nothing of himself, but derived his power from his Father. If he really meant to assert his own power in opposition or distinction to invested or reflected power, then all I can say is—the reflected power manifested greater strength in wonder working than the real and inherent power.

A falsehood may generally be detected by seeing how other falsehoods are brought forward, in order to make it be believed ; but truth needs no support.

So, the falsehood of miracles is exposed, by showing how many other miracles are required to support them.

Shall we "receive that as truth on one side of the boundary line, which simply transferred to the other, becomes falsehood "?

Shall every argument we bring forward to point out an absurdity or an absolute contradiction, be stopped by the cry "A miracle! a miracle!" ?

If so, when shall we see truth ?

When shall fools be convinced of folly ?

Let us see how ignorance and falsehood combined seek to prop up faith relative to the journey of the Israelites through the wilderness. I copy from the answer to the Sixth Essay in the *London Review* :—

"But while the historical basis of the story is admitted, the miraculous events connected with it are denied. Well, time rolled on, the wilderness is traversed, Sinai is reached, when lo, there are discovered innumerable inscriptions on the rocks. Inscriptions ? Impossible ! Yes, sceptic ; look again, examine them well—they are inscriptions ; the work of men's hands.

"But how came they there ? Some solitary wanderer—pilgrims who have reached the sacred spot, have there inscribed their journeys and names. No; they are too numerous for that ; they are deeply and beautifully carved—they cover the rocks for miles.

Thousands of living men must have been here engaged !

" But what could have brought such multitudes to the place, or, when there, how could they have been sustained ?

" Let the sceptic answer. He is silent ; he cannot explain. Well, the believer ventured to suggest that these inscriptions may have been engraved on the rocks by the hosts of Israel when in the wilderness ; but the sceptic, though unable to offer a more reasonable solution, only smiled and looked incredulous. But time, the revealer of all things, advanced, and now, in our day, God has given, to faith and patient labor, the key by which these inscriptions have been deciphered ; and what do we read ?

" The marvellous story of Israel—their deliverance from Egypt, the destruction of Pharaoh in the waters of the Red Sea, the sending the manna from heaven ; and thus, for the confirmation of faith and the confusion of infidelity, after three thousand years, there is read on the stony pages of the rocks of Sinai what Moses wrote on the page of inspiration."

Really this astounding passage quite took my breath away. I, a most decided sceptic on the subject, did really tremble ! Should I, after all, be forced to swallow this monster ! There is a note appended to this passage :—

" We are aware that some writers still reject the

Israelitish origin of the Sinaitic Inscriptions. We would only, however, refer our readers to Mr. Foster's learned and interesting works, "One Primeval Language," with their illustrative plates, to enable them to form their own judgment on the matter."

A few weeks after, I had lent me Bunsen's "Philosophy of Universal History." He is one I find who not only rejects the Israelitish origin of the inscriptions, but *has* offered a more reasonable solution. Baron Bunsen's work was published in 1854 ; and yet the writer in the *London Review*, 1863, would have us believe that all the sceptics could do, was "to smile and look credulous," while the Rev. C. Foster was by "faith and patient labor," guided by what "the believer ventured to suggest"—finding out a confirmation of all the miracles to the "confusion of infidelity." It may, possibly, prove "to the confusion" of "the believer" instead. I mean not the true or reasoning believer, but the false or blind believer.

It is good to see how Baron Bunsen turns the tables on the churchmen, who cry out that philosophy is not to touch their sacred theology.

The language of the inscriptions is proved by philologists to be principally Arabic.

The alphabet was discovered by Edward Beer, of Leipzic, with the utmost care, and so correctly "that Tuch, after the most searching inquiry and with fresh materials," could discover no error. The letters of the Sinaitic alphabet are placed on his (Beer's) tomb, as "a well deserved trophy of this self-sacrificing inquirer, who lived and died in starvation—a martyr to his zeal for truth and science."

Most of the names have a reference to Baal, such as "*Germ el Ba"li,*" "*Sad el Ba'li,*" which means "Fearing Baal," or, the "Fortunes of Baal."

It is proved also that Mount Seir (Sinai, or Serbal), was an object of religious awe to all the Semitic tribes; and pilgrims of all tribes went to worship there. Bunsen goes on to say—"As to the Rev. C. Foster's enthusiastic and fanciful attempts to make out of these inscriptions the journals of the people of Israel, on their way through the Sinaitic peninsula, science can only deplore such unwarranted encroachments of wild imagination and crude conjecture into the *sacred domain of history.* The absolute nonsense which the poor inscriptions are made to produce, when read according to that false key, would be its strongest refutation. A glance at the Hebrew of Moses would at once involve us in a dilemma; either we do not possess a single genuine text in the Old Testament, or Mr. Foster's pretended language is not Hebrew."

Another of the Rev. C. Foster's discoveries is truly wonderful! From an ancient inscription, which he supposed written within 500 years before the flood, he translates these words: "And we believed in the miracle-mystery, in the resurrection-mystery, in the nostril-mystery." These, he affirms, show "the precious central truths of revealed religion." The "nostril-mystery" meaning, of course, "Jesus and the resurrection!"

I continue from Bunsen :—

"I have said nothing about Mr. Foster's former Himyarac dreams, because, I hope he has abandoned them, and because they are forgotten; but, as his recent attempt to ignore what science has gained by the sweat of the brow of her true disciples, to despise method and learning in a domain intimately connected with our religion and our faith, to throw discredit on honest inquiries, it would have been a dereliction of a public duty not to have recorded here my solemn protest against such relapses into a strain of uncritical conjecture, which if not sincerely repudiated, must render all philological researches ridiculous in the eyes of the public."

We have yet to find what great thanks are due to these "true disciples" of science for their discovery of truth.

Theologians do nothing for the advance of knowledge or truth; they are only carried forward on the shoulders of philosophers; and all they do is to cry out and grumble because they are moved about inconveniently. They think it very hard they cannot be allowed to sit still in their old comfortable places.

This is hardly to be wondered at, nor ought the stagnation of the church to be ascribed entirely to the pride, ignorance, or idleness, of churchmen.

We, the laity, bound them only to teach in one way. We would not let them think for themselves, or advance one original idea respecting any mysterious or unintelligible doctrine. We obliged them to preach only, according to the Rubric and the Thirty-nine Articles, the ideas of men who lived many centuries before them, and so many centuries less advanced in knowledge.

A paper in the *Quarterly Review*, on "Training of the Clergy," asserts that "The English mind— whether rightly or wrongly, morbidly or healthily— will not in any province, but especially in religion, tolerate self-conceit or self-origination; it insists upon the clergy walking in old paths."

This has been the rule with regard to church theology, but most certainly in no other province of science do we insist on men "walking in old paths;" and while the clergy were closely bound by these Articles, the laity were bound by them just as much as they chose to be bound.

To those whom we supposed to be our teachers we made it almost an article of faith that they should not think for themselves; but there was nothing to hinder the pupils from thinking what they pleased and saying what they pleased. For them theology was placed on the same footing as every other science, admitting, if they chose to use it, that full and free discussion, by which alone truth was found in every other path of knowledge.

In this path the clergy were forbidden to walk, hence the anomaly that four-fifths of a congregation are more enlightened than the one who is set up as their teacher; and now the churchmen, many of them, have become so reconciled to their bondage, and even so attached to it, that they do not desire, and indeed fear to have it removed. They think they would be falling into the very lowest depths, if they had not the support (or weight?) of their chains.

It is a pity they do not perceive what a disadvantageous position they are placed in. Their congregations have slipped away from the yoke, no power of the clergy can ever bring them back again, while they themselves still continue to wear it, cramping thereby their natural growth and strength, as a Chinese woman cramps her feet.

One cannot but feel sympathy with the men on whom so much obloquy and ridicule is now being thrown, whether they deserve it or not, or whether even they themselves are aware of it or not. Probably those who deserve it most will feel it least, while those who least deserve it feel it most keenly.

We owe the clergy a tribute of gratitude, particularly the lower working clergy, who, for the most part, are, and have been, men of pure and self-denying lives, who have done their best to assist the poor, and comfort the sick and dying. It is curious to remark that on a man's death-bed, be he ever so vile, they give him more consolation than they ever did in his lifetime. Condemn him daily in life, as a child of the devil, but lower him into his grave, and cover the earth over him, "in sure and certain hope of a joyful resurrection to eternal life." And so in the presence of the dead I believe they speak the most christian, and the truest words they ever uttered.

What time have these poor and hard-worked clergymen, even if allowed, to consider or study deeply? and the higher and better paid class we have enveloped in spiritual pride and forced ignorance, by supposing them invested with some mysterious wisdom and sanctity by virtue of "apostolic succession" (flowing mesmerically I suppose, through the fingers) but at the same time refusing them the use of this apostolic wisdom, or even poor insignificant human reason, to advance them a step beyond the wisdom of St. Chrysostom, St. Athanasius, St. Augustine, or St. Jerome.

It sometimes amuses, and sometimes vexes me to have to listen quietly to a lecture, in the shape of a dozen texts from the Bible, generally written by St. Paul, while the lecturer, who has spoken like a parrot the words of another, retires with a proud and self-satisfied air, supposing me completely annihilated. They say to me, " God says this," and " God says the other," but they do not remember that this is the very assertion that I question. I say God never spoke anything but the truth. There are things here not true, therefore God did not speak them. One says, " Recollect Christ's *own* words are, ' he that is not with me is against me.' " I accept this as a truth, and for this very reason I believe what is against love and truth is against Christ, and I follow out my belief not only in words but in deed.

Another says the perfection of a Christian character is to "hope all things, fear all things, believe all things." Now this text from St. Paul is utterly devoid of sense, it is impossible to *hope* all things and *fear* all things at the same time. You cannot hope a thing, you hope *for* it, or hope or trust *in* it, and you cannot hope and trust in or for a thing, and at the same time fear it. And if you believe *all things*, you believe falsehood as well as truth.

Another politely but significantly informs me, " *There are those* who wrest Scripture to their own damnation."

One would imagine that these people supposed I had never heard any of these texts before; I have heard them many times, the only difference is, that they take them without thought, and repeat them by rote, while I *have* thought of them, and endeavored, to the best of my ability, to understand them. So I have come to the firm determination to trust and hope *fully* in God's truth and love, and to fear *nothing*. Yes, I do fear something—I fear pain, fear it in a most cowardly manner.

CHAPTER VI.

WHAT DO WE WORSHIP?

I HEARD read in church the 4th chapter of Judges, in which is related how Jael slew Sisera.

That Sisera being conquered fled to the tent of a supposed friend for rest and protection. That the woman Jael said to him, " Turn in my lord, turn in and fear not." That Sisera, believing her deceitful words, took food from her hand, and in full security of mind, laid himself down to sleep. That then this woman, whom the beaten and defenceless man had trusted, came and murdered him in his sleep. As I sat and listened I said in my heart, Good and merciful God, how shall a so-called christian congregation and a christian people become truly christian, while they hear in their churches this narrative of a vile, treacherous murder, said to be done by the permission and approbation of God ! A murder which, if we should read of in our next Monday morning's newspaper would call down the execration of every right feeling person on the head of the cruel and brutal woman who perpetrated it.

It cannot be said that it is not intended for us to think God approved of this murder, for Deborah the prophetess, and Barak were inspired to utter a song of praise and thanksgiving for it, and the writer of the book of Judges, whoever he may be, was inspired to transcribe it; and the cruelty of the spirit of the song is more vile even, if we only consider it with christian feelings, than almost the murder itself.

We *can* make some allowance for a murder committed in defence of one's country, though God who said, "do NO murder," cannot commend it. But what allowance can we make for a woman, and a warrior, "a mighty man of valor," exulting together over the death of the murdered man? and gloating over the description of it, as in the fifth chapter, from the 24th to 27th verse. They may be beautiful words but the spirit is the very reverse of beautiful.

Shall we say it was good that the woman Deborah should think with savage joy how Sisera's mother would look and wait for his coming; strain her gaze from the window and cry, "Why is his chariot so long in coming—why tarry the wheels of his chariot"? As a Christian, I say it was a vile murder; and the so-called song of praise an insult to God, and a disgrace to the humanity of those who said it. And *I* will not insult the good, the just, the merciful God, by thinking he inspired, or approved

r

of, either the words or the deed; and the sooner such stories are expunged from our church service the better; and the sooner the ears of christian men, women, and children are spared from having them polluted by listening to such an atrocious narrative, the sooner will they become really christian.

If God did not inspire the deed or the song, why is it inserted in what we call God's Word? But if he did inspire it, he is not the God I worship, for that God is a God of love.

And why is it said in the Bible, "God tempted David," or "God hardened Pharaoh's heart"? Of course, it is very easy, by substituting the word Satan for God, to alter the whole meaning of the sentence; but if we alter one inspired word why not another? If we are allowed to expunge the word God and insert Satan, why not in another place take away the word Satan, and put in the word God? Why, indeed? Because we cannot impute evil to God. If so, follow out the rule, and if an evil and wicked deed is recorded in the name of God, refuse to believe it, and trace it to its right source as the offspring of evil.

A magistrate once, by a mere slip of the tongue, said, "By the laws of England, every man is guilty till he is proved innocent." All who heard him knew well that he intended to have said just the contrary, so they only indulged in a laugh at the mistake; but suppose this man had to write down our laws for the benefit of another nation, and continually made the same mistake, writing the maxim sometimes one way, sometimes the other. What would the people think to whom it was sent? Either that the laws were very barbarous, or the person who wrote knew very little of the laws he pretended to instruct them in ; or, he was so careless and inaccurate in transscribing them, that little reliance could be placed in his writings. But how much more would it increase their dilemma if they were told that the words were written from the direct dictation of the law-maker, and could not possibly err ; and, moreover, they were bound to believe fully all that was written in this book of law on pain of being destroyed by the lawgiver. Even granting, that when saying, "God tempted," the writer was in error, and that the " Devil tempted," was intended, it does not greatly improve the matter.

It is said, "God hardened Pharaoh's heart," that he might show his wonders. This is hardly a godlike motive : that he should inflict unnecessary torture on Pharaoh's people, to gain the admiration of the world, or even angels. Or if " The devil hardened Pharaoh's heart," why should the people have been punished with plagues ?

In the 24th chapter of Samuel it is written, " And again the anger of the Lord was kindled against

Israel, and he moved David against them to say, Go number Israel and Judah."

In the 21st chapter of Chronicles it is said, "And Satan stood up against Israel and provoked David to number Israel."

Take either passage separately, or endeavor to reconcile them, I cannot see much good to be extracted from them. Take the first passage: if Israel had committed any wickedness that deserved punishment, could not God have awarded the penalty, without moving David to number the people as a sort of excuse for its infliction? Or take the second text: why should the malice of the devil be suffered to be the cause of punishing Israel? Or take them together: if it was sin to number the people—and it is not said to be sin, and, in order to consider it sin, we have to impute ambitious motives to David, which are not imputed—but if it was, why were the people punished? they could not help it; and God says, every soul shall bear its own iniquity. The truth most probably is: there was a sort of superstitious fear of numbering the people, and from Joab's trying to dissuade David from doing it; most likely, it was thought to be something "unlucky;" and then, when a grievious plague broke out soon after, of course it was attributed to the numbering the people, and David's obstinacy in not taking advice put down to the temptation of Satan.

The great plague of London gave rise to super-
stitions somewhat similar, the inhabitants reckoning
it as a punishment for moral delinquency, instead of
what it really was—the effect of the general filth and
uncleanliness of the city.

To return to David. Look at him on his death-bed;
his last words were, to bequeath several deeds of blood
to his scn and successor, Solomon. Though he (David)
had promised not to slay certain men, who had offended
him, Solomon was on no account to let their grey hairs
go down to the grave in peace. This is the spirit of the
man who is said to be " after God's own heart ;" that
God who says, " If we from our hearts forgive not
our brother his trespasses, neither will God forgive
us ;" but David, as in his life so at his death, went
before God with curses upon his lips : " Curse my
enemies, but bless me, for I am holy," is the substance of his prayers.

The first acts of Solomon were to execute these
deeds of vengeance in obedience to the commands
of his dying father ; and it is implied that for this,
God blessed and greatly prospered him.

David may have been a good man, as far as the
age in which he lived would allow him to be ; and he
was, in his knowledge of the truth, doubtless, greatly
in advance of his contemporaries ; but this need not
make us blind to his errors, either in deeds or words,
and it need not force us to read in our churches

those words which we feel in our hearts to be wrong
and unchristian. Our hearts tell us the truth,
but we are afraid to utter, or even admit the feeling, because our lips are sealed with the word
"inspiration."

What more beautiful, for instance, than the 57th
Psalm ; in it, and many others, David might shame us
by his real trust in the mercy of God : he approaches
Him in sincerity, not thinking it necessary to appeal
to his mercy only through another, or through sacrifice, past, present, or to come. There is a touch of
his unforgiveness of his enemies, even in this psalm,
which displays itself fully in the next. He says,
" The righteous shall *rejoice* when he seeth the
vengeance."

What righteous man should rejoice in witnessing
the punishment of another either in this world or
the next ?

In some places God is openly held up before
our eyes in the detestible character of a liar and
deceiver : " And if the prophet be deceived when he
hath spoken a thing, *I, the Lord, have deceived that
prophet.*" " Now, therefore, the Lord hath put a
lying spirit in the mouth of all thy prophets." " The
Lord " inspired four hundred prophets to speak lies !

Is this God or devil ?

St. Paul, of course, follows in the same steps :
" For this cause, God shall send them a strong delu-

sion, that they should believe a lie, that they all might be damned."

The God St. Paul worshipped had such a desire that "they all might be damned;" that if they would not "believe a lie," naturally, he would "send them a *strong delusion*" to force them to believe it.

A curious sort of inspiration !—from whom, God or devil ?

CHAPTER VII.

LIGHT.

CAST aside, then, the idea of inspiration as a falsehood, if for no other reason than this : that it can never cast out falsehood. It may prop up error, but it can never remove error. It is false, then, because it effectually precludes us from seeing what is false.

It is contrary to freedom, therefore leads to bondage.

It is contrary to light, therefore leads to darkness.

Bondage and darkness are contrary to truth : therefore inspiration is contrary to truth.

" That was the true Light, which lighteth *every man* that cometh into the world."

As every man who enters the world may behold the light of the sun, so every soul into which God breathes the breath of life, may see the light of the spirit—the true inspiration.

The true light is free and universal. But inspiration is particular and peculiar ; therefore not the true light.

It may be said that some men are born blind, or afterwards become so, and in this diseased or abnormal condition cannot see the light; that by the fall of man the minds of all were reduced to a blind and abnormal state, and could only be enabled to see the light of truth by a miraculous inspiration. The fall of man is the very centre pillar of our theological edifice. I wish I had the strength of Samson to shake it, even though I might be crushed beneath the ruins !

CHAPTER VIII.

THE CREATION.

It is curious to remark that in all our attempts to reconcile the Mosaic account of Creation with the scientific one, none have ever taken the trouble to reconcile science with the narrative in the second chapter of Genesis. It has been simply laid aside as something quite out of the reach of human understanding, completely at variance with nature, nothing in science or the known world bearing any likeness to it.

We endeavor to unite the first account with the truths of science, because it shows a semblance of truth, but the second bears no similarity to any truth we are acquainted with, so cannot be united with truth. The principal objection to the first appears to be in the extension of time—instead of a week the Creation must have occupied "a long period." Some make the days to mean long periods; some put the "long period" before the days, and a writer in the *Athenæum* puts the "long period" between the days; there is evidently a long period required somewhere, and it seems to me to matter little where we insert it. All we have to learn from this chapter is, that

God made the world and all things in it, as we see it to this day. That after (perhaps before) the work of Creation was ended, God governed the world by the laws he then made, which remain firm, unshaken, and unbroken to the present time.

That God made the world for man, and man for the world; both in harmony and consistently with one another, and the relation of man to nature and nature to man is the same now as then.

But the account in the second chapter is directly contrary to this. We are there told, that from the beginning the Earth was *not* made as we now see it, but after the fall a supplementary creation was effected, and the world only then became as we now see it. Next, that the laws God made to govern the world were immediately broken and miracles substituted; that, though God by a long process had made the world a fit habitation for man, and man expressly as its inhabitant, it would appear the world was *not* suitable for him, but in some unknown corner of the world a miraculous garden had to be planted to receive him.

Either, then, man was not adapted for the world or the world was not adapted for man; or, being both suitable and in harmony with one another, the visible Creation as we behold it now, was not the Creation God made " in the beginning."

But geology proves that before man set foot on the earth the laws that governed it were the same that govern it to the present time. Then the first man and woman, if like Adam and Eve, were not in harmony with the world they came to inhabit, subdue, and people.*

I defy any one to think of the life of Adam and Eve in Paradise, but in the same way he would consider a fairy tale. Of course it was all very pleasant and happy, and the very height of felicity, but how it was so he cannot imagine.

The meteorological laws must have been suspended, the weather never too hot nor too cold ; the wind never blew, the rain never fell on them.

The animals, whether carnivorous or not, ate grass, and were otherwise tame and peaceable.

---

* I repeat from "The People's Dictionary of the Bible" the fact which Bishop Colenso has made known to the public, of the hand of two different writers being traceable in the so-called Books of Moses. I found this the most valuable part of Colenso's book ; it broke the last chain that fettered me to an implicit belief in the words of the Bible, for to me, and I dare say to many others, this view of the Hebrew Bible was quite new.

Respecting the Mosaic record of Creation, " If we look into the sources from whence the writer drew his account, we may find aid towards a right conception of its import. That they were partly documentary appears certain, equally, that the documents were of a twofold kind. As they are twofold in their nature, so, most probably, had they a twofold origin. Certainly they have produced a twofold description of Creation—a fact of which the reader may satisfy himself. These two leading documents are distinguished chiefly by the names used to designate the Divine Being, who in one is denominated, *Elohim*, in the other *Jehovah*. Other documents may have furnished contributions."

The earth was different, no weeds sprang from it, two wonderful trees grew in it, the fruit of one had the property of giving immortality, the other of imparting the knowledge of good and evil.

Animals spoke, at least one did, and as it does not appear to have excited any surprise in Adam or Eve, we might conclude that others did the same; and, finally, if Adam and Eve continued obedient to one arbitrary command there was to be no death.

It would also be a question how the miraculous garden was fenced or guarded from the outer world, not by the rivers named, as they are mentioned as encompassing different lands; one, "the whole land of Havilah, where there is gold," and the writer naïvely tells us that the gold "is good."

In whichever way we regard the story, fancy must fill up the picture, reality cannot. If there ever was such a place as Eden, it certainly could not have been on this earth, or regulated by the laws of this earth, and, if not on this earth and moved by its laws Adam and Eve could not have had the same bodily structure as ourselves, for we are made in harmony with the laws of nature, and they in harmony with us; destroy one and you destroy the other; and, if not harmony, then confusion and contradiction. And, if Adam and Eve were the inhabitants of another sort of world, how are we their descendants?

This world they could not have lived in, for they were not in harmony with, or adapted to it.

We might imagine that, had not the laws regulating the world been right and good for men, God would not have placed us here, but in another world where the laws would be suitable to us. But in placing the first man not in the world, but in a miraculous garden, would lead us to think that the Creator had made an oversight, and was obliged to put a miraculous patch over one corner of it to remedy the mistake.

We suppose Adam to have been perfect in understanding and yet deny him the first glimmering of reason—the knowledge of good and evil; and, yet, though he had no knowledge of what was evil, he had power to do evil. Deprive man of the knowledge of good and evil you leave him nothing but the instinct of the brute.

Professor Huxley quotes an anecdote of a monkey, narrated by Mr. Bennett, in which a certain consciousness appeared to be displayed, and he concludes, "There was certainly something more than instinct in that action; he evidently betrayed a consciousness of having done wrong, both in his first and last action, and what is reason if that is not an exercise of it?" Here is an argument trying to persuade us that monkeys have more than animal instinct because being able to be conscious of wrong, and by this faint spark of reason are to claim affinity with man.

But we assume that Adam and Eve were superior to the rest of mankind, in not possessing the reasoning power. We take from them all but the instinct of the brutes, in order to make them but a little lower than the angels.

We might think the proof of an angelic or higher nature, would consist in a clearer perception of right and wrong, and before we gain a higher intelligence, we must obtain this fuller knowledge; not to have a perception of good and evil, would be going back, not coming forward, in the scale of moral intelligencies. It is, in fact, putting the progenitors of mankind just where Professor Huxley seeks to place them.

Yet this man (Adam) without the reasoning faculty had the difficult task assigned him of being the originator of language. In naming the animals, Adam must have either been miraculously inspired to pronounce their names, without knowing their different habits or instincts, or he was miraculously endowed with this wisdom, and named them accordingly. He could not have the power inherent in his unreasoning mind; and even with our full human reason, such a work would be the careful labor of years.

I should like to know how all these "heavy beasts"

made their entrance into the garden of Eden, unless they miraculously trod the air, or the soil and plants supernaturally resisted the impression of their hoofs and paws; they must have caused sad devastation. I hope Adam did his best to "tidy it up a bit," before Eve made her appearance.

If Adam named all the animals, to have brought them all before him would have required days, so several days must have elapsed between the creation of the man and the woman, unless it was all accomplished in such an *extra* miraculous manner, that it took no time at all.

It is curious that Adam and Eve should have been allowed to eat in Paradise—for to eat implies them human; they must have had mouths to eat with, stomachs to digest with, lungs to breathe with, hearts to circulate the blood with, blood-vessels, nerves, muscles, in short, bodies like our own. This one touch of the *real* blows away the thin bubble of *fancy*. Eating implies the necessity for nourishment; this necessity implies waste or decay.

Decay and reproduction is the law of our nature, and makes us in harmony with the world in time, and all our bodily organs work to this end; and our bodily organs which work this constant decay and reproduction, in time wear out and end in death. As time itself is mortal, so is man mortal. Adam and Eve living like ourselves in time, and being of the race of man—subject to the same constitutional laws—were mortal. By eating the fruit of a tree, or by any bodily or even mental act, they could never have made themselves immortal, or not subject to death. To have eaten of the tree of life, and lived for ever, would have been the greatest misfortune could have happened to us—tied us to earth for ever, and to such a life of inanity as the one represented in Eden! If I was obliged to put on such a burden in time, I would much rather live outside the garden than inside, where there was some *real work* to be done—something in myself and the world to subdue and conquer—something to look forward to and pro-gress in—something that was firm and sure, to grasp hold of; in a word, not fancy but reality.

I have had great difficulty in writing this chapter; for I found I had nothing to take hold of. It is only when we come to the " Curses " that we feel we begin to touch on the real and the natural. I proceed to investigate how far, as they *are* real and true to nature—how far they are curses: and I would look at them in the manner I conceive to be the only way to elicit truth—by interpreting them either wholly literally or wholly spiritually; not a mixture of literal and spiritual.

G

CHAPTER IX.

THE CAUSE OF THE CURSES.

BEFORE the fall, man, it is said, had not eaten of the fruit of the tree of knowledge of good and evil; and on the day they ate thereof, they were surely to die.

This must either have been a bodily eating or a spiritual eating.

Supposing it the former, how could it injure the soul? If it was a sour and indigestible apple, it would, in all probability, have given them both a stomach-ache, and so brought the natural punishment for their disobedience. Had it been a poisonous fruit, they would both have died; and there would have been an end of them. Had it only been a slow poison, that could not have affected the blood of all the race of mankind afterwards; the tendency of disease is gradually to work itself out of the constitution in the course of generations.

There was, then, nothing in a bodily eating of a visible fruit, to cause bodily death on the human race; death is and was inseparable from the nature of man, not the product of a single sin, either mental or bodily, but the product of an unalterable law working in the world and in man.

Supposing even it caused bodily death on all mankind, which it could not, this would not have touched the soul. Christ's words, when he said "Not that which enters into a man can defile the man," are a complete refutation of this. Considering the crime spiritually—and the fall caused not by the simple eating, but by the disobedience—it is not according to the justice or mercy of God to kill the soul for its first offence. He who said, "Forgive thy brother man his offences until seventy times seven," would not punish his children for ever, or even to the end of time, for one and the first offence. Undoubtedly, every time we sin, we injure and cause disease to our soul, and the effect of the sin punishes us; but the soul is immortal and cannot die—so one sin could not cause spiritual death; neither mental death, for, by receiving knowledge, instead of sinking we rose. Neither did spiritual eating cause bodily death, though by a long and continued course of vice, we may cut short the natural span of our life.

Neither did we lose the image of God in our souls; for that, in Goodness, Truth, and Love, is still with us.

What, then, did we lose?

Do you answer, our Innocence?

You must first define what Innocence is. If it is the innocence of a child, or the innocence represented in Eden—of not knowing evil—it is then, ignorance. But see, now, what if from the innocence of ignorance, we have to ascend up to the innocence of perfect knowledge; must we not, on the way, pass through the knowledge of sin?

The innocence of ignorance is passive, stationary—does not grow; but the motto of world visible and invisible is, "progress"—upward and onward, to perfect knowledge and perfect light! Sin and death are not caused by our desire for light and knowledge; but sin, standing in the path of knowledge, and death, inseparable from our imperfect bodily state.

A knowledge of sin, necessary to our knowledge of the truth.

Death, necessary to our entering immortality.

Without both, we can attain neither.

It is said there must have been a fall, because there must have been a first sin. True; but does a child's first sin completely alter its internal nature and outward circumstances? Does any earthly parent, after a child's first disobedience, curse that child in wrath—discard him from his affections, and make him an outcast in the world? What should we think of such a barbarous and arbitrary parent? All men would cry, "Shame upon him!" And why think that God, because perfect, would act thus cruelly and unjustly?

CHAPTER X.

THE CURSES.

" Now the serpent was more subtle than any beast of the field which the Lord God had made." And he said to the woman, " Yea, hath God said, ' Ye shall not eat of every tree of the garden !' Ye shall not surely die, for God doth know that in the day ye eat thereof then shall your eyes be opened, and ye shall be as gods, knowing good from evil."

They ate the forbidden fruit, and it would appear the serpent had spoken the truth, for they did not die, either bodily, mentally, or spiritually.

The curse pronounced on the serpent was, " Because thou hast done this thou art cursed above all cattle, and above every beast of the field ; upon thy belly shalt thou go, and dust shalt thou eat all the days of thy life ; and I will put enmity between thee and the woman, and between thy seed and her seed, it shall bruise thy head, and thou shalt bruise his heel."

The question that first presents itself is, was this serpent the devil or a real serpent, or did the devil take the form of a serpent, or get into a serpent ?"

In the interpretation of these words there has

been such an inextricable confusion of the literal and the spiritual, it is almost impossible to separate them, and see either clearly. We are sufficiently enlightened to throw aside the notion that the tempter was really a " beast of the field," though it is twice distinctly called so, we spiritualize the words to make them apply to the devil.

If it was really the devil, why was not the curse levelled at him ? but no punishment is mentioned with reference to him. It seems rather unfair to serpents generally, that they should have to bear the penalty of the curse, because the devil borrowed their form, or got into one of them. I suppose they could not help it. The first part of the curse was that they should for ever after progress in what was considered a very uncomfortable and derogatory manner, and always eat dust.

The latter part of the curse is such utter nonsense it is difficult to comprehend it, either literally or metaphorically. Literally I can only understand, that whenever men had an opportunity they would knock a serpent on the head, and, if a serpent could, he would return the compliment, by biting their heels, which really *is* literally fulfilled, though why we are allowed to vent our spite on serpents, because the devil tempted us, it is difficult to know.

With regard to their diet : this part of the curse they appear to have evaded, for they certainly do not live on dust, but prefer chickens and rabbits, and, generally, too, manage to get them or some other animal food. It might be worth while to inquire whether, before the fall, the serpents ever progressed in any other way than they do at present, whether they ever walked erect on their tails or ever had legs.

I learn from Professor Owen's "Palœontology," that serpents belong to the class, *reptilia;* order, *ophidia*—one characteristic of which, being, having no visible legs : some live on worms and insects, others prey on living animals of frequently much greater diameter than their own. The first evidence of these reptiles is in the eocene clay, the lowest stratum of the "Tertiary formation," therefore, before the time of the creation of man. The fossil remains prove them to be of similar structure to those of the present day. "Being endowed with great mobility of the vertebræ, they are enabled, notwithstanding the want of legs, to climb trees, to run with considerable speed on the ground, and to swim rapidly in rivers or lakes," *vide* Knight's "Cyclopædia of Natural History." As thus provided with organs sufficient for the support and protection of its natural life, as "a beast of the field," the appendage of legs would have been quite superfluous.

Applying the curse to the being of evil, Satan, it is impossible for us to know how the "devil walks," either literally or spiritually. St. Paul speaks of him as walking about as a roaring lion; but I do not see how this assists us in comprehending his spiritual mode of progression.

As to his being metaphorically degraded and "eating dirt," if we are to believe churchmen, he greatly extended his power and dominion by the fall; he made himself thereby "The Prince of the World," and the most "delicate pickings" of the world belong to him. There is profane music, and profane pictures, and profane dancing, and profane poetry; he has the lion's share of it all: besides, the greater part of wisdom and learning. I really cannot see that he has anything to complain of in the treatment he receives. Substantially he gets, we will say, two-thirds of the world; with the addition of only a few hard names, which, probably, he does not much care about.

It is very likely, if there is such a person as the devil, he does us all the mischief he can; but how in any way we can injure him, or "bruise his head," I cannot imagine; but, perhaps, this is the reason: because we cannot get at the devil, we are allowed to ill-treat serpents.

Of course, it is said that Christ was the seed of the woman that should bruise the serpent's head. I do not know that I could point out a better illustration of an enigmatical oracular prophecy, interpreted after the manner alluded to in a former chapter.

What real meaning is it possible to extract from these words, or rather, what *imaginary* meaning may we *not* draw from them ?—

" It shall bruise THY head, and THOU shalt bruise HIS heel."

Looking at the subsequent interpretation, based upon a supposed coincidence, what shall we gain ? Christ said, " Hell was *prepared* for the devil and his angels," they were to be punished, because they *had* disobeyed God, not because one of them tempted Eve ; and he also said, men who disobeyed God would likewise be punished.

Whether man sinned or not, devils would have been punished.

Whether Christ came into the world or not, devils would have been punished.

Neither the supposed fall of man, nor the coming of Christ have anything to do with the punishment of devils : they are punished for sins thought to be committed before the creation of man ; and we might imagine their being allowed to roam at large over God's creation, the Earth, and wreak their vengeance on his creatures, might be some slight mitigation of their punishment; nor does it appear that if we go to the place prepared for the devil and his angels, that we are likely to be able to do them any injury.

The curse to the woman is, " I will greatly *multiply* thy sorrow *and* thy conception."

If, then, sorrow was only added to or multiplied, there must have been some sorrow before, or did the just God only apportion a small quantity of sorrow to the woman in Eden, just to keep her in order?

The latter part of this curse I shall investigate in another chapter.

With regard to Adam's curse. If men were sent into the world to subdue the earth, as affirmed in the first chapter, they would have to work and labor to do so; they could not have been sent to subdue what was subdued already. You would say a man talked nonsense if he said he had succeeded in subduing a lamb, or any other meek, subservient animal, who could not possibly offer any opposition.

This part of the curse, "In the sweat of thy face shalt thou eat bread," is completely avoided by the possession of a little gold: as the sacred(?) writer observes, "gold is good"—perhaps, as a sort of hint, that if we only looked sharp and got some of it, a great part of the curse might be evaded.

Next, the ground was cursed.

In this supplementary creation of weeds, briars, and thorns, we make God the creator of what was considered something evil, bad, and noxious. In the 1st chapter everything was "very good," as all God's works *must be ;* but here He called into being that which was not good.

What means the assertion that "God had not

caused it to rain upon the earth ;" when it is proved,
that as soon as there was a sun above and water
below there must have been rain?

Or how shall we believe there were no weeds till
after the fall?

In the Palæozoic period, when Hugh Miller
describes the earth as a perfect hot-bed of rank vegetation: in this luxuriant and tangled mass of growth,
were there no weeds, think you?—no thorns, no
thistles, till after God had cursed the ground He
had previously blessed?

In the first place, we have to define what a weed is.

What is useless, or a weed, to us, may not be so to
an animal (donkeys, for instance, are supposed to be
fond of thistles); and if not of use to an animal, it
may be so to an insect: in all probability, there is
no plant quite useless.

We may, on the other hand, call any plant a weed
that springs up where it is not wanted. A tuft of
wheat is a weed in a garden flower bed, and flowers
are weeds amongst a crop of corn. A weed may,
then, be considered, as any plant growing out of
its proper and alloted spot of ground. It would
appear, then, that in the garden of Eden—however
different the outside world—the vegetation was not
affected by the natural laws governing earth, air,
moisture, heat and light; but the Lord God acted as
a gardener, and planted it with plants, wherever a

plant was to grow; and Adam had nothing to do but to trim these plants, as no labor could be required to keep them free from weeds. Also, a miracle would have been requisite in order to prevent the wind from carrying seeds of weeds either over from the outer world, or even from one spot to another in the garden itself. If so, the air would have been stagnant and not fit to breathe.

The plant, of all others most useless, either to man, or, as far as we know, to animals, and also one most difficult to eradicate, is the fern; no animals care to eat it, and to our knowledge, no insect lives on it; but traces of fern in the Carboniferous rocks are more numerous than any other; and not only this, but Hugh Miller mentions poisonous and noxious plants as existing in the Palæozoic period. The existence of weeds, therefore, before even the creation of man, is proved; and if not in Eden, they must have been kept out by a miracle.

Professor Owen says, " This science (Geology) has shown that from the inconceivably remote period of the deposition of the Cambrian rocks, the earth has been vivified by the sun's light and heat, and has been fertilized by *refreshing showers*, and washed by tidal waves; that the ocean not only moved in orderly oscillation, regulated as now by sun and moon, but was rippled and agitated by winds and storms; that the atmosphere, besides these movements, was healthily influenced by clouds and vapours, rising, condensing, and falling, in ceaseless circulation. With these conditions of life palœontology demonstrates that life has been enjoyed during the same countless thousands of years, and that with life, from the beginning, there has been death."

If man, then, from the first creation, was not mortal, he was not in harmony with the world around him or even with his own body.

The idea of man immortal, and nature mortal, puts me in mind of a note of my harmonium, which, owing to the damp, when once struck, persists in continuing to sound for an indefinite period after the hand has been removed, and while my fingers play different notes, chords, keys, it goes on dinning, producing discord enough to drive any one wild. Any one who takes up in his hand a bit of coal, with a fern impression on it, holds, in it, a most convincing proof that before the fall there was death in the world, and also weeds.

CHAPTER XI.

CHRIST *OR* ST. PAUL.

IN the 1st of Genesis it is written : "And God said let us make *man* (not *a* man, but the race of man) in our image, after our likeness, and let *them* have dominion over the fish of the sea, and over the fowl of the air, and over the cattle, and over all the earth, and over every creeping thing that creepeth upon the earth. So God created *man* in his own image, in the image of God created he him (the race of *man*) male and female created he *them*. And God blessed *them*, and God said unto *them* : Be fruitful and multiply, and replenish the earth, and subdue it, and have dominion over the fish of the sea, and over the fowl of the air, and over every living thing that moveth upon the earth."

There is not a sentence in either of these three verses that does not apply equally to male and female, neither could a command, or a permission, or a blessing be pronounced on *them*, if both had not been created.

In the 5th chapter of Genesis, 2nd verse, it is written : "Male and female created he *them*, and blessed *them*, and called *their* name Adam (from *Adamah*, 'the Earth') in the day when *they* were created."*

Adam, then, was not the name of *a* man only, but the name of the race of mankind.

In the 2nd chapter of Genesis it is written: "And the Lord God planted a garden *eastward in* Eden."

It would appear by this that the so-called Paradise was not Eden, but only a small portion of it—a garden in a place or country called Eden.

Cain, after he had killed his brother, went into the land of Nod, " on the *east* of Eden." †

Was this on the *east* of the country of Eden, or the garden, at the *east* end of which was placed " Cherubims, and a flaming sword, which turned every way to keep the way of the tree of life ? "

What has become of the garden in Eden, and the cherubims, and the flaming sword, and the tree of life ?

---

* *Pyrrha* (the Eve of the Greeks) was nothing but a name of "the red earth."—*Max Müller.*

+ " *Arabia*, a Greek word formed on a Hebrew one ; whose meaning may have the idea of darkness for its basis, and so set forth Arabia as the unknown land ; a character which it still, to a great extent, retains."

" *Arabia* is a name which, in a wide sense, was unknown to the Hebrews. This country, to speak of it in a loose way, they termed 'the East'—'the land towards the East'; and its inhabitants, ' the sons,' or ' natives of the East.' "—*People's Dictionary of the Bible.*

They all look uncommonly like Joe Smith's gold plates and triangular spectacles!

In the garden God put "*the man* whom he had made." In the 1st chapter the expression THE MAN or A man is NEVER used, but only *man*.

Whether this second chapter is written with regard to time or not, it is evident, that all the animals were brought to Adam to be named before the appearance of Eve, it would seem also, that Adam was created before the animals, according to the letter of the text, which is a contradiction to the 1st chapter; but this difficulty is got over by affirming that no chronological order of events is attempted in the 2nd chapter.

This excuse cannot be admitted in the point to which I allude, the supposed formation of language by Adam, because all cattle, and every beast of the field, and fowl of the air, were brought to him for the double purpose of being named, and being shown to Adam, to see if from amongst them he could (or God could) find a help-meet for him.

Besides the time that this would have required, *naturally*, there are also one or two other questions to be answered on the subject.

To show how important is this first beginning of language, I quote from Max Müller's "Science of Language." It will be seen that the Professor is a firm believer in the biblical account of its origin.

" If you consider that, whatever view we take of the origin and dispersion of language, nothing has ever been added to the substance of language, no new root or radical has ever been invented by later generations. If you bear in mind that in one sense, and in a very just sense, we may be said to handle the very words which issued from the mouth of the Son of God, when he gave names to all cattle, and to the fowls of the air, and to every beast of the field."

If no new root has been added since Adam (who I suppose meant the Son of God) * first spoke, how did the fishes get names? or if Adam named them also, how came they into the Garden of Eden?

The question is so obvious as to be almost ridiculous. Nevertheless it requires a more conclusive answer than " somehow." Also, this man being the " Son of God," his superior intelligence giving him by a look an insight into the habits and dispositions of all the animals, would have known that God was only mocking or insulting him by offering him a beast or a fowl for a " help-meet."

Though in the 1st chapter God had blessed mankind and pronounced them good, and all nature

---

* On a second reading it appears possible that Max Müller may mean by the " Son of God" the man Jesus—" the Word" alluded to by St. John in the beginning of his gospel. But till "the Word" was made flesh, it could not have the fleshly organs of speech, or be heard by fleshly ears.

H

good, that is, perfect and sufficient, and in harmony one with the other, in the 2nd chapter he found something not good, for man was alone and had no companion.

It would seem that the Creator perfectly understood the making of animals, and made them male and female together and at the same time; but in the creation of man there was certainly an oversight, and when the work of creation was ended a man stood alone.

To repair this error there appeared to be one of two ways. First, to look among the brute creation for a mate or companion suitable for him—none was found, but had Adam chosen one, some animal would have been in the same predicament as Adam was; the man, or the Son of God, would have taken the animal's mate, and the animal would have been alone, and without mate, or companion. So, I say the looking among the animals would have been a farce and mockery. This method not succeeding, the other plan was to cause a miraculous sleep to fall on Adam, during which he was deprived of one of his ribs, and therewith a woman was formed. If Adam was at first created good and perfect, this abduction of one of his bones, made him imperfect. When Adam saw the woman he said, " This is now bone of my bone, and flesh of my flesh : she shall be called woman, because she was taken out of man. Therefore shall a man leave his father and mother, and shall cleave unto his wife, and they shall be one flesh."

This sentence could hardly have been spoken by Adam, who knew no father or mother, but was, probably, inserted by the writer; the words " They shall be one flesh," spiritually or metaphorically alluding to the inseparable connection of man and wife, and the very literal story (of the first wife being made out of the first man's bone) added to verify the *words*.

It has been suggested to me that the reason why the man was first alone, and the animals offered him to choose from, was the one indicated by Milton. That not till Adam felt in his own mind it was not good for him to be alone, and also, not until he was perfectly convinced that no animal companionship was sufficient and proper for him; in fact, till the want was suggested or forced upon him by his own feelings, the gift was withheld.

I would answer by a counter proposition.

We may take it for granted that God, in the creation of mankind desired the happiness of the race he had made—the happiness of the female half as well as the male half; some, perhaps, may be inclined to doubt this, nevertheless, I will assume that such an intention only is consistent with God's justice and mercy. If then, it was advisable for Adam, before he was presented with a wife, to be perfectly sure that he wanted a wife, and sure also that no animal would suit him for a wife, why was it not equally desirable that Eve should be allowed time to understand that she wanted a husband, and that none of the animals were suitable for her as a husband? but without giving her freewill or choice she is presented to her husband (such being the Jewish custom of marriage). The very thought of offering her an animal is revolting : but why more so than when applied to Adam, who was supposed to be more nearly allied to God and created more in his image, therefore higher removed from the brutes ?

As far as I can discover, from the marginal references to the Bible, the only time in which Christ alluded to the creation of man, was in reference to this subject.

In the 19th Chapter of St. Matthew, the 4th verse, it is written :—" Have ye not read, that He which *made them at the beginning made them male and female.*" And said, " For *this* cause shall a man leave father and mother, and shall cleave to his wife, and they twain shall be one flesh."

In St. Mark, 10th chapter, 6th verse, it is still more clearly expressed :—" But FROM THE BEGINNING OF THE CREATION God made them male and female : for *this* cause," &c.

These two verses are a confirmation of the first account of Genesis, and a complete contradiction to the second.

But what says St. Paul, overlooking the words of Christ, and taking the second account in Genesis as the right version; he declares, (1st Timothy, 2nd chapter, 13th verse) :—" For Adam was first formed, then Eve."   But if one was made before the other, how could God have made them, male and female, "*from the beginning* of the creation."

In the Epistle to the Corinthians he writes :—" For the man is not of the woman, but the woman of the man.   Neither was the man created for the woman, but the woman for the man."

This all assumes that "*from the beginning* of creation," male and female were *not* created together, but one *after* the other, and one *for* the other.

In the 5th chapter of the Epistle to the Ephesians, it is affirmed, that the relation of the church to Christ is the same as that of wife to husband, being " Members of his body, of his flesh, and of his bones."

Evidently this alludes to Eve being made out of Adam's rib, and so bone of his bone, and flesh of his flesh, and, the same as in the 2nd of Genesis, he declares :—" For *this* cause shall a man leave his father and mother, and shall be joined to his wife, and they twain shall be one flesh."

But Christ says :—Because " God *from the beginning* made them male and female, for *this* cause

they should be one flesh." But St. Paul says:—
Because Eve was one of Adam's bones, "for *this*
cause they should be one flesh."

Which is correct? Both cannot be; for they are
direct contradictions.

At the risk of being tedious I will again repeat
the two arguments :

1ST CHAP. OF GENESIS, *and Christ's words.*

Both show, that the race of man, male and female, were from the beginning created together, and had equal dominion over the rest of creation; and being *thus* jointly created, and joint rulers : for *this cause*, they two should become as one.

2ND CHAP. OF GENESIS, *and St. Paul's words.*

Both show, that not a race was created at the beginning, but only one man alone; after some length of time, one woman was made out of the man, not having equal privileges or dominion, but subject to the man, and being of the bodily substance of the man : for *this cause* they should be as one.

I do not wish those of the one sex, who may read
this, to accept the first argument because it is agreeable to them, or those of the other to reject it because
disagreeable ; but both to investigate for themselves

which is the truth : and it is equally to the advantage and interest of both, truly and fully to learn what is the truth.

The evils produced by adhering to St. Paul's words, and his reasons for them, as set forth in the the 2nd of Genesis, are many. On one hand, causing men and women to look upon each other as natural enemies. Many, particularly at about middle life, most cordially and thoroughly hating and detesting one another; or, on the other hand, preventing a free and healthy action and reaction. The two sexes are not as they should be, mutual helps and mutual checks in every department of life's work ; but one is forced to stand still while the other advances, and one follows the other.

That the relationship between men and women should be more equal, free, and just, and that for their mutual benefit, is beginning to be seen and acknowledged by the most clear thinking men of the day.

NOTE.—I am tempted to depart from my original intention, and to write in this note as a woman. Having listened to a sermon lately preached, upon some silly rubbish of St. Paul's, relative to the moral and religious necessity of women covering their heads while "praying or prophecying," and that women have power on their heads "because of the angels." The clergyman wasting his time in endeavoring to extract sense from words in which no sense could possibly be found, and the congregation having their's wasted in listening to such nonsense.

St. Paul's argument is wonderful logic. "Nature herself teaches if a man have long hair it is a disgrace to him."

What *does* nature teach? I used at one time to think that a short fringe of hair was all nature bestowed on men, but, on inquiry, found somewhat to my astonishment, that if nature was allowed her free course, men's hair would grow just as long as women's.

How, then, does nature teach that for a man to have long hair is a disgrace to him?

Do we mean to say that God giving men long hair was disgraceful, or intended as a disgrace to them? if so, what for? Do men keep their hair close cut because they feel nature gave it them as a disgrace? Did Milton think himself, or do we think him, disgraced for wearing his own natural, long, curling hair?

Because men artificially keep their hair short, St. Paul says nature teaches that it should be short. It might as well be said that because some foolish women compress their waists to within an inch of their lives, "nature herself teaches" that a woman should have a small waist. But even supposing that, naturally, men's hair was short and women's long, I should imagine the lesson nature taught would be, that as women's hair was given as a covering for her head, there was no necessity for an artificial one as well, nature having already provided one. Men have beards given them by nature. Suppose I say, then, "nature herself teaches" that men's chins should be covered; why don't men tie up their chins in bags when they go to church? because praying or prophecying with their chins uncovered dishonoreth their chins, for that is "all as one as if they were shaven," and "nature herself teaches" it is a disgrace to a man to be shaven. For my part, I think it *quite* disgraceful that men don't cover up their chins and upper lips in church, and so do what St. Paul implies, "nature herself teaches"

It is high time such an antiquated piece of absurdity was held up to public ridicule, and not solemnly discussed by a clever clergyman, before a sensible congregation.

If we really want to discover what "nature herself teaches," let the minister take the votes of his congregation, and see how many husbands would object to their wives cooling and relieving their heads by laying aside their ugly tall bonnets, and if the men would honestly ask themselves whether they would feel their dignity in the slightest degree infringed by such a proceeding, or their head-ship in any way questioned thereby. And, if they are not offended, we may be quite sure "the angels" will not consider themselves insulted.

An enlightened congregation ought to be ashamed to continue to consider it a part of religion that women should be forced to give themselves a stupifying headache by remaining in a close bonnet or hat in a hot suffocating church, either for the sake of proclaiming by the covering of the said bonnet or hat, that the man was the head of the woman, or " because of the angels."

I appeal to any one whether it would not be more natural, as well as more beautiful and devotional for all mankind, to bow before God with uncovered heads.

CHAPTER XII.

RIDICULE.

BEFORE I proceed further with my subject I would say a few words respecting the propriety of using ridicule or sarcasm upon subjects spoken of or affirmed in the Bible. I have been advised to strike out those touches of ridicule, which in some of the previous chapters I have applied, for fear I should be thought to be trying to imitate the style of Tom Paine or Voltaire. Upon consideration I have decided not to do so for the following reasons:— Never having read a page of either Tom Paine's or Voltaire's books, or, as far as I can remember, not having even seen a quotation from either, I do not see how I can imitate them. Ridicule and sarcasm, when legitimately used, are powerful weapons; if they are in my hand why should I throw them away, because others may have wrongly applied them?

Ridicule, it is allowed, is legitimately used against folly and nonsense; I do not think I have directed it against anything in itself good or sacred.

I have never made any straining attempt to be, or be thought "witty"; anything I have said, showing the ridiculous, has arisen naturally with the subject.

I have merely put a few plain every-day facts in juxtaposition with a monstrous, impossible, nonsensical legend—the visible incongruity of the two has produced the ridiculous.

If the laugh arose spontaneously I did not check or suppress it. If any one else is induced to laugh so much the better.

Some people seem to think that when one begins to talk of religion the orthodox pulpit style ought to be assumed, and every smile banished from the countenance. I am told by many that my style is too light for the subject. I do not see why I should try to make it heavy, or why I am expected to put on a solemn air and a forced gravity, when really I feel exceedingly merry and joyful. My religion is not a Sunday religion only, that is obliged to be dressed in its best clothes, and looking remarkably stiff in them. I would rather feel that I am dressed in my ordinary everyday garments, in which I can converse easily and naturally on the subject I love best, and imagine I am talking to the reader or writing to a friend.

Ridicule is a fine test of truth—no amount of ridicule or sarcasm can throw discredit, or even raise a smile against Truth, Love, and Joy.

Though men and women, when they are as it is called, "in love," or when foolishly excited by joy or pleasure, may act in a ridiculous manner, and cause *themselves* to be laughed at, there is no laugh at the God-like attribute of Love or Joy, and as to Truth, no effort could make that appear ridiculous.

The man who always acts and thinks and speaks the truth, is always dignified, and, in a measure, even sublime; he need never fear what society he enters, or what subject he handles, Truth shall make it become good and pure in his hands.

Discussions and arguments on the Bible, it is said, ought to be carried on in seriousness and without levity from reverence to its great age, but those who urge this plea do not own the Bible to have the weakness and feebleness of old age: they say it is as strong in youthful vigor as in the beginning, and will remain so to the end of time. The Church says, " have respect to the aged ; do not bind the old man's hands." Then, immediately you turn away it rises with the strength of a giant and seeks to bind you again in a closer bondage.

Where a subject admitted of argument I believe I have, and shall, I hope, continue to treat it with the utmost seriousness, and, at the same time, without fear.

But on a subject like the Garden of Eden it is impossible to find anything to build an argument upon. I had only to place the natural and unnatural, the real and imaginary, side by side, and let the truth work its own work.

Religion is to most people a solemn and awful infliction, and a sort of heavy responsibility they would gladly be rid of, if they only knew how to do it with safety. There is no reason why to *any one* religion should not be the most beautiful, the most glorious, the most joyful part of their whole lives.

CHAPTER XIII.

THE RACE OF MANKIND.

THE origin of species and the origin of the human race, now occupies the attention of scientific men, both naturalists and philologists. It would be absurd for me to attempt to look at the subject at the head of this chapter, in its scientific aspect. I regard it merely as a church doctrine ; and what little my common sense or reason will allow me to glean from the Bible, or any works on the subject that are within my reach, I select and join together, either to prove or disprove the doctrine. It is not just, however, to say, " prove or disprove," because I have now no intention of doing the former, neither the latter, or trying to disprove what I conceive to be an error.

I begin with the Bible, and see how far it bears out its first assertion : that all mankind are descended from Adam and Eve.

Cain, according to the 4th chapter of Genesis, was the first man born. No daughters are mentioned as having been born to Adam and Eve—(it is no convincing proof that there were none born, because the birth of daughters was not recorded by the Jewish historians unless some particular circumstance was connected with their history; but we might imagine that the natural birth of the first woman would have been a sufficiently remarkable event to cause it to be noted). "And Cain went out from the presence of the Lord, and dwelt in the land of Nod, on the east of Eden; and Cain knew his wife." This wife, if all men were descended from one pair, must have been Cain's own sister. Or, if she was a native of the land of Nod, the descendant of another pair.

Cain had a son named Enoch, then "he builded a city." Either Cain alone, or he and his wife and infant son, built a city! Enoch also must have married one of Cain's daughters, his own sister, or one of Adam's daughters, his own aunt.

"Unto Enoch was born Irad, and Irad begat Mehujael, and Mehujael begat Methusael, and Methusael begat Lamech." As before, all these men must have taken to wife their near blood relations.

These atrocious and criminal unions, would, as all physiologists know, have ultimately produced degeneracy, disease, and finally, extinction.

The 5th chapter contradicts the 4th. In that Seth is mentioned as the first child of Adam—there is no record of Abel; Seth begat Enos (but another name for Enoch), Enos begat Cainan (the same as Cain, the termination *an* added), Cainan begat Mahaleel (4th chapter, Mahujael), Mahaleel begat Jarad (4th chapter, Irad).

Then another confusion appears : Enoch again makes his entrance into the world as the son of Irad, and to Enoch is born Methuselah (4th chapter, Methusael), and to Methuselah is born Lamech.

Here are two contradictory genealogies—one from Seth to Lamech, the other from Cain to Lamech; in one Cainan (or Cain) is a descendant of Seth, in the other Cain is born before Seth.

With but a very slight alteration, the names in both genealogies are the same, and follow in the same rotation.

The beginning of the 6th chapter is written :— " The Sons of God saw the daughters of men that they were fair." By the " Sons of God," doubtless are meant the descendants of Adam and Eve, the favored of God, from whom the Jews owned their descent. " The daughters of men" were evidently of another origin, and considered by the " Sons of God" an inferior race.

Such an arrogation of superiority finds its parallel in every nation. To the Greeks, every other nation but their own was " Barbarian ;" to the more modern Jews, all other nations " Gentiles ;" to the Mahomedans, all other people are " Giaours," or " Kaffirs." Every one considers his own religion the true one, every ancient nation considered their's the primitive and most ancient nation in the world, and their language the one first spoken by man ; so there is nothing at all singular in the Jews considering their ancestors "the Sons of God," and the progenitors of every other nation the sons of men : but that very touch of arrogance proves the existence of another race of a separate origin, as much as the assumption of a true religion proves the existence of others supposed to be false.

We must now go back to the expulsion of Adam and Eve from Paradise.

This unfortunate couple after having been coddled up in the miraculous Garden of Eden, were turned out naked and defenceless into the outside world of reality ; and now, when they really had to do battle and subdue the earth, and labor for their daily bread, God took from them (or him) their (or his) superhuman intelligence, and left them so pitiably ignorant that they could not make a covering for themselves. Had they really been thus cast alone into the world, all they could have done would have been to lay themselves down like the poor babes in the wood, and died in the "forest primeval."

A kind Providence helped them, it will be said. Doubtless ; but how ?

Did he come bodily into the world, and become a planter of gardens, and a builder of houses, and a maker of coats ? We do not sufficiently remember that a spirit has not flesh and bones as we have ; that material work requires material weapons—that

I

to make coats from animal's skins, requires hands; and to strip the skin from the animal, requires not only hands, but some sort of weapon, if only a sharp stone, or a stone hatchet. What right have we to call for miraculous power for such trivial work?

We suppose God rested from all his work on the seventh day, but if he had to supply all Adam and Eve's daily wants, his work was only begun!.

Is this God-like work?

Suppose God had sent a few angels to assist these poor creatures, he must have temporarily given them bodies—something with eyes and mouth, hands and feet could alone have been any service to them! But if man was made for the earth, and to remain on the earth, why not have made them together as a race to assist one another?

The same argument applied equally to those animals, like ourselves, of gregarious habits, whose very existence almost depends upon mutual assistance; shall we imagine that God sent a few angelic animals to help them, when a few of their own kind, to whom the work and the life was suitable and intended, would have done as well? And why not, for the same reason, make many men as well as many animals?

It required no greater power to make twenty couples or three hundred couples, from the earth, than to make one; and then all necessity for miraculous interference would have been avoided.

But Cain was a tiller of the ground, and a builder of a city : he must have been a wonderful man, to plough the earth and to build a city without tools! Before he could have cultivated the earth in the rudest manner, he must have cleared his spot of ground from the weeds, and briars, and thorns, and then, to till the ground, must have required some implements, however rude : and as to how he was to build a city single-handed, without tools, is rather more astonishing; or does it mean, when it is said, " Cain builded a city," he only constructed a hut or wigwam for himself and his wife : if they were the sole inhabitants of the land of Nod, that was all they required; though it must be owned it is somewhat an exaggeration to call this building a city !

No one can help feeling, on reading the 4th chapter of Genesis, that from the 1st verse, when the one solitary pair are mentioned, to the latter part, a semicivilized nation is spoken of. In the time of Jabal (fourth generation from Adam), tents were made, and tent-making involves many other arts in preparing the materials for tents. But, not reckoning Adam with them, there were only seven men in that part of the world : viz., Cain, Enoch, Irad, Mehujael, Methusael, Lamech, and Jabal.

Another son of Lamech constructed a harp and an organ; and a third (Tubal Cain) was " an instructor of every artificer in brass and iron."

So, according to this, in the fourth generation from the creation of the first pair, the use and preparation of metals was discovered—metal tools constructed and musical instruments invented.

How does this agree with the discoveries of science ? I write from Sir C. Lyell's " Antiquity of Man " :—

Many eminent antiquaries and naturalists " Have succeeded in establishing a chronological succession of periods, which they have called the ages of stone, of bronze, and of iron, named from the materials which have, each in their turn, served for the fabrication of implements."

Heaps, or accumulations, where stone instruments are found, are called by the Danes Kjökken-mödding (or " kitchen-refuse-heaps ")—" Scattered all through them are flint knives, hatchets, and other instruments of stone, horn, wood, and bone, with fragments of coarse pottery, mixed with charcoal and cinders ; but never any implements of bronze, still less of iron. The stone hatchets and knives had been sharpened by rubbing ; and in this respect are one degree less rude than those of an older date, associated in France with the bones of extinct mammalia. .   .   . No traces of grain of any sort have hitherto been discovered, nor any indication that the ancient people had any knowledge of agriculture. .   .   . What may be the antiquity of the earliest human remains preserved in the Danish peat cannot be *estimated in centuries*, with any approach to accuracy. In the first place, in going back to the bronze age, we already find ourselves beyond the reach of history or even tradition. . . . The next stage of improvement, or that manifested by the substitution of iron for bronze, indicates another stride in the progress of the arts. Iron never presents itself, except in meteorites, in a natural state, so that to recognize its ores, and then separate the metal from its matrix, demands no small exercise of the powers of observation and invention."

It matters not to my subject whether Sir C. Lyell has proved the antiquity of the human race to be much greater than that recorded in the Bible. But it is quite sufficient to prove that if Adam was the first man upon the earth, the fifth man from him could not possibly have discovered the use of the metals, brass and iron; or, had Tubal Cain been a worker of metals, particularly iron, he must have lived in an age when the world was thickly peopled, and very far removed from the original inhabitants of the earth. If a churchman, a believer in the inspiration of the Bible was asked, "Do you believe Adam was really the name of the first man in the world?" he would, doubtless, answer, "Certainly I do." But that is not possible, for *Adam* is a Hebrew word, and Hebrew is proved not to be the most ancient language. The Hebraic is the second branch of the Semitic family of languages ; and this Semitic family is but one of three that have yet to be traced to their source.

"What prevented, however, for a long time the progress of the science of language, was the idea that Hebrew was the primitive language of mankind, and that, therefore, all language must be derived from Hebrew. The fathers of the church never expressed any doubt on this point. . . . . . . After much battling between theologians, and men of science, when books after books had been written to show how Greek and Latin and all other languages were derived from Hebrew, and when not one single system proved satisfactory, people asked at last, why then *should* all languages be derived from Hebrew?" —*Max Müller*.

The theologians were defeated, the scientific men conquered. But the most curious thing I observe is, after the theologians have been worsted, they turn round and smile, and rub their hands, and say, "oh, it's not the slightest consequence, this does not in the smallest degree interfere with the theory of inspiration." What, but a short time before, they have tried with might and main to put down as heresy, when they find it will not be put down, they quietly appropriate it to their own side, and say, "see how wonderfully science bears out inspiration!"

and the majority of the laymen have hitherto suffered themselves to be bound hand and foot till the next great scientific fact again bursts the fetters. The discovery that Hebrew is not the oldest language, involves the acknowledgement that God having called the first man's name *Adam*, is false. (I must repeat again, for fear of misconstruction, that I mean, man spoke falsely in the name of God.) It is mere shuffling and prevarication to say, as in this or other palpable errors, that it is a proof of God's condescension, for Him to speak to us in language we can understand. God would never condescend to speak falsely for such a purpose, if he speaks to our minds, he speaks the truth, for what is not the truth misleads, and has misled, which true inspiration never could do.

Look at the books on books wasted to prove an error. Read this paragraph from Max Müller's " Science of Language :"

" It is astonishing what an amount of real learning and ingenuity was wasted on this question during the seventeenth and eighteenth centuries. It finds, perhaps, but one parallel in the laborious calculations and constructions of early astronomers, who had to account for the movements of the heavenly bodies, always taking it for granted that the earth must be the fixed centre of our planetary system. But although we know now, that the labors of such scholars as Thomassin were, and could not be otherwise than fruitless, it would be a most discouraging view to take of the progress of the human race, were we to look upon the exertions of eminent men in former ages, though they may have been in a wrong direction, as mere vanity and vexation of spirit. We must not forget that the very fact of the failure of such men contributed powerfully to a general conviction that there must be something wrong in the problem, and thereby solved it."

What is to blame for this waste of life and energy in a wrong direction, but belief in these words of the Bible? And what hindered the progress of scientific truth but the theory of inspiration?

If men would but open their eyes, they might see from this fact, of giving the first man a Hebrew name, that the story is nothing but a Jewish legend.

According to 2nd chapter of Genesis, Adam is the first inventor of language; but the name *Adam* is given by God to the man before the naming of the beasts and fowls, therefore we are to imagine that *Adam* was the first word spoken; and as that word was spoken by God, it ought to be a root, not a derivative—but taking the general acceptation of the word, it is derived from *Adamah*, "the ground;" so the word *Adamah* is older than the name *Adam*: neither is this word a root, but a branch, and derived from many sources. I should like very much to be able to trace the word philologically to its original root, but am not able. I learn from a Hebrew scholar, that *ad* is "witness," "a memorial," or "time;" but neither of these express primitive roots. *Adam* also means "red"—either "red earth," or, symbolically, "red blood," which the Jews thought to be the life.

"In whatever sense we take the word *Adam*," adds my informant, "it means the original of all substance."

Adam could not have been the "original of all substance;" but the Jews might have considered the ground to be so. In the oldest known family of languages (the Aryan), the root from whence the earth is named is *ar.* "A more primitive formation of the root *ar* seems to be the Greek, *era,* 'earth;' the Sanskrit, *irâ;* the old High German, *ëro;* the Gaelic, *ire iriouu.* It means, originally, 'the ploughed land,' afterwards 'earth' in general. Even the word *earth,* the *airtha* (the Anglo-Saxon, *oithe),* must have been taken originally in the same sense of 'ploughed' or 'cultivated land.'"—*Max Müller.* It is evident, then, that in the Aryan language, at least, the earth could not have been named, till it had been ploughed or cultivated.

What originated the name or root in Semitic I am not able to trace.

It is taken as a great proof of the authenticity of the Bible, that philologists lean to the idea that the different families of language may, in the end, be traced to one source ; but even if they should, it does not at all follow, because they might prove that, at one time, all the earth was of one speech, that one pair were the originators of that language. Max Müller allows this. I must quote one more passage from his work, with which he terminates his lectures : " If inductive reasoning is worth anything, we are justified in believing, that what has been proved to be true on so large a scale, and in cases where it was least expected, is true with regard to language in general. We require no supernatural interference, nor any conclave of ancient sages, to explain the realities of human speech. All that is formal in language is the result of rational combination—all that is material, the result of mental instinct. The first natural and instinctive utterances, if sifted differently by different clans, would fully account both for the first origin and for the first divergence of human speech. We can understand not only the origin of language, but likewise the necessary breaking up of one language into many ; and we perceive that no amount of variety in the material, or the formal element of speech, is incompatible with the admission of one common source."

Now if we require no supernatural interference,

how could one man be the originator of language? Language is the product of an inward want or necessity, the necessity for communicating thoughts or ideas. Firstly, relating to corporeal wants; secondly, to mental wants; and they must be communicated from one person to another person, one individual alone has no necessity for speech.

But if Adam created the germ of language when alone on the earth, to have had the necessity for speech, he must have either conversed bodily with God, or an angel, or with beasts.

But God is a spirit, has not flesh and blood, nor bodily organs of speech; he speaks to our spirit only, and through our spirit only can we converse with God. Shall we then give animals organs of speech?

If we do, we remove the greatest barrier, perhaps the only one, which divides man (as an animal) from the beasts of the field; and also to account for their subsequent loss of the faculty of speech.

There have been two or three experiments to endeavor to discover the first dawn of language in man.

They have proved the utter impossibility of one man, or even a pair, inventing a word. (The two, indeed, did speak one word, but it is supposed to have been merely the imitation of the bleating of a goat).

But because this experiment failed, it does not at all follow that two or three hundred people together, could not have contrived, by a few words, to communicate their thoughts.   Though the words might be few and meagre, if they were able to take the first step, the proof would be sufficient; for a language, or perhaps even the root, is the growth of centuries. It seems to me that roots or radicals are like the first elementary rules of a science; though apparently simple in themselves, they have taken years to discover, but when found, cannot be departed from, and a magnificent structure is built upon their foundation;—but I must leave this subject, I find I am wandering much beyond my depth.

I have "half a mind" to cut the chapter out, it is so poor and meagre, but if I did, I could not write it any better; and the other half of my mind thinks the quotations I have inserted may serve to add to the conviction of those who, like myself, are unscientific, and who may not care to read the books from whence I have drawn them.

I say nothing of Darwin's theory, as it is yet but a hypothesis, but if we are to accept the development theory, there is no reason why several as well as one pair might not have been developed.   The author of the answers in the *London Review* most "solemnly protests" against the ideas of Messrs. Darwin and Huxley; and politely hands over all such disreputable animal connections to those who claim kindred with them.   Of course! men shan't have gorillas for their ancestors if they don't like it.

CHAPTER XIV.

ANALOGY.

It may be said, that in doubting the truth of the story of the Garden of Eden, I have been fighting against a mere shadow—that no one, even the most orthodox, believes in the story literally, but it is considered, because perfectly unintelligible, to have a profound spiritual significance, and to make it appear consistent, one part is taken typically, and another literally ; for instance, no one hardly thinks it was the real eating of a fruit that caused God's wrath, but the curses that follow this sin, whatever it might be, are taken most literally ; we have bodily death, bodily labor, bodily pain. It might be enough to satisfy any one, that these curses were not God-sent punishments, because the great, the wealthy, the powerful, the wise, (in as far as they *are* curses) do not feel them at all, but they fall entirely on the poor, the weak, the helpless.

No punishment sent by God would fall so unevenly and unjustly.

I am informed by the same Hebrew scholar to whom I before referred, that throughout the Old Testament, the word *Elohim* is plural, and should be translated THE GODS. That *Jehovis*, or *Jehovah*, is but a name for the superior God, as Jupiter was the first of the Greek Gods.

I do not advance this with any certainty, not knowing a word of Hebrew, but I received it from one I believe thoroughly conversant with the language, himself a Hebrew.

The first Commandment of the Lord God (or Jehovah) tacitly admits the supposed existence of other Gods. " Thou shalt have none other Gods but me."

I also was told that in the 2nd chapter of Genesis, when it is said, " and there was not a man to till the ground " it should be, there was no *slave* to till the ground (or none to slave the ground). These interpretations, if incorrect, can be easily refuted.

It is very evident we have received but a very garbled and imperfect translation of the Hebrew Bible, and it has been made, as far as possible, to fit in and coincide with the New Testament.

Should the latter interpretation be correct, it is no excuse for slavery, no more than other parts of the Bible are an excuse for polygamy—both are a disgrace to a christian people—but it proves, from what a very unenlightened, an *un*inspired source, we have derived our religious faith. Christians may say they do not build their faith on the Old Testament, but on the New, but this legend of the Garden of Eden, which is *false* in fact, *false* to nature, *false* in spirit, *false* therefore in every way to truth, has tainted the whole Bible, from the 2nd chapter of Genesis to the last chapter of Revelations.

Taking the legend literally, word for word, as written in the 2nd chapter of Genesis, we cannot fail to see it is utterly impossible and unnatural, therefore, false in fact ; and yet we think to extract a spiritual truth from it. An analogy, to be true, must be built on the foundation of a truth in nature, if the foundation is crooked, the superstructure raised upon it will also be crooked ; I can explain my meaning better by an illustration.

In a paper on " Training of the Clergy " in the *Quarterly Review* of April, 1862, I read the following presumptuous and false assertion :—" Constituted as the Church of England is, with the full possession of all divine truth, that truth composed (if the phrase may be employed) of polarized and seemingly antagonistic doctrines."

Though this sentence is extracted from an old paper, it is still an orthodox church doctrine, and the differences in the belief of its ministers are still accounted for as the polarization or two sidedness of a truth. I therefore take this sentence to analyse, as a church which professes to stand still, having full possession of all divine truth, is not likely to think differently in the year 1864 to what it did in 1862.

There is a metaphor, or analogy, or spiritual meaning, introduced into the foregoing sentence by the word *polarized*, and upon that metaphor the whole of the sentence really hangs or depends. The parenthesis is only a sort of apologetic way of bringing in the words.

The metaphor is drawn from the known property of the magnet or magnetic needle, of polarization, by which one end points to the north, the other to the south; one the positive, the other the negative end.

The conclusion derived from this principle of polarization is, that seemingly antagonistic doctrines, are not really so, but as the needle, or magnet, is one thing, having two sides or ends; so these apparently contradictory doctrines of the Church of England are but as the two sides of one truth. And also, as the church thus possesses both sides, or ends, or faces of the truth, it is in full possession of all truth.

There is the same idea introduced in another page : " It (the church) has, like all truth, two faces, one silver the other gold"—(this, by the way, has nothing to do with the idea of polarization ; silver and gold are two metals merely, of greater or less value, that value depending on greater or less scarcity)—"every part of it has a double polarity. . . . The distinction of High Church and Low Church can never be obliterated, without narrowing conditions which a divine hand has fixed,—without abandoning some portion of the whole body of truth which he has committed to our keeping."

In the middle of this sentence, after " High Church and Low Church," is this parenthesis :— " Oh, that the names could be utterly abolished !" Does the writer mean the names or the things ?

If the latter, he has just proclaimed them part of the whole body of truth, then the things must be good in themselves ; and if good, why quarrel with the names ?

A metaphor, or an analogy, or parable is the clearest and most self-evident way of proving a truth ; but if the metaphor be not a correct metaphor, or the analogy not really drawn from a fact, it is most dangerous, if received without due consideration, and insensibly leads us into error; but, on the other hand, if thoroughly analysed, and found untrue, becomes most clear and self-evident in discovering falsehood.

An analogy is an abstract thought made appreciable to us as far as our senses are capable of seeing it, by being based upon, or compared to a known fact. If the supposed fact is incorrect, or a wrong inference taken from it, the idea is, in all probability, a fallacy. The endeavor to prove the church doctrines all true, by analogy to the loadstone's property

K

of polarization may be proved a fallacy by a few sentences.

Truth is given us to show us our way to God and heaven, and points but one way.

The magnet we use to direct us on our course to another country; and we use the loadstone's known property of polarization to guide us on the way when we have no other means of finding it.

If a mariner wishes to sail north by the positive point, will he reach his destination by taking either the positive or the negative point; or will any point, taken indifferently between north and south, lead him right?

If a man desires to gain heaven by following the truth, will he gain it by following indifferently one theory or another?

There is truth in the illustration derived from polarization as far as this: that both ends point truly to two opposite poles :—Positive, north; Negative, south. But to say, whether you sail north or south, you are travelling to the same pole, is false ; and it is upon this false drawing of the metaphor, a supposed true theory is based.

If one ship sails north to the north pole, and another, south to the south pole, they certainly cannot be said to be sailing the same way. If High and Low Church, are as the north and the south poles, and proceed by opposite, or polarized, doctrines, they are certainly not likely to meet at the same destination. The two poles are—

NORTH.	SOUTH.
Positive.	*Negative.*
Good.	Bad.
Truth.	Falsehood.
Love.	Hate.
Trust.	Fear.
Joy.	Sadness.

Whichever way you turn the needle, these two points can never meet, or direct the same way.

Produce the lines mathematically, and they diverge more and more ; they never join.

To say God loves all His creatures, is a universal affirmative ; and is true.

To say God hated Esau, is a particular negative ; and is, therefore, and must be, false.

This is not the two ends of one truth, but one truth and one falsehood ; they can never join.

St. Paul's argument, therefore, based on this falsehood, must also be false.

But the idea of the churchman is, that at some time the two polarized ends of truth, shall, in some way, be mixed and jumbled up into one " harmonious whole." God forbid ! There would be no harmony in it, but discord, confusion, and destruction. In the centre the magnet loses all power of attraction, or polarization, therefore points nowhere.

If the two ends of the needles were doubled up and met in the middle, it might be made to point either up into the sky or down into the deep; neither of which can be looked upon as the proper and ulti-mate course of ships. And if the two poles of the church are made to meet and join in the middle, either all power of direction is lost, or we may be led up into the sky—and that is not heaven, but the clouds of imagination, fancy, and dreams—or down to the earth.

Suppose a vessel trying to reach the north pole sails either east or west, it may sail round the earth for ever, it will never reach it. If the church steers between the poles, it may wander round the earth for ever, and never find truth. We have seen, then, that as the two ends of the pole point differently, and can never both point in the same direction, so must it be with polarized doctrines : and if the two points or the two doctrines are left, and the middle sought, it leads nowhere. But the *power* that guides the needle is not antagonistic in the sense of one end being attracted to, or repulsed from a certain point.

" The force which determines the direction of the needle is neither attractive nor repulsive, but simply directive. If a small magnet be placed on a cork floating in water, it will first oscillate, and then gradually move into a line virtually north and south. But if the surface of the water be quite smooth, the needle will not move either to the north or south."

By analogy, this is directly opposed to dogmatic teaching, which would forcibly lead the mind.

But the power exercised by truth is neither attractive nor repulsive, but simply directive. If the reason is working, moving, alive, the poles of the mind will gradually, after oscillating, gain virtually its true direction. But if the mind be idle, stagnant, dead, the directive power of truth is suspended.

I ask pardon of the reader for dwelling so long on this subject. I do so because sentences of this sort are likely to lead us blindly into error, not only by a false analogy, but by introducing another which may be true, and the mind is led to suppose the two illustrations are connected together, and one being correct, so must the other be also ; as for instance, in this illustration of two metals of different value, color and properties, and which you *can*, in any way, amalgamate, and between the poles of the magnet which can never be united or amalgamated, unless by destroying the very property for which it is of such incalculable value to mankind, there is no connection, though one is implied.

From the loadstone may be drawn a full and

beautiful analogy to truth, and it is like truth also in this particular, wherever you point to a truth, you invariably point to a falsehood as its opposite.

If a person has recounted to him two contradictory reports of some phenomenon in nature, or of a quarrel between two people, he is inclined to think the truth lies somewhere between the two accounts : this may be if they are both somewhere near the truth, but cannot be if they are both directly contrary statements. The reason why we give this sort of judgment is either because we are quite ignorant of the facts, and so have no clue to guide us, or if we have a clue, we are too lazy to make use of it ; it is much easier to say, " I suppose the truth lies somewhere between the two."

If a jury are called upon to pronounce a verdict upon a man, the plaintiff says he is guilty, defendant, not guilty. Shall the jury take the "happy medium," and say he is neither, but something between the two ?

We must remember that in many and conflicting statements regarding one simple fact or proposition, there can be but one true, and every other false, to discover this let the mind *work* for the truth ; one truth a man finds out for himself by mental labor is worth more than twenty given to him without work.

This was the belief of Socrates, " No man can teach another, but he may help him to learn." To borrow the ideas of another was not to learn ; to guide oneself by the arguments of another was blindness. The sophists, who pretended to teach everything, could teach nothing, and their ignorance was manifest in the very pretension. Each man must conquer ·truth for himself, by rigid struggle with himself.

We do not yet know all truth, for we have not yet sufficiently worked for it.

In a sentence I before quoted, it is said, the magnet gradually moves into a line which is *virtually* north and south.

It is not really north and south, but only near it.

All those who know anything of magnetism have read of the unaccountable variations or perturbations of the magnet, of the dip of the needle; in the northern hemisphere the north pole dips, in the southern the south pole.

The intensity of the magnetic force is very unequal: " Lines drawn on a globe through all the points⁻ where the magnetic intensity is the same, are so complicated that it is scarcely possible to convey an idea of them in words."—*Mrs. Somerville's Physical Geography.*

I do not intend to enter on a minute investigation of the subject, indeed it would be as great a trouble to me to write as to the reader to peruse. I only desire to show that from some unknown cause, the magnet does not point true north and south, and this cause is, at present, completely unknown to science.

Besides these invisible influences, there are sometimes local ones, such as iron of a ship, &c.

These unknown agents, are not any inherent fault in the magnetic needle; but our ignorance of the causes which affect it, prevent us perfectly adjusting it, so as to make it free, or clear, from these disturbing influences. So is it with truth; not knowing all the laws respecting it, we have arrived at no perfect standard of truth—we are drawn one way and the other, by some unknown attractions, and we are perplexed, weary, sad, disheartened, and say—what is Truth?—almost as if it were but an *ignis fatuus*, tending more to deceive than to guide. Why is it so? If not but for this reason : that we assume we already comprehend all truth?

Would the sciences of magnetism and electricity ever become perfect sciences, or even advance, if scientific men should take upon themselves to declare they knew all respecting them? It would, therefore, be useless to seek further, and not only useless, but dangerous, because it might possibly tend to upset what they had already gained.

It seems to be now an accepted theory, that truth is advanced by being held back. Mr. Farrer says, " Under the overruling of a beneficent Providence, antagonism is made the law of human progress." The meaning of this sentence appears to be, that antagonism, something in itself evil, and rising up to conquer truth, is overruled by a higher power for good.

I do not see why we cannot draw our analogy from nature in this as in every other thing. I continue with an illustration from the magnet. Though a commotion, or movement, on the face of the water can alone enable the needle to gain its right position, that movement is in no way antagonistic to the magnet; on the contrary, it enables it to fulfil its directing mission—neither is there anything wrong or contrary to natural laws, in the agitation of the water, for the health and vitality of water depends on constant motion; immediately water is still, it stagnates, becomes poisonous, and endangers human life. The purification of water by motion again depends on the atmosphere. But this is not antagonism.

Life, whether of mind or body, depends on motion. Everything must be active, or it dies.

We place bands and fetters round truth, and when it has advanced, and grown strong, it bursts these barriers; and then we think the struggle of truth to effect its escape has *caused* its advance. Were there no bands there would be no antagonism, but only natural action and reaction.

Emerson has a similar expression of polarized truth, that every fact has two sides—that everything "is and is not" at the same time. They may be at the same *time*, yet not in the same sense—but a bodily and spiritual sense.

When Aristotle said, "My book is published and not published;" it involves no contradiction, if understood in two senses—it was published to the world by being written, but mentally, his ideas were published to no mind which could not comprehend them.

After all, such aphorisms are but a sort of sophistical quibbling, and if taken literally, induce error and confusion. Socrates uses the same figure of speech, but he explains his meaning, "Men differ, but men also agree : they differ as to what is fleeting, but agree as to what is eternal. Difference is the region of opinion; agreement is the region of truth."

The moral of one of Æsop's fables is, "Every truth has two sides;" because a mule boasted that its sire was a racer, then afterwards remembered its dam was only a donkey. This fable might also serve as a good illustration of "polarized truth"—producing, after all, only a miserable hybrid, incapable of reproduction.

In conclusion, I must briefly recapitulate my argument. Truth cannot be polarized, in the sense of having one-half the truth at one end, and the other half at the other end of the poles; because one is contrary to the other.

If there are contrary doctrines in the church, they can never be united.

If there are contradictions in the Bible, they can never be united.

But as there are contradictions in both, neither the Bible nor the church contain all truth, but part truth and part falsehood.

To find the one point of truth, all falsehood must be eliminated; we must not vacillate between one or the other, or seek a compromise between them. Truth must be worked for—freely, openly, without let or hindrance, or fetters of ignorance or dogmatism. If we assume we know all truth, we shall never find it.

CHAPTER XV.

MODESTY.

"A good tree cannot bring forth evil fruit, neither can a corrupt tree bring forth good fruit."

In the last chapter I have gone rather a roundabout way to illustrate the assertion that no true analogy or spiritual meaning could be built or founded on anything that is false in fact.

I have endeavored to show how untrue are the facts narrated in the legend of the Garden of Eden. I will now try to prove how untrue, also, is the spiritual meaning.

Such a subject as the one now before me is generally ushered in by some such sentence as, "and now we approach delicate ground, or a ticklish subject." It comes with a sort of apologetic simper, and is, really, the most indelicate way of introducing it. I care not to think whether what I write of is delicate or indelicate; I remember only there is folly, and crime, and misery, and would, if I could, discover and remove either.

All sins appear to me indelicate and shameful; only we consider sins more immediately connected with our bodies are more indelicate to mention than those more referring to the soul.

It is said, immediately the fruit of the tree of knowledge was eaten, Adam and Eve knew they were naked. I wonder what this means? That they just then, for the first time, discovered their bodies were not covered with fur or feathers, like the bodies of beasts and birds?

That all the animals had natural clothing, but, for some unexplained cause, when their "eyes were opened," they found, to their shame, they had not.

It is very curious, certainly, that there should have been such a serious omission, if omission it was, in the Garden of Eden. But if eating the forbidden fruit taught them it was right to hide their bodies from a lascivious gaze, it taught them true modesty.'

The tree of knowledge, then, furnished them with the beginning or clue to all wisdom and virtue, knowledge and modesty. How, then, can either produce death, mentally or bodily? and, if the tree yielded such good fruit, why call it evil?

Is there really any harm in our bodies being naked? Do we put on clothes as a sort of tacit reproach to our Maker, because he did not cover them with fur or feathers? I have heard of some women so foolish as to refuse to wash their bodies, because they were ashamed to see their own bodies. Is this modesty?

Modesty is not shame of the body, but purity of

thought. Foolish shyness, mock modesty, squeam-ishness, are usually the very reverse of purity ; and when you see the one you may generally argue low thoughts and a vicious mind.

But because I condemn squeamishness, do I advocate boldness or vulgarity ?

Modesty, both in man and woman, is a mental virtue, not a mere outside show, and one who pos-sesses real purity will neither be vulgar nor squeamish in thought or action.

The fruit of the tree of knowledge, if evil, induced us to cover our bodies out of squeamishness, or hidden vulgarity, and is then the *evil* fruit of an *evil* tree.

But if we put on clothing, besides for the reason of keeping ourselves warm, from an innate love of purity as a protection from licentiousness, it is then the *good* fruit of a *good* tree.

. It would be as well to bear in mind, what is modesty, and what is vulgarity.

What is vulgarity in anything but the attempt to display your goods, your riches, your learning, or your beauty, for the sake of exciting the envy and cupidity of others ?

If a man is constantly thrusting his wisdom in your face, you say he is a vulgar pedant.

If a person can talk of nothing but his aristocratic connections, or displays his wealth ostentatiously, you say he is a vulgar snob.

Yet there are some who make a really vulgar display of a small portion of their bodies: vulgar, not
in the act itself, but from its motive; yet have such
a false shame of the rest of their bodies as to blush
even to look at a naked statue. They talk of the
shocking indecency of nude statues: what should a
statue be but nude ? We possess each one of us in
our own bodies, if not diseased or deformed an object
of the greatest beauty the Creator made on this earth.
We see nothing daily of this beautiful form, but only
ugly coats and trousers, and ugly balloons. We do
not want to see in a statue a copy of an artificial
covering, folds of cotton or cloth, but a sight of this
glorious beauty; which, partly the effects of a cold
climate, and partly our own licentiousness, have
deprived us of. How much joy we lose by losing so
much beauty : not the joy of passion, which is a fire
and a curse, but the joy of purity, the gratification of
the pure, intense, unsatisfied longing for beauty:
beauty of the body, or any other beauty ; not an end
in itself, but a means of educating the mind to love
beauty, and to be beautiful. How dark the world
would be if we shut out the light of our countenances
from one another.

CHAPTER XVI.

WORK.

THERE was a reward offered some years ago for the best written paper on the advantages of the Sabbath Day. Several papers were sent in, one written by a poor Scotch girl, called the "Pearl of Days," was considered very praiseworthy, perhaps the best of the lot, but as the reward was not offered for the competition of both sexes, the judges could not award her the prize. The book was, however, published by subscription.

The paper for which the prize was allotted was called " Heaven's Antidote to the Curse of Labor."

Labor a curse ? Work a punishment ? Impossible. Why, God works ! and the very antithesis of work and God, is stagnation and death.

Vitality *is* vitality only inasmuch as it is constant and unceasing work.

Our bodies, both voluntarily and involuntarily, work constantly.

Our minds, both sensibly and insensibly, work constantly. To stop working is death.

With labor, to us, is attached the idea of weariness,

because our bodies in time are mortal, and are not capable of continued labor.

Weariness proceeds from decay, every action of the muscles and every thought of the brain cause some particles of the body to decay—mental work causing more exhaustion than muscular labor. Decay is constantly tending to death, the final stop to all earthly work.

Rest in heaven is work without a shadow of weariness—life and vitality, without decay and death. Labor a curse ! Why, no grain of good can come to us without labor. We receive only what we stretch out our hands and take. Whether it be bodily health, or mental strength, or moral good, all come to us by labor, and as the just payment of our work—the fair hire of the laborer : for we are free laborers, not slaves to have gifts given us for which we have not striven, or from the caprice of the master.

As we strive, so we gain.

Work is Health, Joy, Life, Immortality !

Where, then, is the curse ?

Indolence, the mother of mischief, bears the curse, not labor. The Sabbath Day is an antidote to our bodily weariness of labor. Work and rest are not contraries, in this sense, as applied to ourselves : work is an act, rest a feeling ; both may exist together, and in another life accompany one another.

L

Work and stagnation or inertia, rest and weariness are contraries.

A day set apart for rest is not peculiar to the Jewish or Christian religion. It is observed by nearly every nation.

It is a physical, as well as a moral *necessity*, for every industrious nation to set apart a certain day for rest. It is only savage tribes, that live upon the spontaneous productions of the earth, and do no work, who have not a Sabbath; they do not require it, any more than does a child before it has begun to learn feel the necessity of, or a desire for, a day of rest; simply because it has not commenced work. We sometimes try to force it upon children by withholding the childish amusements—force upon them what they have no necessity for, and so make it a day of weariness instead of a day of rest. But in every nation where work enters, a day of rest *must* also enter; for men cannot continue working without it.

In France, where the attempt was made to abolish the observance of Sunday, and men tried to do without it; after a little while it was found necessary to set apart one day in ten for rest, thus proving its physical necessity—necessary, both to mental, moral, and physical health, as much as our nightly sleep. It is indispensable both to health and life. It is, therefore, impossible, that any ancient nation could have become even physically great and strong without a Sabbath Day.

Dr. Farre, before a Committee of the House of Commons, thus shows its necessity, both for *man and beast* :—

" Although the night apparently equalizes the circulation well, yet it does not sufficiently restore its balance for the attainment of a *long* life. Hence one day in seven, by the bounty of Providence, is thrown in as a day of compensation, to perfect, by its repose, the animal system. You may easily determine this question as a matter of fact, by trying it on beasts of burden. Take that fine animal the horse, and work him to the full extent of his powers every day of the week, or give him one day in seven, and you will soon perceive, by the vigor with which he performs his functions on the other six days, that the rest is necessary to his well-being."—*Taken from* " *The Oasis*," *a Tract for the People*.

Nature then points out the necessity of a Sabbath quite clearly enough, without the aid of revelation or inspiration.

And from what do we derive the name of our day of rest, Sunday ? the Sun's day, a day set apart for Baal, or the worship of the sun.

But because the unenlightened worshippers of Baal had also the blessing of a day's rest, is it any desecration to our Sunday ?

"The Sabbath was made for man," that is all mankind, not for one nation, the Jews only: so also were *all* God's good and perfect gifts given to all mankind; and as much as they worked for them, they obtained them.

Ought we not rather to admire and thank the God of mercy in giving a day of rest to both man and beast, and not only to one nation and people, but to all mankind, and from the beginning of the world.

But a life of sabbaths, in the sense of cessation from work, would be unendurable weariness, even in the body when the decaying members are a heavy clog to our efforts, how much more, then, when the vital spirit was free? Heaven would be a prison to the soul, if condemned in it to eternal inactivity. Can we say, then, labor is a curse, when it is the very life of heaven? How often do we find this in our experience, that something given us which we at first dislike, and call evil, we afterwards find has been "a blessing in disguise." That is, what God always gave us as a blessing, but we, in our foolish ignorance, saw not the good, and called it evil and a curse.

It is a false idea to suppose that what God first pronounced as a curse, He, in His mercy, changed into a blessing, for that is making God a liar. That He said cursing, when He meant blessing. If labor is always rewarded, it is blessed, for blessing is the reward of a good deed done.

Christ says, " Blessed are the pure in heart, for they shall see God." (I apply the text both to this chapter and the one preceding.)

He does not say, purity of heart, though the cursed fruit of a cursed tree will, in the end, cause you to see God. Neither does he say, labor, though a curse, shall in the end prove a blessing, and in the kingdom of heaven make you fellow-workers with God.

CHAPTER XVII.

DEATH.

I must add a few more words on this subject, for I find though men are convinced that in all the rest of the earthly creation in time, mortality was the rule ; they are slow to accept the belief that men also from the beginning were intended to die, and were under the same law.

The author of "Creation's Testimony to its God" triumphantly says, "We seek in vain for any appearance of the reign of death over *man* before the Adamic period." If by this, he means, "I defy you to say any man died before any man was born or created," I really think we must grant that ; but if he means, no traces of man's death are visible before the period assigned by the Bible as the time of man's creation, according to Sir C. Lyell there are proofs of death without number, previous to that period, witness the Neanderthal and Engis skulls.

The former writer continues, "The simple statement of scripture would lead us to believe, that, in his created condition of purity, man's bodily constitution was either exempted from the law of progress towards dissolution, which belonged to inferior animals, or that there was, in the fruit of some 'tree of life,' an antidote to that progress, continuing in innocence, and feeding upon which, he might live for ever; or pass out of that into a higher state of being, without separation of body and spirit, which is usually denominated ' death.' "

Now look at this *feeding*, which must be by our mouths upon the *fruit*, a vegetable production, composed of sap drawn from the earth, of a *tree*, grown in the ground, receiving from that ground the same materials that nourish the grass and other herbs upon which animals feed, and upon these earthy materials a tree becomes (on the " somehow " principle) the *tree of life*, and man by eating it, and feeding upon it, is made to *live for ever*.

The tree, in fact, elaborated from the ground, the famous *elixir vitæ!*

My dear reader, if you had the *elixir vitæ* to-morrow, what blessing could it be to you?

If there came a person to me, holding in one hand the power of instant death, and in the other life to the end of time : I would say, " Death is the blessing; to live for ever, in my present state of existence, would be the curse."

Such an idea seems vaguely to strike the writer—so must it every one—that earth, in *no* condition, could be our final rest. It would appear to be a sort of optional matter whether men chose to continue eating the fruit, and living for ever, or they might leave off eating, and "somehow" "pass out of that"(?) with their bodies, into another and higher state.

Suppose it was said to a donkey, or any other animal, "Bye and bye you shall have given you a man's soul and a man's mind, a man's speech, and a man's desires; you may either die and quit your donkey's body, and take then a man's body, or if you dread death keep your body, and it shall be a most perfect body of its kind, full of health and perpetual youth, and of perfect beauty, according to the beauty of an ass." How could such a spiritual man and bodily donkey be received among men?

Much in the same way as an angelic spirit with a man's body would be received into the world of spirits.

In a note, the writer quotes from a work by Professor Hitchcock:—"I maintain that God, in the beginning, adapted every other being and event in the world, to man's character and condition, so that there should be entire harmony in its system. And since, either in the Divine appointment, or in the nature of things, there is an inseparable connection between sin and death, the latter must constitute a feature of the system of the world; because a free agent would introduce the former. Death would ultimately exist in the world; and, therefore, all creatures placed in such a world must be made mortal, at whatever period. *For mortal and immortal natures could not exist in the same natural constitution ; nor could a condition adapted to undying creatures be changed into a condition of decay and death without an entirely new creation."*

One would imagine the conviction expressed in this latter sentence, would be sufficient to banish the belief in the statement in the story of the Garden of Eden, of death being introduced as a curse, but he makes it fit into the legend in this manner:—" The certainty of man's apostacy might have been the grand reason in the Divine mind for giving to the world its present constitution, and subjecting animals to death."

The former writer makes it coincide in this way : " Farther, we should remember, that our first parents were naturally *mortal,* but God covenanted with them for immortality, as a matter of favor and upon particular conditions."

Surely men's minds must have been dreadfully warped and twisted by folly and falsehood, to imagine, or think to instruct others, by showing such a distorted vision of the good God !

Christ told us to judge of our Creator's goodness to us by examining our own conduct in love to one another : " Will a man, if his son asked bread, give him a stone ? "

Let us examine evil by the same rule, and if we

know what is evil in the conduct of one man towards another, be sure God acts not so towards his creatures.

A nobleman of enormous wealth and power, takes hold of a little country lad, who has never mounted a horse before, lifts him on one, pats him on the back and says, "Now my lad, you take this horse and leap over that chasm there, and if you can do it, I will give you a thousand pounds and make a man of you for life."

He turns to his friends and says, "He can't possibly do it, my money is quite safe; the lad must be killed, so I have got his coffin all ready for him, and I shall punish all the rest of his family, because he did not do it."

In all probability the bystanders would exclaim, "what a cold-blooded villain!"

But we say, in such a manner God acted with men. He covenanted with them to give them immortality on one condition, but, by his foreknowledge, was so certain they either could or would not keep the covenant, he prepared all the rest of the world as a grave for them, and cursed the world and all things in it, because the two people, with whom he made the covenant, did not keep it. A covenant is a mutual agreement between two parties. How, can it be called a covenant between God and man, when the latter had no voice in the matter?

What contradictions, inconsistencies, falsehoods, evil thoughts of God's truth and love, has this miserable story occasioned! Will any one show me, from the words of Christ, one sentence that can lead to such a gross idea of injustice on the part of God, as is involved in the story of the cause of the fall of man?

Dr. Cumming has suggested that all pre-Adamic death was the consequence of the angel's sin! This is certainly a brilliant piece of wisdom. The monstrous injustice of such a thought must strike any one who has a particle of truth in his mind.

I must again advert to the idea that "There is an inseparable connexion between sin and death." I say there is NO connection between the sin of the soul and the death of the body. It was quite a Jewish belief, that both death and bodily disease were produced by sin. We in these days ought to be able to understand, that holding to the belief in the connection of death to sin, is equally foolish as the idea that disease was the effect of moral pollution, and a token of God's displeasure.

The quotation from Professor Hitchcock contradicts itself. Man, he says, *must* have been made mortal, even before man sinned. Mortality is but the daily death of some minute particles of our body, and is daily, by decay, hastening to the death of that body; but if sin be the *cause* of death, how could death have commenced its operations *before* the entrance of sin ?   How could the effect precede the cause ?

Animals die ; plants die.   Neither have sinned ; but, in conformity with their organization, they die.

Man sins, and his soul does not die—it is immortal —but his body dies, as every other animal dies, and by and through the same laws.

Suppose the body lived for ever in time, that would not be immortality ; for immortality cannot be lived in Time, but only in Eternity.

If you desire immortality, you must pass out of this world into the region of immortality.

How, then, will you accomplish it ?

Will you take with you your body—your poor, weak, eating, and drinking body, that lives off the the ground, and is of the ground ?   Or, will you leave it here, and rise to immortality a free, pure spirit ?

This is death.

But is there in this anything so very dreadful—so very fearful ?   That we shrink from the idea of laying our bodies quietly down upon the ground, and letting them crumble back again into the earth ?   Would we, instead of this, choose rather, like the foolish animal I imagined, to carry our bodies with us ?

To take them with us, is to clothe the spirit in a body of death in heaven.

To leave them here is to die the last death, and be for ever after free from death.

To talk of a spiritual body is as erroneous as to talk of earthy water, or watery earth ; you can have neither but by spoiling both. Earthy water would only be thick, dirty water : watery earth would only be a soft muddy quagmire.

A spiritual body, would be spirit spoiled by body; and a bodily spirit, if we can imagine such a thing in heaven, would feel itself very uncomfortable— nothing solid to support it, nothing to walk upon, nothing to eat; in fact, I think it would feel in heaven very much ashamed of itself.

My dear reader, can you not see, that death, as every other natural law of God, when rightly understood, is no curse, but good, and beautiful, and lovely. It is only men's idea of it that makes it ugly, foolish, ridiculous, sinful, and cursed.

CHAPTER XVIII.

MARRIAGE.

"Ye fools and blind, whether is greater, the gift or the altar that sanctifies the gift?"

THIS chapter was at first written as a conclusion to Chapter IV., but I divided it, and preferred writing down a few intervening chapters, to serve as stepping-stones to the subject I have named at the heading of this chapter.

It will be said, that by doubting the truth of the immaculate conception, an aspersion is cast on the moral character of the human father and mother of Jesus. This need not be; we might, instead, ascribe the story to a monkish legend, or even an evangelical error, in order to make the birth of Christ to coincide with the supposed prophecy in Isaiah.

Before examining this text, I would point out an instance where, in two Gospels, one evangelist appears to take a Christian view of one of Christ's speeches, the other falls back to the preconceived Jewish idea.

It relates to the sign of the Prophet Jonas.

Consider first, that Christ likened the Jews who

sought after a sign, to an *evil* and *adulterous* generation. *Evil*, in wishing him to break God's laws, in order to induce them to believe, by showing them a manifestation of his power by unnatural, that is, unlawful means; and "adulterous," because they were not satisfied with what could be worked by those laws, but desired the birth of a *monster*, by other laws, or no laws.

In St. Luke it is : " There shall no sign be given it but the sign of Jonas the Prophet. For as Jonas was a sign unto the Ninevites, so shall also the son of man be to this generation. The men of Nineveh shall rise up in the judgment with the men of this generation, and shall condemn it, for they repented at the preaching of Jonas, and behold a greater than Jonas is here."

To the men of that generation whom Jesus rebuked for seeking a miraculous sign, no hint of any miracle respecting Jonas is given in this Gospel; the true sign was from the *preaching* of Jonas to the *preaching* of Jesus. That because the Ninevites listened to the preaching of a mere man, and repented, Jonas should condemn those who refused to listen to the preaching of the Son of God. In this warning, or rebuke to the Jews, the idea of Jonas being three days and three nights in the inside of a whale is not even remotely alluded to, nor is it required.

But St. Matthew, when he came to record the same

narrative, remembering the allusion to Jonas, connected the sign in his mind, not to the preaching of the prophet, but to the improbable story, or legend, connected with his name, and that this sign was typical of Christ remaining three days and three nights in the ground; but such being the intention of the sign proves itself an error, because Jesus was *not* three days and three nights in the earth.

With respect to the prophecy in the 7th chapter of Isaiah, if the reader will take the trouble to read it, he will find that, in order to make the 14th verse appear a prophecy at all it is completely isolated from what precedes and what follows it. Taken in conjunction with the events to which it alludes and rightly belongs, he will find the text is really no prophecy at all, but only a sign given that a prediction should be fulfilled.

It was told Ahaz that his enemies should be destroyed before him, and as a sign, Isaiah said, one who is now, " A virgin, shall conceive and bear a son. . . Butter and honey shall he eat, that he may know to refuse the evil and choose the good. For before the child shall know to refuse the evil and choose the good, the land that thou abhorrest shall be forsaken by both her kings."

The latter part of this verse is the prophecy or prediction, and the sign given was, before a child of the prophetess by Isaiah should grow to a reasonable age, the events predicted by the prophet should come to pass.

In the 8th chapter the same prediction is repeated: " For before the child shall have knowledge to cry ' my father and my mother,' the riches of Damascus, and the spoil of Samaria, shall be taken away before the king of Assyria."

It is impossible to separate the text from this narrative, and if it is affirmed that Isaiah did not mean, one who was then a virgin should bear him a son, we must suppose that an immaculate conception occurred twice.

But even if the story of the immaculate conception be not an apostolic or monkish legend, and we suppose that the earthly father and mother of Jesus committed sin, it is a less vile idea to me than that of the conception by the Holy Ghost, which is a frightful profanation of the spirit. Besides, to assert that the mother of Jesus bore a child " conceived by the Holy Ghost," and afterwards children by her husband Joseph, is accusing her of another and worse crime, to which the Holy Ghost is a party.

What is sin in respect to the connection of man and woman ? Is it violation of the marriage ceremony, or violation of the law of God ? The breaking of the law made in " the beginning," when God made them male and female, or the violation of a vow made at a church ceremony ?

M

The law of God is, that one was made for one, that two might be united as one. The sin is in separating what God thus joined, not by a ceremony, but by a divine law, existing prior to the ceremony.

Perhaps it is imagined, that the Son of Man avoided a human conception, because the natural conception of male and female is in itself sin.

What do we impute to God by this assumption?

That for every man that must be born into the world, its parents are *forced* to commit sin.

That the very act that unites them together, and that God enjoined when He said "be fruitful and multiply," is sin. It is not the church ceremony that joins them together.

Every man who, by this law of God, joins himself to a woman, and every woman who thus joins herself to a man, are *one* in the sight of God as long as they are on the earth together. And if they are not united together by holy love—love of the mind, as well as of the body—it is adultery, whether before or after marriage.

Anything that is holy in the sight of God does not require a church ceremony to *make* it holy, and surely if God made and commanded it, it is holy; but if it is in itself an unholy act, does the church ceremony make it holy?

We call adultery, a sin committed after marriage,

but Christ said a licentious look, before or after marriage, was adultery.

We say, a sin committed before the marriage ceremony, therefore *only* violating the holy natural law of God, is of less magnitude than the same act committed after the church service.

" Ye fools and blind," whether is greater the church ceremony of marriage, or the law of God, upon which that ceremony is based, or instituted ?

I do not say the church service is useless. It is necessary as a protection of the innocent against the guilty—of the virtuous against the vicious.

It is only to be deplored that the laws of our country are not more stringent—more powerful to protect the weak against the strong, and not, as many of them are, but acts to give a legal right to injustice and oppression. But, how far are either the church ceremony or the laws a check to vice ?

Unless the holiness of the law of God enters the heart, the service is utterly nugatory and vain, so can only act as a preventive to bodily or temporal injury.

Were we perfectly obedient to the law of God, and perfect Christians, no such human ties would be required. God forbid that I should even be thought to advocate sin or licence. The moral depravity of social life I read of in England at the present time, is to me perfectly appalling, but even with this staring me in the face I have faith in the ultimate perfection of mankind, and that even now we are tending to it.

What we now see is only the outward form of a malignant disease, long working in the social body, and when men are brought to know how destructive this disease is; how the very shadow of death hangs over it, they will begin to try and rid themselves of it, and, in order to do so, they must first discern where lies the root of the disease. They must clearly distinguish where and what is the sin : they must find the cause before they can remove the outward effect.

Oh, that I could speak but a word to further this noble work! what matter if I incur the risk of having my words and thoughts misconstrued, Truth shall justify me. I believe, even, that the love of Truth is so inherent in the minds of men that my sincere and earnest desire for Truth shall justify me to them.

I do not desire to shelter myself under the mistaken idea that the end justifies the means; on no account would I add a line to support such a false doctrine.

Truth only can justify Truth.

If I have done wrong or spoken wrong, that wrong can never be productive of right or good.

But, if I have spoken the plain truth, for the sake of Truth, then that truth *shall* be productive of good, and *cannot* be productive of evil.

CHAPTER XIX.

THE DEVIL.

IT is curious, but most certainly true, that mankind generally have a greater personal fear of the Devil, hobgoblins, and ghosts, than they have of God.

They have a sort of notion that devils and ghosts may sometimes be uncomfortably near them; and that the latter may, perhaps, appear all in white, and frighten them terribly some dark night. That some hideously ugly invisible creature, they call the devil, is perhaps standing close beside them (take care!), whispering in their ear, breathing his hot breath in their nostrils, or he creeps behind them, and they dare not look round; they have a sort of creeping sensation in the small of the back, and across their shoulders, that he is going to make a grab at them (ah!!). Really reader I cannot help laughing.

Only imagine if any one with long sharp finger nails should steal behind you while you are sitting alone some evening between light and dark, while your mind was becoming uneasy with unearthly feelings, and should suddenly claw hold of you, with a howl between the laugh of an idiot and the whoop of a New Zealander. I really think if you are a nervous debilitated female, with no appetite, you certainly would go into fits.

We have no unpleasant sensation of this sort with regard to God. He is conjectured to be far away in heaven, and not likely to make such a sudden, rude, and horrible attack upon us. I have been endeavoring for some time to arrive at a satisfactory conclusion with regard to this dreadful person, as to where he came from, where he is going to, and what business on earth he has to do with us.

The conclusion I have arrived at is perfectly satisfactory to myself, and that is—there is no such person; but I am afraid I shall have some difficulty in offering any convincing argument to my reader. If I can, in any manner, either from the nervous female aforesaid, or others, remove a supposed cause of fear, what I have to say on the subject may be worth while reading and looking into.

The sun is the most perfect analogy of God we can point to. It is the earthly giver of light, heat, rain, color, beauty, health, joy, life itself, to every creature—without it the world would become a death mass : the grave of all living.

When the half of the globe we exist on, turns from the sun, and night and darkness prevails, do we for one moment fancy that a huge body of blackness in the heavens causes it ?

It is curious that philologists have not found the meaning or derivation of the word *God*.

Bunsen, speaking of the meaning of Biblical words, says, " And what of *God*? not the *good*, though its meaning is unknown. *Deus* (and all the cognate words, as shown in what precedes) is the bright Ether." The devil has several names which have somewhat different meanings, but all tending to the same idea.

The devil, or principal devil, I would premise, appears to control our mental nature ; the devils, or secondary imps, our corporeal nature, afflicting us with bodily diseases, insanity, dumbness, &c., at least, according to Jewish belief, they did so in the olden time ; but they have not tormented us since witchcraft was abolished. Allowing even that we were delivered from the power of witchcraft and demoniac possession by the advent of Christ, we might inquire why, when he sent the little devils out of the world, he did not send the big devil also ? But I really must leave off joking, it is certainly highly improper to laugh at his " Satanic majesty," as he is denominated.

Does any one think I am *irreverent* for ridiculing the supposed power and pretension of the something we call the devil ? Does any one say, as did John Wesley, when the power or existence of witchcraft was called in question, " No devil, no God " ?

Does any one think the existence of God depends on the existence of the devil?

Does any one think that belief in God, rests on belief in the devil? or that we cannot have one without the other? I should think not.

If disbelief in the devil, as a being or power of evil, cannot touch the existence of God, or our belief in that God, let us examine, without fear, his pretensions, or rather, the powers we have imputed to him.

I take the theological belief, and interpretation of the term *Devil*, from a Biblical Cyclopedia, published by the Religious Tract Society, which I therefore conclude to be quite orthodox : "*Devil*, derived from the Greek name, *diabolous*, which means, 'a calumniator,' or 'accuser.' "

Satan (Hebrew), "adversary," and from the notion of an opponent in a court of justice, comes also to mean "accuser." "*Abaddon* (Hebrew), *Appollyon* (Greek), both mean 'destroyer.' " I do not find throughout the Gospels, the devil spoken of as our accuser.

John v. 45—"Do not think *I* will accuse you to the Father; there is one that accuseth you, even *Moses*, in whom ye trust." Luke xi. 32—"The *men of Nineve* shall rise up in the judgment with this generation, and shall condemn it," &c.

John viii. 7 and 10—"So when they continued asking, he lifted up himself, and said unto them, He that is without sin among you, let him first cast a stone at her. . . . . •Woman, where are those thine accusers, hath no man condemned thee ? "

In the first of these texts, Christ alludes to himself as an accuser, but declares he will not be, but that the truths of the Bible written by Moses, in whom the Jews trusted, would accuse the Jews.

In the second, better men than themselves.

In the third, Jesus would not suffer, or even listen to the accusers of the woman, because he considered them as sinful as she was.

An accuser, therefore, will not be one even as guilty as ourselves, still less one more guilty.

Then God cannot suffer the devil to be the accuser or condemner of men.

In the words of Christ, sin is spoken of as Beelzebub, Belial, The Prince of this World, The Spirit that worketh in the hearts of the disobedient, The God of the World, a murderer, a liar.

Turning to the Cyclopedia for these terms, I find *Beelzebub*, or *Baalzebub*, " An idol God of the Ekronites, and was probably worshipped as the patron deity of medicine."

If this be correct, it would have been the reason why the Jews accuse Jesus of casting out devils by Beelzebub, that is, curing disease by the aid of a heathen idol god. He was one of the chief gods of

the heathen, and hence the prince or chief of the
devils. Such a term would be easily understood by
the Jews, who were taught to regard all idols as
devils.

The " People's Dictionary of the Bible " says :—
" A new doctrine was imported into Judaism after
the exile, from the Zoroaster Chaldaic philosophy,
in the distinction between good and bad angels,
forming a celestial and demoniacal hierarchy ; becoming a sort of Judaical polytheism ; and, like all
polytheisms, interfering with the due recognition of
the sole Creator and Preserver of the universe.

So also _Belial_ meant originally, " lowness, base-
ness." In Psalms xii. 8, the words translated _an evil
disease_, literally meant, a " word or thing of Belial."
With that tendency to personification which marked
the Jewish religion, when, in its decline, it fell under
rabbinical influence, the word came to be an epithet
of Satan. " Under the influence of a corrupt oriental
philosophy, a system of doctrines of devils, demons,
was introduced, and spread throughout Judea, and
other western countries. This system made a complete infernal hierarchy, setting forth the rank, order,
and giving names to their respective chiefs. Our
Lord, who, adopting the popular phraseology, speaks
of Beelzebub, ' the prince of the devils.' We might ask,
why did Jesus adopt the popular phraseology of a
polytheistic doctrine, which interfered with the due

recognition of the sole Creator and Preserver of the universe ? "

Baalzebub must have been derived from Baal: " Baal, Bel, Belus, were the names by which the sun was worshipped. Human victims were offered to Baal. The worship of Baal prevailed through all ancient Scandinavia, and is supposed to have been general throughout all the British Islands. The worship of Baal was a besetting sin of the Hebrews."

The worship of the sun under the name of Baal, we may conclude, was the earliest form of idolatry, and also, the most universal. *Belial*, from Bel and Belus, means "worthless," and is connected with the idea of everything filthy, corrupt, and lewd. Idolatry and licentiousness may well be spoken of as the god of the world, being now, even, the most prevalent and destructive vices, both of soul and body. Well might Christ say they had nothing in him. This idea, then, of the person of the Devil, or Satan, or Beelzebub, can be traced, as we have seen, to the worship of the sun, and the inhuman and horrible rites attendant upon it. But the idols were neither gods nor devils—nor a temptation of any devil, but proceeded from ignorance, which prevented men from knowing the one God of Truth.

St. Paul says, " We know that an idol is nothing." He also says, " We cannot say we are tempted of God, when we are drawn aside by our *own* lusts and enticed." Here again we notice the confusion there was in the minds of the Jews between God tempting and the devil tempting. In fact, the Jews could hardly prevent this confusion from arising in their minds. Their form of worship was little above heathen worship.

The God they worshipped was a God of fear and vengeance, that required a daily bloody sacrifice, as an atonement or propitiation for his wrath ; their worship of him was only better than heathen worship, in that it did not offer human life as a sacrifice. Nor even are they quite free from that idolatry.

If the reader will look at the 32nd chapter of Exodus, he will find that to propitiate the wrath of God, because Aaron had made a golden calf, and the people had worshipped it, Moses said, " *Thus saith the Lord God of Israel :* Put every man his sword by his side, and go in and out from gate to gate throughout the camp, and slay every man his brother, and every man his companion, and every man his neighbor. And the children of Levi did according to the word of Moses, and there fell of the people that day about *three thousand* men."

Also, in 2nd Samuel, 21st chapter, it may be read how to propitiate the wrath of God " For Saul and his bloody house." Seven of Saul's sons were given up to the Gibeonites to be slain, and for this act, a famine was stayed.

I think both these instances look very like human sacrifices offered as a propitiation; but whether to God or the devil, both we ourselves and the Hebrews might find it difficult to determine. It is curious that this confusion has even crept into the Lord's Prayer: we say, "Lead us not into temptation." Can anything be more contradictory than first addressing God as "Our Father," and then begging him not to *lead* us into sin. Suppose a little child being led home by the hand of his earthly parent, and having on the way to beseech him not to lead him over a precipice, or into any other danger; we should say of such a one, he surely could not be a loving and affectionate parent; but we say this in the Lord's Prayer to our heavenly Father.

We are, however, more Christian than to believe what the words in this prayer, and in the other church services, would imply. We are not really so cruel as to believe or wish the curses put into our mouths, nor so ignorant as to have a reasonable faith in some of the petitions we utter; which is a great proof, perhaps the greatest, that church theology and church creeds are not consistent either with reason or Christianity, or the advance of the age.

So in the petition of the Lord's Prayer, no one really believes the words he repeats—no one, I hope, thinks that God leads us, or even connives at our

being led into sin or temptation, but that our own
unchecked passions lead us unto sin.

Still, though we know God does not lead us into
temptation, we are content to repeat the words,
hardly knowing what they mean, certainly, without
knowing that the words are a remnant of idolatry,
when "a God," or "a devil," or "an idol," were
almost synonymous terms. But when this is shown,
do we do right to continue the words? It is a pity
to spoil such a beautiful prayer by suffering such an
error to remain in it. We should pray, "*Leave* us
not *in* temptation, or *let us not be led into* temptation,
There is but little difference in the words, but much
in the sense. It is, that our Father would not leave
us where we have ourselves weakly yielded to temptation—that he would help us to deliver ourselves
from the two besetting vices of humanity—idolatry
and licentiousness.

One, the depravity and lowering of the body.

The other, the depravity and lowering of the
mind.

And these two, *are* the devil, in *ourselves ;* and
these our punisher, and accusers, and destroyers.

There was a wise man who said to his children,
"My sons, you will never see anything worse than
you see in yourselves."

So, after all, there is a great deal of truth in the
joke with which I commenced this chapter, and

sometimes we really do frighten ourselves with our own shadows.

I do not mean that such a feeling proceeds from wickedness, it usually arises from nervousness or weakness.

But it is true that evil is near us, and in us, and not anywhere or anything outside of us ; and though God is near us always, it is to do us good and not evil—not to frighten or terrify us, but to lead us to approach him in love without fear.

It may be said here again, that I have been seeking to destroy what has long ago been destroyed.

Even the orthodox writer, the Rev. Thomas Ragg, denies the existence of the devil as a being of evil; he says, "When men talk gravely of a Satan as a personification of the principle of evil, and write his name 'D'Evil'; I proceed, then, to show that these notions are fallacious, and that the existence of such a principle of evil, equally infinite with the principle of good, is an absurdity and an impossibility."

But if enlightened men, and even orthodox churchmen, see the absurdity of believing in a being of evil, called Satan, or the devil, why do we preserve such a false notion in the Bible ?

And if they know, as Thomas Ragg says, there is no such thing as a devil, for these reasons :—"Firstly, The existence of two infinite beings is impossible. Secondly, That if two such infinite principles were contending, and had been contending from eternity, the result must have been, that nothing would ever have been produced or created. Thirdly, That under the supposition of the existence of such a malevolent principle, evil would not be evil. Fourthly, That evil is *not a principle at all, but rather, a defect or imperfection*."

I ask again, if we acknowledge this, why keep the name of the devil in our Bibles and our creeds? and pray to be defended " against the world, the flesh, *and the devil*," when there is no devil *but the flesh*.

This again we have to thank INSPIRATION for; we dare not alter it, though we know it causes error.

We well know that no ignorant man can take up his Bible without reading of the devil, and that he cannot help believing the devil to be a great, and mighty principle, or Being of Evil; and what right have we to continue to keep and foster this ignorant and idolatrous belief, and thus allow a stumbling-block to remain in their way, when we know it ought to be removed? And why should we frighten the minds of our children with such a false, vicious idol?

But, instead of this, what are they doing? Now, this old devil is nearly defunct, some foolish, though, I daresay, well-meaning divines, are trying to dress up another devil for us, which they call Antichrist, or rather, St. Paul gave them the name, and they are straining their wits to work to find out something to fit to it.

It does not seem quite settled what this something is, whether man or thing, another name for the old devil, or for a new devil, or the diabolical essence of all the devils and human evil together.

It would appear to be rather a difficult cap to fit. They can find plenty of " scoffers," that is, those who, in these last days, doubt and question the falsehood of inspiration ; but, instead of these scoffers, walking after their own lusts, they are men of pure and irreproachable lives.

I think it is a great misfortune that talent which God has given men, to make known his *love* to mankind, should be so misapplied, to preach, instead, a doctrine of *terror* and *fear*. They do, indeed, lead captive, a great many silly women, and not a few silly men as well, laden with their sins, and very heavily laden indeed they are, poor creatures, with the load that has been bound on to their backs—a burden too heavy to be borne, and which they who put it on would not touch with one of their fingers, to help to lift it off.

It is very odd, people, who ought not to quote scripture, still continue to do so, and more curious still, that it is for the purpose of trying to cast out a devil, by the word of truth. From whence do we

N

derive our doctrine of the devils being fallen angels, who fought with God in heaven! and were then turned out of it? And why do we suppose "the serpent that was more subtle than any beast of the field" to be one of the devils?

I can find no answer to either question in the Bible. I think our ideas on the subject are gained principally from Milton. The doctrine is alluded to in some of the Epistles, and the writers of them derive their *inspired* information from an apocryphal book, called the Book of Enoch. And this Book of Enoch, why is it not amongst those we choose to set up as our canonical scripture? We might suppose the writer of this book, who had such wonderful and extra inspiration as to allow him to view the interior economy of the heavenly life, hid from every other human gaze, to behold this curious and anomalous scene of confusion, rage, and deadly hate in heaven, ought to command from us even a greater amount of veneration and respect. But if this Book of Enoch proves itself, by its absurdity, to be a tissue of lying fables and legends, why do St. Paul and others quote from it, and are we obliged to receive these quotations as infallible truths?

CHAPTER XX.

HELL.

We pray, "Lord of all power and might; thou that art the author and giver of all good things, graft in our hearts the love of thy name." But how can we believe God to be all powerful, and that he is really the giver of all good things, and, at the same time imagine that the devil has the largest share of power over men, and also that he must be self-created, then really a God, or that God created evil; or, how can we in our hearts truly love Him, when we think this all powerful God suffers the devil to tempt, accuse, and finally destroy us?

The belief in the devil, as a person or being, is nothing else but a remnant and rotten rag of idolatry.

What now is the idea of our future connection with the devil or devils? That they are to torment all, except the "select little flock," for all eternity!

We might suppose God hated man, instead of loving him; that He created the greater number of men, not only to be tempted and tortured by devils in this world, but gave them the privilege of continuing the torture for all eternity. We may quibble, and try to explain it away as much as we like, but if we believe God all-powerful, and to have perfect foreknowledge of the fate of all His creatures, in our hearts we must think that He hates man, and as long as we believe this, we shall, in our hearts, hate God.

I have some outline engravings, drawn several years ago, for the London Art Union, to illustrate "Bunyan's Pilgrim's Progress": there is a picture of demons tormenting lost souls in hell. The devils appear to be taking it very coolly, considering the hot place they are in; the atmosphere seems to have become a sort of "native element" to them; it is only the poor human beings who appear to be suffering: the devils are employed in making hideous grimaces at them, and adding, by all means in their power, to their torture; one imp, with an expression of diabolical satisfaction, is quietly gouging out the eye of a woman—bah! it is a disgusting picture; let us turn over another page.

It will be seen that the idea of hell as a place of torture is also derived from heathen worship. I take from the Cyclopedia,—"The word *hell*, is the representative of the Hebrew word *sheol*, 'the grave,' and *hades*, 'darkness,' and another Greek word, which is also translated *hell*, literally means, 'the Valley of Hinnom,' where the most abominable idolatries were practised, called also, Tophet, from *toph* 'a drum,' because that instrument was used there to drown the cries of the victims."

This picture, and the one in the " Pilgrim's Progress " would match very well together.

Though *sheol* means " the grave," it has been translated sometimes " the grave," sometimes "hell," according, I suppose, to the will of the translator.

1st Kings ii. 9—" Thou shalt bring down his hoary head to *(sheol)* the grave with blood."

Psalm xlix. 14—" Like sheep they are laid in *(sheol)* the grave."

Psalm ix. 17—" The wicked shall be turned into *(sheol)* hell."

Prov. xxiii. 14—" Thou shalt beat him with the rod and shalt deliver his soul from *(sheol)* hell."

Psalm xvi. 10—" For thou wilt not leave my soul in *(sheol)* hell; neither wilt thou suffer thine Holy one to see corruption."

It does not appear that the Hebrew word *sheol* meant anything further than death or annihilation; but David, in this last text, showed a belief in the immortality of his soul, that it should not be left in *(sheol)* the grave, and that God would not suffer his holy one (himself the man after God's own heart) to see corruption.

I suppose from this translation of *sheol* into hell, our creeds say Christ descended into hell, and we imagine that his earthly body did not see corruption, but with that coporeal body, he ascended into heaven, and is living there still in a human body.

The word in the New Testament translated hell, is *hades*, " darkness."

The devil as a being of evil, or hell as a *place* of punishment, are both heathen idolatrous ideas. There is no devil but in our own hearts, and no hell but in the worm of remorse and the fire of unchecked passions; neither will any one punish us but our own selves.

Because I say there is no devil, no hell, and that God will not punish us, it does not follow that the just and the unjust shall alike be rewarded, or that the wicked shall go unpunished.

Mr. Mill speaks of the necessity of obeying God, " because God is stronger than we, and able to damn us if we don't." Though we may dislike to put it into such strong language this is really the secret feeling of our hearts. But it is an unjust and hard thought of our Father. We say *all* things are possible with God, but at the same time, say it is impossible for Him to pardon our sins without propitiation of his wrath.

There is nothing unjust in granting pardon.

It is unjust only to allow criminals to be at liberty to cheat, defraud, and ruin others.

We deny God the power of doing the first—of giving to all men a free pardon—because we say it would be contrary to his justice. We say he did the second, by allowing guilty devils liberty to cheat, defraud, and ruin innocent men.

Which would be the greater injustice ?

God does not, nor will not punish us—we punish ourselves.

If we disobey the physical laws, and injure our constitutions, we bring disease on our bodies, for having infringed the law of our bodies. We cannot say God sent the disease, we brought it on ourselves— we punish ourselves.

The same with the soul, if we break the moral laws, we bring disease on our souls, but we cannot say God brought the disease, we brought it on ourselves ; we punish our own souls. Should we consider it just to healthy people to force them to be contaminated, by living with people infectiously diseased ? We know we would not.

Neither would it be just that God should force pure, holy spirits to be united in eternity with impure and unholy spirits.

Where, then, is punishment ?

We have learnt the great, and holy, and merciful lesson, that punishment is vicious and cruel, unless used as a means of reformation. Be sure God's punishments are not vicious or cruel, and the lesson we have learnt is a lesson of love, which is God.

God's punishment, therefore, will be for reformation. We know not how : but what if to walk up our weary way again through the world till the spirit is purified and enlightened, and fit for heaven ?

This would neither be inconsistent with justice or mercy. Eternal damnation *is* both unjust and unmerciful. If God is really a God of Love, it is impossible he could have joy in heaven, knowing that millions of the creatures he had made were suffering tortures. Does it improve the idea to say, God will not look at or heed these millions, but completely shut them out from his omnipresence, as we should turn our backs upon our poor relations, and while we were feasting in pleasure and luxury, try conveniently to forget they were in being, and were starving and in misery?

Is this the God of Love we worship?

God loves every creature he has made, and never created any for eternal damnation; but each one shall work his way up to the heaven for which God created his soul. It would be no light punishment to be sent back to begin life anew. In a measure we follow out this principle ourselves in convictism; we prevent criminals doing mischief to others, and at the same time give them a second chance of regaining their lost station in the world; for a time we keep them in bonds to break them off from the *habit* of vice, and induce the *habit* of work. They are then again *free* to choose either the one or the other, and in nine cases out of ten, they choose the latter, and advance by it to an honorable position in the world.

Suppose it was possible for this world (the earth) to disobey or break away from the laws of attraction that hold it in its place. It would fall. Should we say, God thrust it down?

But what do I say: it would fall?

There is no such thing as falling. There is no where to fall to. If the earth fell from under our feet here in New Zealand, the people of England would be mounting up into the skies; and if it fell away from the people in England, we should be mounting up into the skies.

It is equal nonsense to talk of its wandering off into infinite space : which way? Up or down ; right or left? It must take either, and what should guide it? In all probability the nearest heavenly body that had power to attract it.*

If attracted to the sun, it would most likely be consumed, and injure no other world.

If attracted to the nearest planet, by the collision it would ruin both itself and the world with which it came in concussion. Would the just God suffer a world that continued obedient, to be ruined by one that had disobeyed and broken loose from his laws? Surely not.

* I am supposing the world would cohere together without attraction, which it would not ; but without the force of repulsion, the same rule which applies to the whole would apply equally to the invisible atoms.

Would, then, God suffer man, who had not dis-obeyed, to be ruined by fallen angels, who had disobeyed?

And who are fallen angels?

Not former inhabitants of heaven, the abode of the perfect God.

No created being is good by nature; *that* belongs to God, and to God only.

All created beings must have struggled and worked up to goodness, as we are now doing.

If those whom we call angels fell, it must have been before they reached heaven, or perfection. Heaven would not be heaven if it were possible to sin there; and the constitution or government of the Eternal Heavens will not be altered or improved because man's salvation is completed.

If angels were originally created good, they could never have had free will; then would they have had no *power* to disobey or fall: and if they never had power or free will to choose between good and evil, they would have been forced to good. Heaven would then have been a despotism, and God a despot, and all under him slaves.

But man is made for freedom, educated in this world by free will, and finally to attain the perfect freedom of heaven.

By such a plan only can created beings become good, perfect, and still free; not slaves under a despot. "Truth can never be guaranteed unless error has had a fair trial."

This is the secret of human free will, or power of sin ; because goodness and perfection can never be sure and stedfast, and yet free, till even evil has been tried and condemned.

We suppose man a fallen creature, under the wrath of God. Why this fierce wrath upon us ?

We are placed in a state in which it is impossible for us not to sin, that is, disobey *the perfect* law of God. We are in a transition state ; we cannot help being imperfect, till we have reached perfection, and we cannot reach perfection till we have been convinced of sin ; and till we have had a knowledge of sin, we cannot be convinced of evil ; and till we are convinced of sin, we cannot be convinced of righteousness.

Then only can man be convinced of judgment between good and evil—convinced that sin is evil, and righteousness good.

Thus only can we be *sure* and *firm* in perfection in heaven.

That there cannot be an eternal hell is demonstrable.

There are but two states : good and evil.

Hell cannot be good, therefore must be evil.

Then hell, if eternal, would be the perpetuation and immortalization of evil, sin, and pain.

There cannot be immortality, or eternity, apart from God, for they are the very nature of God, and all eternity *is* God.

Then God's own nature must be divided into part eternal sin, and part eternal good.

To imagine a devil having power to give immortality to evil is to say he is God; " eternal death " is a contradiction in words. It is *dead life*, which is impossible.

When perfection is reached, eternity is reached; for perfect good cannot gain more good, neither can it be less good.

Immortality is the same yesterday, to-day, and for ever.

If hell is eternal, it is also the same yesterday, to-day, and for ever; for eternity is *one*, and has not, like time, a past or a future; if so, hell is equal to heaven, and the devil to God—the devil the creator of immortal evil, and God the creator of immortal good.

This cannot be, for two equal forces neutralize one another.

So, then, there cannot be any eternal sin, or eternal hell. Sin belongs only to this world of mortality and change, and has, in time, a beginning and an ending.

If there is no place of eternal punishment, men cannot be eternally punished.

And as there is but *one eternity*, the place of the *One Eternal*, all men must reach that eternity.

And when ?

When they are perfect.

There can be no skip, or short-cut, to heaven by the imputed merits of another, for that can never be *our own* which we have not worked for.

CHAPTER XXI.

THE DEVIL'S WORKS.

THEOLOGIANS will not have the saying that "Evil is only good in the making," though in other words they affirm the same thing, namely, that good has been made out of evil. Some of the most useful inventions and discoveries which have resulted in the utmost benefit to mankind, have been supposed to originate from the devil.

Luther styles him "God's deacon upon earth."

By the same idea (in a sentence before quoted), Mr. Farrar says,—"Under the overruling of a beneficent Providence, antagonism is made the law of human progress."

Both Luther's and Farrar's words have the same meaning, that from an unholy thought and unholy thing, what was evil was produced, but God, working on this base of an unholy thought and an evil thing, changed it to good.

Now, I say that to affirm, "Evil is only good in the making," and that the "devil is God's deacon upon earth," is blasphemy. When shall we comprehend justly the meaning of these three texts?—

"Can Satan cast out Satan?"

" A good tree cannot bring forth evil fruit, neither can a corrupt tree bring forth good fruit. By their fruits ye shall know them."

" Every good gift and every perfect gift is from above."

Those, however, who think with Luther, say a thought or discovery which causes evil to be cast out; which proves itself by its fruits to be good, did not originally come from Him who gives every good gift, but from the power of evil. Is not this blasphemy? I will take one instance, the invention of gunpowder, which, I suppose, would rank first in the estimation of most people as the work of the devil.

God gave, through the reasoning mind of a man, the thought, which, by the industry of man, gradually produced the most perfect means of self-defence and control over the animal creation, which it was his work to subdue. It gave him the means not only of protecting his body from danger, but also, what is far greater, the power of protecting both mind and body from the unholy usurpation of tyranny.

The means were no more evil in themselves than the teeth and claws of a lion, which are his weapons for protecting himself and procuring his food.

But our artificial weapons are so powerful, that by arming the few with them, the many are preserved from danger, to follow, unmolested, a higher path in the pursuit of truth, in philosophy and science.

We are not obliged, as are animals, every one to make use of his own natural strength for defence, and fight one against the other, as before the invention of gunpowder and firearms was, in a great measure, the case : prevented only in proportion to the perfection of the artificial weapons men could command, such as bows, arrows, spears, &c. ; and as every weapon increased in efficiency and power, so far did man, in this manner advance above the brute, and the brute necessity of fighting. We can even trace this fact as far back as the earliest records of man yet discovered, where the stone, bronze, and iron weapons, lie side by side with the bones of the men who lifted them, and witness to their gradual rise and improvement.

There is sin only when we take this good and perfect gift; given us for protection and freedom, and make it subservient to wrong purposes, to gratify our private malice and revenge, forgetful of the God of love, who trusted us with the gift.

The theological bugbears of hell and devil, are useless, and worse than useless—mischievous. They have never deterred any man from crime, but have only substituted one crime for another; for open vices, cowardice, hypocrisy, Phariseeism ; but the best, the noblest, the boldest, most courageous spirit, they have vitiated, and turned to reckless crime.

There are some who say, come death, come hell, I will KNOW! Some are so miserable in this life, that no fear of hell can keep them in it; they kill themselves to escape their misery. Would they do so, if they knew that to run away from their present life would only be to have to go back, perhaps to come again to that very rock upon which they struck, and be forced to mount over it?

There is no more fertile producer of crime than fear.

Look at smuggling, as an instance.

What an amount of crime was perpetrated in pursuit of this contraband trade. And what caused it? The trade itself was caused by *antagonism*, by the attempt of the law to restrain the freedom of commerce. The crimes following in its train were caused by fear of punishment.

"When any of the numerous smugglers were taken, some of them were hanged, some broken on the wheel, some burnt alive."

None of these atrociously cruel punishments prevented smuggling, but only made those who embarked in it, reckless, dissolute, and immoral.

"These men, desperate from fear of punishment, and accustomed to the commission of every crime, contaminated the surrounding population, introduced

o

into peaceful villages, vices formerly unknown, caused the ruin of entire families, spread, wherever they came, drunkenness, theft, dissoluteness."—*Buckle's History.*

Yet, but for smuggling, a French author declares, trade could not have been conducted, but must have perished, in consequence of incessant interference. Duties were levied on exports and imports: all branches of industry that flourished, therefore, those which the country showed it wanted, were heavily taxed; while others that declined, which the country showed it did not want, were tried to be propped up by bounties.

Here is no evil producing good, nor good coming of evil. The good desire for progress in commerce, producing free trade, called then smuggling, because carried on in spite of foolish and unjust laws.

The sins of smuggling were caused by evil laws, and immorality, by fear of punishment.

When the laws were repealed, and the fear removed, the crimes ceased.

Mr. Mill remarks, that "antagonism of influences is absolutely necessary to progress."

It may be necessary to, but cannot be productive of, progress. Antagonism is not the law of progress, but of check and stoppage, preventing progress going ahead too fast; so, keeping order in the march of progress.

It throws back the ball, when it might otherwise overshoot the mark. This is simply action and reaction.

In Mr. Darwin's book on "Natural Selection," the writer says, "That all organic beings are exposed to severe competition." But this competition, or antagonism is not the *cause* of advance, but the necessary stop to over-production, by the destruction of one species by another, as in another page he says, "Although some species may be now increasing, more or less rapidly, in numbers, all cannot do so, for the world would not hold them. . . . Hence we may confidently assert that all plants and animals are tending to increase in a geometrical ratio, that all would most rapidly stock every station in which they could anyhow exist, and that the geometrical tendency to increase must be *checked* by destruction at some period of life."

Antagonism, or competition, is not, then, the law of progress, but of the counter-check to over-progress or over-growth.

CHAPTER XXII.

SELF-LOVE.

SIN is the bending of the spirit, or soul, to the worship of the flesh or body, which is idolatry and disobedience to every law of God.

The only worship God desires is our love.

To love him with all the strength and power of mind and soul, and to love our neighbor as ourselves, is God's command, and also nature's command.

Now, here are three injunctions, not two only:—

> The love of Self.
> The love of Man.
> The love of God.

In this is comprehended *all* the law and prophets.

If self is not to be loved, how can it be put as a measure whereby we are to love our neighbor?

If we do not love self, how can we love our brother? By the same rule as, if we love not our brother, how can we love God?

Here are three links not to be divided, and each must be kept whole and perfect; but ignorance prevents our preserving either perfectly.

Surely, the reader may say, " I know how to love myself perfectly." I think not.

Selfishness is not self-love : selfishness is the greatest evil a man can inflict on himself—makes him wretched in himself, and hateful to others. This, therefore, cannot be the fruit of love, but of ignorance. A man who loves himself perfectly will endeavor to protect himself from bodily and mental injury ; and this only he can do fully by understanding the physical and mental laws ; and by knowledge of the former can we alone interpret the moral or spiritual laws.

Disobedience to any of these laws produces unhappiness.

A man who indulges in drunkenness and debauchery does not love himself wholly and entirely, but shows partiality to one bodily sense, sacrificing to that one, every other sense ; and not only his bodily senses and physical strength, but degrades to that one taste his mental and moral powers. Thus by a want of true love to self, gross ignorance produces great wickedness.

By abstracting one of the bodily senses or feelings, calling it sin, and endeavoring to weaken or root it out, we destroy the due balance of the body, as much as by pandering to one, and causing that sense to be overpowerful. To destroy the balance of power in the body is equally dangerous as to destroy the

balance of power between nations—conquer one
and another will usurp its place; or as ill-judged
as to destroy the balance of parties in a state.

The prime mover of the world is self-love.

In the animal kingdom self-love has been the
mover upwards; the intense desire for self-preserva-
tion blindly followed; the self-love of another species
as blindly followed, coming in contact, and checking
in each undue usurpation or over-growth.

Political economy follows in the same steps, is
built on the principles of self-love—stigmatized unjustly as selfishness. But in political economy we
have not to follow self-love blindly, but to work
out its principles by the clearest light of our
reason.

Could we fully comprehend these principles, antagonism would end; there would be peace, not only
amongst nations but individuals.

It has been observed, that in reckoning on perfection in enlightenment, we do not take our passions
into consideration. Allowing that all human passions are good in themselves until they usurp more
than their due share of power, it is a question merely
of the cause of this usurpation. Passions becoming
vices must, in a great measure, be the effect of bodily
or mental disease. Knowledge would go far towards
removing this.

Action and reaction also work eternally; remove

ignorance ever so slightly, you remove prejudice
and vice. The removal of vice, which has hitherto
blinded the eyes, again, further opens the mind to
enlightenment. Self-love will remove selfishness,
and selfishness being removed, will tend to perfect
self-love.

The very first measure of political economy was
to show how self was injured by the attempt at
selfish appropriation; and through self-love to build
prosperity on the wider basis of love to man.

When it was believed that the accumulation of
gold by one particular country constituted wealth,
each nation sought to draw off, or appropriate, the
gold of another nation; hence endless quarrels and
wars between one country and another, and between
rival tradesmen and merchants, and real impoverish-
ment to themselves. But when men were fully
convinced that this selfishness was destructive to
prosperity, the principle of freedom was established.

"When these great truths were recognised, all the
old notions respecting the balance of trade, and the
supreme importance of the precious metals, at once
fell to the ground. The result is, that the commer-
cial spirit, which formerly was often warlike, is now
invariably pacific."

By freedom there is no destruction to the balance
of trade, but it thus naturally finds its own balance,
which interference, instead of assisting, prevented.

It is the business of every individual to advance his own interests, position, and rights, in this world and in the next.

I might say, this is his duty only and solely.

This is self-love, not selfishness.

It will be acknowledged in the end that every atom of good one man has selfishly appropriated, either for his body or his soul, in an exactly equal proportion he has deprived self of good.

Another error the age is beginning to learn is, the mistake of giving. The whole system of private and public charity is rotten, and productive of more mischief than good. It is as impossible to give to, as it is to teach, another.

By giving, you only impoverish self, wrong the industrious and weaken the indolent.

The motto of men should be, " Never give, never steal," but work up in your own groove; raise yourself, but never push another down, or you fall yourself. Help another to raise himself if you can, but never lift him, or he will fall lower than before.

CHAPTER XXIII.

BODY AND SPIRIT.

THERE is a Trinity in our Godlike nature. Soul, body, and mind, or reason, which connects soul and body, and is the only medium of communion between spirit and flesh.

Soul is not mind, but above it.

Body is not mind, but below it.

Mind stands between, and unites both.

Spirit cannot communicate with body but through reason, or mind, neither can body communicate with spirit but through the mind.

We say in the creeds that we believe in the resurrection of the body. *Possibly* it may rise again on the earth, but it is impossible for it to ascend into heaven.

The writer of the "Answers" to the "Essays and Reviews," says, "We have been accustomed to think that the great hope of mankind, as brought to life in the Gospel, is the resurrection of the flesh, but now it appears we believe 'in such a form of immortality as may be consistent with union with the spirit of our Eternal Life-giver.' This has a very Brahminical sound."

If this is one of the Brahminical doctrines it only proves how much more enlightened they were than the Jewish doctrines, and also than church doctrines.

We forget that the body is only a machine, made for a certain purpose, for a certain time, and worked by a certain means.

It is nourished, or kept alive, by the blood, and that blood is made from the matter and material of the earth, and could not be produced in an immaterial world.

How can corruption inherit incorruption? Decay and decomposition go on every instant in our bodies; every breath we exhale, by passing through our lungs, has become impure, and not fit again to be inhaled. The heart, the lungs, and the digestive organs are made expressly for the purpose of effecting this constant decay, and also constant renewal, by converting the material of the earth into nourishment.

Of what use, then, the lungs, if the impurities of the venous blood had not to be removed?

Of what use the heart, if a fresh supply of blood to counterbalance loss, was not required?

Of what use the digestive organs, if no food was required to be digested for nourishment?

Of what use the muscles, which are made to combat resistance of matter, if no matter to resist?

Of what use the skin, and pores of the skin, whose

principal office is to carry off impurities, if there were no impurities to carry off?

The body, then, and the complex organs to carry on the functions of the body, would be utterly useless and unnecessary in any other state of being, but this life on earth, and if useless, then only an incumbrance to be cast away.

And how can we rise again, *every one* with our own body?

Our bodies are but the cast-off materials of the bodies of our forefathers—but the repetition of former bodies. The men of past generations, who have died and been buried, by the decomposition of the constituent particles of their bodies have been resolved into their several elements, and those elements have again passed into our bodies. We have taken up these atoms with every breath we inhale, we have imbibed them in the food we eat. The wheat we make our bread of has drawn up some of these atoms from the ground; the animals we eat have partaken of these atoms in the fresh meadow grass. The sun has drawn up exhalations from many a church-yard, which the clouds have returned again to crops and pastures, and the same moisture has filtered through the earth to the water we drink. Who shall claim a prior right to this bone and flesh, which nature has passed through so many bodies?

Do you call it a "horrid idea," reader, that you are

daily receiving into your body, and that that body is partly formed and nourished by, the same identical elements that constituted the bodies of both men and animals before you?

It but shows that we are all of one and the same substance. Our bodies are neither more or less than the bread (food) we eat! Professor Owen remarks, " Everywhere in organic nature we see the means not only subservient to an end, but that end accomplished by the simplest means."

Where would be the means subservient to the end in carrying about a useless body in elements not fit to assimilate with it, or construct it? But body, that would be an encumbrance in another world, is an assistant here, and must be carefully preserved. I have felt vexed and angry with myself that I could not fix, and bring into words, thoughts that seemed glancing and flitting in my mind. I thought by fasting and retirement I could make the body more ethereal—more like spirit to discern spirit, ; but instead, I only found I brought it more to decay and earthliness. If I refused food, or society, or exercise, instead of finding my thoughts clearer, I had no thoughts at all—thought had vanished; I only apprehended a feeling of corporeal weakness and suffering.

I found if I desired to think well and healthily I must study to keep up the full pulse of strong vitality ; to eat, drink, sleep, walk, in moderation, not excess, for the health of the body ; and laugh, play, sing, dance, or indulge in some other amusement, for the health of the mind, to force it sometimes to quit the all-absorbing thought, and by temporary excitement force the mind to feel other emotions.

By the first, I gained strength of body to continue bodily labor; by the second, in breaking off the strained attention to one object, I found I acquired more power when I returned to it. I feel thankful sometimes to a person or a book that can make me laugh heartily. It does me good for a week; it is as refreshing as looking at a beautiful bouquet of flowers—for are not flowers Nature's smiles and laughter ?

I love to have them on my table while I write, to refresh me when I look up from my desk or book, that my eyes may have joy in looking at their fresh, bright colors. Often, in New Zealand, I have wandered alone into the deep forest, where, in all probability, never before had the foot of man trodden. How calm, solemn, magnificent ! These great trees had grown by God's eternal laws ; had never asked or received anything from the hands of men. No man had planted them, reared them, tended them ; the eye of man had not even looked on them, or his finger touched them. I almost involuntarily uncovered my head, and felt in that solemn stillness something almost holy.

Can any one follow me in imagination into this dark, solemn forest, and then, after a while, realize what a sense of weight comes over the mind; he gives a sigh of oppression, the solemnity becomes gloom, the magnificence terrible, the silence insupportable. With what a sense of relief he emerges into the sunshine, and sees and hears the bustle and life of the homestead!

Sometimes, when I have remained till the shades of evening have darkened round me, and the damp chill has penetrated my body, the gloom has amounted almost to horror. I can easily imagine how, in solitude, a man, by constantly dwelling on one string of ideas which required a stretch of the mind's powers, may become visionary, and at last mad.

So may we explain the excitement which leads, by means of fasting and macerating the body, to supposed supernatural sights, and visions, which borders on madness. Remove the bodily shield or protection, and madness or idiocy is the result; weaken it, even, and mental aberration will ensue.

The result of such morbid excitement, I consider the Book of Revelation to be—the effect of solitude on the sensitive mind of St. John—engrossed by one idea, wound up to the highest pitch of religious fervor. To an affectionate nature like his, the loss of companionship must have been fatal to his reason.

These mental aberrations need not be caused by bodily fear or a guilty conscience; but the thoughts in which the mind is absorbed, penetrate it deeper and more forcibly than the mind can bear.

I have often had occasion to ride home alone on a moonless night, and in pouring rain, through a forest track, so dark that I could not discern my horse's head, or where I was being carried, splashing through mud and rain, my horse occasionally plunging knee-deep into a mud-hole, one hand held before my face to ward off the branches of the trees that came across my path. I never felt fear, or the slightest degree of oppression, my thoughts being entirely occupied in guiding and checking my horse, sticking to my saddle and keeping my face from being scratched.

The absurdity of imagining a spirit, either God or angel of eternity, entering this material earth and living in time, is equally foolish as trying to make the body spiritual, or a tenant of a spiritual existence.

It is like a painter trying to embody his ideal of an angel, by giving him the shape of a man and the wings of a bird. The flying appendages are stuck on, no one knows how, or how they are to be moved, or if able to move, how they could raise the heavy body from the ground, is equally difficult to comprehend.

The artist draws only the muscles of the arms and shoulders, and chest, intended to move the arms and shoulders, if he attempted to insert muscles to move the wings, he would draw a deformity.

We forget that no amount of wings could lift us above the material elements. The body of a bird poised in the air by his wings, remains aloft only by the resistance of the air under them. Carry one up in a balloon, where the atmosphere becomes more rarefied, he finds no support, and drops like lead. The law of gravitation asserts its claim to all earthly bodies, and none but those of earth can live on earth.

How or where can the artist express his ideal? Not in the body; in that he can show only the perfect man in the well-developed muscles, the erect and graceful carriage, telling of work and resistance overcome and to be overcome; in the angelic expression he can succeed in imparting to the countenance, can he only pourtray the angel. The glory of the spirit shining on the mind, and through the mind lighting up the countenance.

CHAPTER XXIV.

THE LORD'S SUPPER.

I HAVE long thought, long before the publication of "Essays and Reviews," that the simple words of Christ were all a Christian was bound to believe. I now think a man is not *bound* to believe anything he *cannot* believe. This is certainly an undeniable proposition, but one we are slow to accept.

There is no more possibility of there being a sin called *heresy*, than there is, or ever was, a sin called witchcraft: believing or disbelieving is no more under our control, and to be forced or commanded, than is loving or hating.

The words of Christ, and the words of the prophets of the Old Testament, being handed down to us by fallible agents, requires our reason to discriminate between the word of God and the word of man.

We have, in some measure, done so, by the light of science; and when the false covering or "protection" of inspiration is removed, and truth is free, science will enable us to do so, quickly and surely.

Had we never read a page of the Old Testament, or the Acts of the Apostles, or the Epistles, I believe we should have been better and more enlightened

P

Christians than we are at present; because, by the chain of inspiration, we have been bound to them: bound to a gross and material worship, which has been suffered to obscure a more pure and spiritual one. Nearly all our church doctrines we have received from St. Paul. It would seem that Jesus, by choosing poor fishermen to hand down his words, took those who were least prejudiced by the Jewish doctrines of the Scribes and Pharisees and teachers of the law, men who would simply receive his words, and hand them down as simply, without dogmatizing or doctrinizing upon them.

Thus would the words of truth surely and insensibly have freely worked upon the mind.

St. Paul completely subverted this intention; he destroyed freedom of thought.

A man of strong mind and fierce energetic temperament, brought up from his youth by the strictest sect of the Pharisees, though wonderfully modified and softened by christian truths, could not wholly throw off the effect of the educational moulding of his mind, and the power and desire of mental usurpation in his disposition, so by and through St. Paul principally, have we received the Jewish shadow and tinge thrown over the christian faith, and a certain cruelty and fierceness grown up together with it. Most certainly, though unintentionally, St. Paul was an enemy to Christ, or love, in so doing.

Yet, though St. Paul certainly taught what Jesus did not teach, by his means, principally, was the Gospel made known to the world. We hear of religion being revealed only to simple unlearned men; but none of these unlearned men have handed it down to us. Abraham was a man of this simple faith and piety, but it was Moses, a man fully instructed in the wisdom of the Egyptians, who formed the Jewish religion, and it was by succeeding in grafting this Egyptian wisdom on to the Hebrew morality that, in a great measure, constituted it the noblest religion of that age. So, though the disciples were with Jesus in his lifetime, and were instructed by himself in his religion, not one of these men succeeded in gaining more than a local and life-interest for that religion. But St. Paul, a man learned both in Greek and Hebrew wisdom, has stamped the faith and love of Jesus into the church religion of the present day.

Jesus supposed that Peter would be the great founder of his religion; but the world has received little from him. The Roman Catholics indeed constituted him their principal apostolic head, but only because Jesus affirmed that "the keys" should be given to him; and this power they would willingly receive for being counted as his rightful successors; but they, no more than ourselves, build their church doctrines on his words,

We read of St. Paul's travels, of his unwearied zeal in spreading the Gospel. St. Peter's name occurs at the beginning of the Acts of the Apostles, but St. Paul's fills up the remainder, and to him all the primitive churches appear to have applied for instruction and guidance; and for his faithfulness, unselfishness, and carelessness of poverty, pain, danger, and death, for the sake of Christ, no one can withhold a just tribute of admiration and respect.

A writer, the Rev. R. Taylor, in a book called "The Diegesis," published in 1844, is much less *respectful* to the character of St. Paul than I am. He says, "Paul of Tarsus, whose fourteen Epistles make up the greater part of the bulk of the New Testament, repeatedly inculcates and avows the principle of deceiving the common people; talks of his having been upbraided by his own converts with being crafty, and catching them with guile (2nd Cor. xii. 16); and of his known and wilful lies, abounding to the glory of God (Romans iii. 7). Accessory to the avowed and consecrated principle of *deceit*, was that of *ignorance*. St. Paul, in the most explicit language, had taught and maintained the absolute necessity of extreme ignorance, in order to obtain celestial wisdom, and gloried in the power of the Almighty as destroying the wisdom of the wise, and bringing to nothing the understanding of the prudent, and purposely choosing the foolish things, and the weak things, and the base things, as objects of his adoption and vessels of his grace."

There is, undoubtedly, truth in both these accusations against St. Paul, though rather broadly and exaggeratedly stated.

We may take the Lord's Supper as an instance where his influence has been exercised for evil. This ceremony is often regarded with superstitious reverence by some, and utter neglect, principally through fear, by others.

The catechism says this and the Sacrament of Baptism, were " ordained by Christ himself;" surely, then, we are not wrong in referring to the words of Christ to ascertain what he really did ordain.

Let us read the records of the Evangelists; I shall insert the words, as perhaps the reader may not care to take the trouble to look for them, if I only mark the references:

Matt. xxvi. 26 to 29—" And as they were eating, Jesus took bread, and blessed it" (the margin says, " Many Greek copies have, *gave thanks*," which is much more consistent than that Jesus should bless the inanimate bread) "and brake it, and gave it to the disciples, and said, Take eat; this is my body." " And he took the cup and gave thanks, and gave it to them saying, Drink ye all of it; for this is my blood of the New Testament, which is shed for many for the remission of sins. But I say unto you, I will not drink henceforth of this fruit of the vine until that day when I drink it new with you in my Father's kingdom."

St. Mark is almost word for word a repetition of St. Matthew, except that it is written, "blessed" instead of "blessed *it*," as in St. Matthew, referring to what the church calls one of the "sacred elements." St. Luke is somewhat different in his account.

St. Luke xxii. 15 to 20—"And he said unto them, With desire I have desired to eat this passover with you before I suffer: For I say unto you, I will not any more eat thereof until it be fulfilled in the kingdom of God. And he took the cup and gave thanks, and said, Take this, and divide it among yourselves: For I say unto you I will not drink of the fruit of the vine until the kingdom of God shall come. And he took the bread, and gave thanks, and brake it, and gave unto them, saying, This is my body which is given for you; this do in remembrance of me. Likewise, also, the cup after supper, saying, This cup is the New Testament in my blood, which is shed for you."

St. John, the beloved disciple, who leaned on the breast of Jesus at supper, makes no mention of this occurrence as a ceremony, but relates instead the spiritual ideas it was intended to inculcate. Beginning with the words, "A new commandment I give unto you, That ye love one another," and ending with "Arise, let us go hence."

St. Matthew and St. Mark both agreeing that the sacrament was the last act of Christ before singing a hymn and going to the Mount of Olives. St. Luke narrates, without regard to time, the conversation which gave rise to the lesson of humility told by St. John in the outward act of washing the disciples' feet. A discussion as to which of them should be greatest. And Jesus answered in word and deed, "Whether is greater he that sitteth at meat or he that serveth, is not he that sitteth at meat? but I am among you as one that serveth."

Why might not the outward, visible sign of the inward and spiritual grace of humility be construed into a ceremony or sacrament, as well as the outward sign of the spiritual grace of love.

St. Luke is the only one who gives the slightest clue to the idea that Jesus intended in any manner to institute a ceremony, by the words, "This do in remembrance of me."

What, then, does "*this*" apply to : but that whenever they broke bread they should call to remembrance their lord and Master. There was nothing unusual, or more than ordinarily sacred in the breaking of bread at this last supper; he gave thanks, called a blessing, as was always his custom, before taking meat; he did so when he fed the multitude with the loaves and fishes. He gave thanks when he handed the cup of wine before supper; but it would seem he did not partake of it himself, telling his disciples, to divide it amongst themselves, as he would drink no more wine while on earth: then he could *not* have partaken of the cup it was the custom to pass round after supper, which we call the sacramental cup.

The two other Gospels imply the same: in St. Matthew, it is "Drink *ye* all of it. . . But I say unto you, I will not drink henceforth of this fruit of the vine." And in St. Mark, "When he had given thanks, he gave it to them, and they all drank of it. . . Verily I say unto you, I will drink no more of the fruit of the vine."

The only passage bearing any similarity to this in St. John is, "Hereafter I will not talk much with you, for the prince of this world cometh, and hath nothing in me."

It would seem that at this last supper, Jesus partook of no wine, but desired to meet his end with a calm, quiet, and composed spirit. That they who had accused him of being a gluttonous man, and a wine-bibber, would find nothing of Beelzebub or the prince of this world in him.

The words, "Take, eat, this is my body," and, "Drink ye all of it, for this is my blood of the New Testament," will present a different aspect to every mind that strives to comprehend them. I can only offer the meaning which is suggested to me, which may not be satisfactory to others: according as the mind is constituted, the words may be interpreted from the lowest materialism to the purest spiritualism.

I would first premise that the more we spiritualize a truth, the more we elevate it, and the nearer we approach to God, who is a spirit, and must be worshipped in spirit. The emblems of the bread and wine are somewhat different; it is, 'bread is my body, but the wine is not *my* blood, but my blood *of the New Testament*, or the New Testament sealed in my blood.'

Bread and wine are taken as the emblems of the body and *spirit* of Jesus Christ, not the flesh and blood. Bread is *the* body, comprehending both flesh and blood. Supposing the wine intended to signify the blood would be but a repetition of a part included previously in the whole.

This is my interpretation. Jesus took bread, and brake it, and said, "this is my body;" this bread, (or food) which has nourished my human body, and is composed like bread, of earthly materials, is, like it also, to be broken, and crumbled into dust. "Take eat," in token that your earthly body and my earthly body are one flesh, and one nature; not the flesh only (as Shylock imagined he could abstract the flesh without the blood), but flesh, blood, and bones.

In the emblem of wine, we may read a deeper significance—an emblem of Christ's spirit, and the spirit bequeathed to us in the New Testament, the spirit of love and joy.

Drink ye all of this wine, which makes glad the heart of man, and see in it a type of the truths I have told you, which shall be full of love and truth and joy to the hearts of all men. He did not partake of it, for his soul was exceeding sorrowful unto death. He gave joy to them, but met suffering himself, and gave his life for the truth.

When on a previous occasion the Jews murmured at Jesus, for saying he would give them his flesh to eat, and said it was a hard saying, or one hard to be understood, he said, "my words are spirit and they are life," and "THE FLESH PROFITETH NOTHING," and yet we say that flesh and blood takes away our sins; but Jesus says, the *flesh* was of *no profit;* not the *bread* profiteth nothing, but the *flesh* was not to be regarded.

It is idolatry to say that Christ's human body can sanctify our souls.

The spirit is far above *any* material body.

Our souls are above Christ's earthly body.

Christ's body was purer than our bodies, and his spirit infinitely holier than our spirits, but *no* body can purify spirit, or be above spirit or soul. The body is but dust, and the body of Jesus was as our bodies, made of the earth, and fed from the earth, and returned to earth, but the spirit is everlasting, and returns to God.

To turn this last supper which Jesus partook of with his disciples into a church ceremony, we must refer, as far as I can see, not to Christ's ordination, but to St. Paul's interpretation.

It is possible that the Jewish converts might have considered it as a substitution for the feast of the Passover; such an inference would naturally arise in their minds, from its being instituted on the same day, and during, or rather, after its commemoration. Christ, however, neither says nor infers such an idea, and we, as Christians, have simply nothing to do with Jewish observances.

The Passover was celebrated at a particular time once a year; but Christ's supper was to be held in remembrance whenever the disciples met to break bread and drink wine. Its being connected in the minds of the Jews with the Passover, gave the idea of its being the celebration of a sacrifice, that it was a commemoration of the death of Christ; but it appears to me it was to be eaten more in remembrance of the life than the death.

The words of Jesus are, " This do in *remembrance of me*;" therefore, not what *was* to occur, but what *had* occurred. Though on the second meeting of the disciples to break bread they could not fail to connect with it the recollection of his death also ; but on this first celebration it could only have been in remembrance of the life, that after his death his disciples might call to mind how he had walked, and talked, and eaten with them in love.

The church commemorates the death of Christ in the sacrament, and in all her doctrines this is more prominent than the life, because the outward suffering of the crucifixion is more apparent to our bodily sight, while it is not considered how much greater and more difficult was the constant, uniform, daily, and hourly endurance shown in the life, than in the comparatively momentary, though sharper pain of the death.

The first thing that strikes a person who desires to partake of the Lord's Supper, when he opens the prayer-book to read the service, is, that the introduction to the feast of love is full of threats, of curses, and anathemas.

Most clearly we receive these from St. Paul.

The exhortation saith, " So is the danger great, if we receive the same unworthily. For then we are guilty of the Body and Blood of Christ our Saviour; we eat and drink our own damnation, not considering the Lord's Body : we kindle God's wrath against us ; we provoke him to plague us with divers diseases, and sundry kinds of death."

These curses are drawn from the account of the

parable of the marriage supper, and the fate of Judas, who, it is supposed partook of the last supper.

I cannot see that either have any connection with it. The last supper was the touching and melancholy feast of parting on earth. The parable was a representation of the kingdom of heaven; the feast of the fullness of joy when Christ should drink it new, or in a new manner, on the occasion of the marriage, or everlasting union of Christians, Christ, and God. The one when the bridegroom was about to be taken away, the other when the bride and the bridegroom were to be joined for ever. The man cast out from the feast—one who had not on the marriage garment of Christian Love.

The sop given to Judas was not during the feast of love; to imagine so would be to desecrate it.

A careful reading of the four Gospels convinces me that Judas was not present at all at the last breaking of bread or the taking of the last cup.

I have before remarked that both St. Matthew and St. Mark place the dispensing the commemoration bread and wine, as the last act of Jesus before singing a hymn and leaving the house. St. John says *immediately* Judas received the sop he went out, probably either from shame, or fear of being recognized. This occurrence is placed by this Evangelist, after the washing of the disciples' feet, and before giving the new commandment to love one another, which I suppose to be the words spoken by Jesus during the outward act of the last supper. St. Luke, in his narrative, takes no account of time, nor does he mention the recognition of Judas as the traitor.

By St. Matthew it would appear that Judas asked Jesus the question, "Master, is it I? and he said unto him, thou hast said," *before* the last breaking of bread.

St. Mark the same, though Judas is not spoken of. The betrayer was one who sat at meat with them at their ordinary supper, and dipped out of the common dish. None but St. John observed that Judas left immediately after the sop; probably he slunk out so secretly that the others did not notice the moment of his departure. But if he left directly after receiving the sop, the sop was given before the sacramental bread and wine, and Judas did not then remain to partake of the sacrament.

We might even think that Jesus showed that he was aware of the treachery of Judas, purposely to cause him to leave, that he might take this feast of love only with those who loved one another, and who loved him.

Moreover, the devil had entered into the heart of Judas before even the commemoration of the feast of the Passover. The crime of betrayal had been meditated and partly carried into execution, when he covenanted with the Pharisees for thirty pieces of silver, therefore could not, in any way have been caused by receiving the bread and wine.

What right, then, has the church or St. Paul, or any other man or men, to thrust curses between us and the participation of the love of God in Christ?

Did Jesus pronounce any curse ? I cannot see it.

Did Christ say, as he gave the bread and wine, he who eats and drinks unworthily shall eat and drink his own damnation ? I cannot find it.

It was the custom at first to assemble to break bread in the name of the Lord every evening; but this assembly soon became riotous, one was hungry and another was drunken, and, in a disorderly manner they seized each one his own supper. This was in every way acting contrary to the spirit of the Last Supper, though if it could have continued as part of the daily life, it would have greatly purified the life.

What so great a check on rioting, gluttony, and drunkenness, as taking the last meal, when these vices are most likely to be indulged in, in loving and joyful fellowship, but with a thankful remembrance of Jesus.

Perhaps, as did Moses, so the Apostles were obliged to divorce it from the daily life, for the hardness of men's hearts. For this cause, affirms St. Paul, "many are weak and sickly among you and many sleep." It could not be the mere fact of not discerning the Lord's body that caused sickness and death, but because the new converts were intemperate, gluttonous, and disorderly. St. Paul had also to condemn their licentiousness; here was quite sufficient cause for their being weak and sickly, and disease would have been induced whether they partook of the communion or not.

I think we misapprehend the character of Jesus by applying to him the text from the Old Testament, "He was a man of sorrows and acquainted with grief."

The Gospels are tinged by the Evangelists with the gloom which their own hearts felt after his departure, and at the persecutions they endured, perhaps also, slightly disappointed that Jesus was not to be what, during his life-time they always looked for, an earthly king of the Jews. And from them we fail to see any joyousness in the life of Christ; we think smiles and laughter would be quite unpoetical, and out of keeping with our ideas of Christ. But one or two texts show that Jesus was not a man plunged in grief and melancholy.

The sneer of the Pharisees that he was gluttonous and a wine-bibber shows that he was in no sense an ascetic, and he, perhaps alone of all noted teachers, adopted no peculiar or isolated mode of life. We read of Levi making a great feast for him, that Martha was cumbered with much serving when he visited the house of Lazarus ; that the Jews accused him of eating and drinking with publicans and sinners—all seemed glad to entertain him at their houses—and they would not have done so had he been a gloomy, unbending, and stern man, who could have no fellowship with their mirth and gaiety.

His immediate followers, or converts, went beyond their master in this, and from moderate enjoyment, descended to license. Had they always eat bread and drank wine, carrying a remembrance of their beloved Lord and Master, who had made them free both in innocent bodily pleasure and spiritual joy, they would have continued to receive both in moderation.

For this reason, I say, that those who, perhaps, once a month, according to the ceremony of the church, receive the holy sacrament, in the spirit of purity and love, do well ; but they who could carry this spirit into their daily life and daily enjoyments, with a thankful heart, would do better. This would be a better test against drunkenness than any tee-total pledge, for the religion of Christ does not require the sacrifice of any one pleasure that the world can give, which can be indulged in without sin ; and sin is the unlawful and inordinate indulgence in any one pleasure to the sacrifice of our bodily or mental health, or the well-being of others.

Q

This is the very spirit of the freedom of Christ, the Son of Man, who came "eating and drinking," not to consider the natural gratification of the senses God has given us to be sinful, but only the excessive indulgence of them.

Whatever is good for the health of the body is not only allowable, but right, and mirth, joy, laughter, are in every way conducive to health, both of body and mind. To endeavor to crush out the sensual feelings, is following, in principle, the monastic and ascetic rule, which is both mistaken and wrong, for God gave both body and spirit. The drunkard, and any of those who are intemperate in pleasure, well know that to abstain entirely, is easier than to take in moderation: a man who has formerly drunk to intoxication, and then has taken the pledge, cannot allow himself one glass, or he relapses; but until he has acquired strength to drink in moderation, you cannot be sure that he is really reformed.

So, moderation requires the greater strength and self-denial, and to *put the cross* on our *intemperate* desires, more difficult, and more commendable, than to utterly crush out the desires themselves.

It is marvellous how the church has contrived to cast out the light of love, by thrusting in the shadow of fear. It reminds me of the story of the sultan, who, seated by a beloved sultana, who also dearly loved him, said, in a thoughtless moment, "Only think, if you were to offend me, if I chose, I could have this little head cut off."

Did love fly away, think you ?

The church says, draw near to receive this blessed sacrament, as pledges of the love of Christ—but mind if you take it unworthily, you shall be damned, both body and soul !

Surely the Christian is hedged round with curses.

If he does not believe the doctrine of the Trinity, as St. Paul and the church interpret it, *without doubt* he shall perish everlastingly !

If he does not come to the Lord's Supper, he " provokes God's indignation against him," and " sore punishment hangeth over his head," and if he does come, there is every probability he will be even more sorely cursed !

Then he must believe all the other doctrines of the church, regeneration, justification, atonement, &c., &c., besides every impossibility recorded from the first chapter of Genesis to the last chapter of Revelations, or he is certainly doomed to everlasting perdition in hell !

But even if he does believe, it is very doubtful if he is saved, for salvation, which it is said Jesus came to procure for every man, was never intended but for the " select small flock." There is not one of these so-called fundamental doctrines of the church, which cannot be traced to the story of the Garden of Eden;

for "**Man is a fallen creature**" is the very foundation of them; and, what are all these doctrines if
investigated?

Nonsense covered over with *Mystery*, inscribed
above *Inspiration*. Not to be touched. Not to be
looked at too closely!

But the truths of God, like the works of nature,
will bear the most searching and microscopic investigation, and the more we look and examine, the
more beautiful and perfect will they appear—the
more consistent and in harmony one part with
another.

There is one injunction of St. Paul's that is omitted
by the church, that in respect to cleanliness; he en-
joins that those who approach to receive the Holy
Communion should have their "*bodies washed with
pure water;*" and it is as much a command as the
one preceding it in the same verse, a "true heart in
full assurance of faith," and "hearts sprinkled from
an evil conscience."

The full assurance of faith, and the *sprinkling*
of the conscience is insisted upon, but the bodily
cleanliness is omitted; the holiness or faith is supposed to do for both. "Examine your own con-
sciences, *and so* that ye may come holy and clean."

It is an insult to God to approach his table with
unclean bodies; the cleansing of the heart ought to
be done, but not the cleansing of the body left

undone. Also, as the sacrament was in the time of St. Paul received daily, he commanded a daily washing with pure water. I recommend this particularly to the attention of orthodox bishops and divines.

It is useless to say, his command was only intended for inhabitants of warm countries, for in reality cleanliness is even more necessary in a cold than a hot country, for the latter produces free perspiration, which cleanses the pores of the skin, but in the former this is not naturally effected; also the injunction is more necessary in a cold country, for in a warm one it is a luxury, and needs no command.

Cleanliness is not only next to godliness, but is a part of it, as much as temperance and moderation.

Respecting the Sacrament of Baptism, I would say a few words, though not on the vexed subject of baptismal regeneration, but on the outward ceremony. Where shall we find in the words of Christ, or even of the Apostles, authority for the ridiculous and lying farce of godfathers and godmothers?

I say lying farce advisedly, for what else is it to make three persons stand at the altar, and utter most palpable falsehoods? To say of the poor little crying infant before them—who, if it is capable of any ideas at all, thinks the whole affair exceedingly uncomfortable and annoying—that when it grows up, it shall renounce the *devil* and all his works, the pomps and vanity of the world, and all the lusts of the flesh, and believe all the articles of the Christian faith.

What *can* this be but a falsehood ?

According to the church doctrine, salvation is only for the few, and " The World" belongs to the devil; how, then, can we know the baptized child is not one of the devil's children ? but, not reckoning this danger, who is to say the child will not grow up a profligate, an atheist, a Papist, or a Mohammedan ?

I observe, in the baptism for adults, the person baptized—to the question, "Wilt thou then obediently keep God's holy will and commandments, and walk in the same all the days of thy life ? "—answers, " I will endeavor to do so, God being my helper."

But the god-parents, answering the same question for another, whose after life they cannot possibly foretell, say boldly, "I will."

What is to absolve from this oath ?

Are they guiltless, because the child, when it comes of age, is *bound* to perform what they have promised for it ? Is any one *bound* to keep an agreement signed for him, without either his permission or knowledge ?

Baptism, like many other Jewish ceremonies, was derived from the Egyptians. " This use prevailed among ancient, and especially oriental nations, who practised washings and lustrations of various kinds. Tertullian states that in Egypt, disciples were initiated into the religion of Isis, and of Mithra, by means of washing, and that the gods themselves were subjected to ablution. They everywhere absolved by water, which they carry round and sprinkle upon villages, houses, temples, and entire cities. Men are dipped at the Appollonarian and Pelasian games. This, they think, sets them free from their perjuries, and accomplishes their regeneration."—*People's Dictionary of the Bible.*

Let us take into our religion again, the duty of ablution, where, from the most ancient time, it rightfully held its place, but was, in later ages, cast out, because it usurped the place of the higher moral purity; cast down, indeed, so low, that, by many, the religion of being extremely dirty was substituted.

Constant and thorough bodily cleanliness would certainly gain better health, and with better health, better temper; and how much happier the world would be, with only a *little* more good health, and a *little* more good temper.

To many lazy, indolent, and untidy natures, the duty of personal purity requires to be enforced as a religious duty, where no motives of comfort, appearance, or health are sufficient to overcome the natural sluggishness of disposition.

CHAPTER XXV.

DOUBT.

"If you begin to doubt you may doubt your own existence."

"I should respect a man who would complete the circle of dubitation, own himself a thorough sceptic, and say he doubted his own existence."

"How do you know that you are not dreaming at this very moment?"

These three sentences formed the basis of an argument I heard advanced by a gentleman in conversation with another, to, or rather at, a Unitarian who had the day before honestly stated his disbelief in certain articles of our faith, and had given reasonable grounds for so doing.

I have heard a similar objection and dislike to doubting, expressed by many, and for the same reason—that if you allow yourself to begin to doubt you cannot tell where it may ultimately lead you. It may involve the mind in such a maze of uncertainty that you may end by doubting your existence. We cannot be certain that at the present moment we are not dreaming; so, as everything about us, around us, and in us, is in such a perilous state of uncertainty, or rather, unprovableness, do not suffer yourself to "begin to doubt."

Doubt what? It is not "do not begin to doubt the Bible," but "do not begin to *doubt*,"—do not allow the dreadful habit of doubting to get possession of you, or it may lead to awful consequences, that most dreadful of all dreadful consequences, doubting your own existence!

It has a fearful sound, no doubt, but even if such a termination should, or could occur, I do not see that the effects would be anything so *very* dreadful—we should continue to exist notwithstanding. Doubting our own existence, even were such a thing possible, (except in words,) would not cause our death or annihilation. If a man declared, positively, he did *not* exist, would that necessitate his vanishing away into thin air? Not even St. Paul, nor any of the holy apostolic fathers have declared, that if a man disbelieved his own existence he should, "without doubt," perish everlastingly, though, I have *no doubt*, if they had been made acquainted with such a metaphysical subtlety they would have been delighted to have done so; but, as it is, I do not see that it need be such a bugbear to us.

"I should respect a man who would own himself a thorough sceptic," said the speaker; "doubting, itself is wicked, doubting a little is both wicked and contemptible, but go the length of doubting your own existence, and I respect you."

Where would be the respectability?

Certainly it would require some courage, or rather, impudence in a man, boldly to proclaim himself a simpleton, which the assertion that he denied his own existence would decidedly prove him to be ; but, how such a proceeding could gain any man's respect I cannot imagine : but our respect is always granted, whether voluntarily or involuntarily, to any man who truly and reasonably follows up and acts according to his own convictions. It is, however, impossible for a man to act according to his conviction that he does not exist, therefore he proves himself unreasonable.

Notice, also, another contradiction, for doubt and disbelief generally, there is invented a sin called heresy ; and dreadful punishments are threatened to those who commit it, but for the very end of doubt and disbelief, beyond which no man can go, there is not and cannot be any punishment, either bodily or spiritual, which, indeed, is sufficient of itself to prove that there is no such crime as heresy ; the very last phase of it not being punishable. The fact is, doubt is involuntary and not under our control, the first beginning of doubt dawns upon our mind we know not how or when ; unexpectedly a thought strikes us, or some palpable contradiction is suddenly made apparent to us, or some trivial action in an instant gives our mind a distrust of a person. We can no more avoid receiving a doubt than we can avoid seeing an object before us with our eyes open. Therefore it is as inconsistent and as unjust to punish us for doubting as for seeing.

"How do you know that at this moment you are not dreaming?" is always a 'poser,' because, though a man might give many reasons for proving himself not dreaming, still, he feels it very possible that some day he may wake up and find it *all* a dream; but, what connection has this inability to demonstrate our *waking* existence? (for the dreaming sleep of life implies existence as much as waking); what connection has it with believing or disbelieving the Bible? If we burnt and destroyed and disbelieved every word written therein, our existence would not be any more unexplainable or unprovable than it is at present; or, if we swore to believe every word and syllable it contained we should be no more sure of our existence, or be able, certainly, to affirm that we were *not* dreaming.

Existence is the most general of all abstract terms or ideas. It is predicated of the whole world and all things in it. It is the attribute of all nature, and it is an attribute we must *grant* before a step in the investigation of nature can be commenced. To doubt the fact of existence is to doubt nature itself.

Mr. Mills tells us that, " The conclusion in which the best thinkers are now for the most part agreed, that all we can know of Matter, is the sensation which it gives us, and the order of concurrence of those sensations, and that while the substance Body is the unknown cause of our sensations, the substance Mind is the unknown recipient."

It is curious to think that Body, though the most outward part of man, is not conscious ; Mind alone is conscious, body is not conscious of body ; it is the mind only that informs us of, or makes known to us, the body.

There is a great difference between doubting a thing because contrary to nature, and doubting nature itself. Those who doubt many of the alleged facts of the Bible do so from the *first* cause ; would-be metaphysicians through a cloud of words and confusion of ideas pretend to doubt, from the *second.* Those who doubt the Bible do so from the very fact of having a firm belief in nature and her laws ; these metaphysicians, not willing to accept this preliminary standing ground are at a loss, and lose themselves in confusion. Euclid could not have written his problems, or any other thinker have worked them, had he not laid down at the commencement, and had accepted without question certain propositions.

The fact of our own existence and of the existence of a God, or first cause, must be first accepted as unanswerable propositions, and we work upwards from thence, and every truth we discover serves but to prove the truth and strength of our foundation. It is belief in falsehood only, that shakes the belief in the sure foundation of our lives; believe a lie and you recede further from truth, and further from faith in your own existence, for your existence depends upon God, the cause of your existence, and that first cause is Truth.

It is impossible to arrive at the knowledge that a certain thing we had hitherto believed in as true, is false, except by commencing to *doubt;* with regard to alleged facts, or to the truthfulness and honesty of a person's character, we say, " I begin to *doubt* such and such a thing :" " I begin to *doubt* such a person's truth and honesty." It is the first glimmering light that breaks in upon a man's mind—that tells him all is not right. The mischief of the habit of doubting is, when we suffer ourselves to remain in this preparatory state of *doubt*, and are either afraid or too lazy to work in the direction of the doubt till we arrive at a satisfactory evidence as to whether we have doubted rightly or wrongly.

We all know how trying it is to begin to doubt the truth of a friend, or the honesty of a trusted servant. In the first case, the pain often mounts to an agony of heart, and from sheer cowardice of suffering, by being made fully sensible of a friend's insincerity and untruthfulness, we foolishly try to suppress and hide the doubt; but it is useless, the more we hide and thrust it back, the more oppressive it becomes.

It is this natural feeling that has given *doubt* a bad name. For we generally give little thanks for being told what we would rather not know : but it is better to be aware of the dishonesty of a servant or the untruthfulness of a friend, than to continue all our lives to be cheated and duped. When a man discovers that he has been duped by a false friend, there usually arises within him, a feeling of bitterness to the rest of mankind ; he foolishly says, or thinks, that because one has cheated him, all the rest of the world are equally untruthful, and he *doubts* all mankind. So, for a similar reason, we think if we begin to doubt what is said in the Bible to be true, we must inevitably be led to doubt all truth.

I think I can show that this need not by any means follow.

In the first place, a man who bitterly doubted all mankind because one had been untrue to him, would show himself very weak-minded, incapable of reasoning, and wrongly suffering himself to continue in doubt; being completely under the dominion of his feelings, not his reason, and unjustly and wickedly permitting his feelings to conclude all men guilty without investigating whether he was right or wrong in pronouncing such a sentence of condemnation.

Doubt must always be followed up by reason. If in one case we doubt, and will not carefully sift the cause of doubt because we dread to find the truth, we increase in our minds the weight and pain of doubt. But, on the other hand, if we refuse to investigate because we do not wish to find *ourselves* in error, we are guilty of moral deception to ourselves—guilty of ill-judging our fellow-creatures, and, most certainly, the bitterness it engenders punishes ourselves.

In the second place, though the proved falsehood of one man might cause us to doubt all men, the same natural unlimited extension of doubt would *not* occur in doubting the Bible. We doubt all mankind because one of mankind has deceived us, but we are not obliged to doubt God and all truth because men have deceived us in the Bible. It is not God who has deceived us, but men; so, though we may doubt their words, we are not forced, or even naturally inclined, to doubt the truths of God.

Doubt is naturally a most uncomfortable state of mind—a feeling that instinctively every man would avoid if he could; it makes him uneasy and restless. It is not from pleasure that a man begins to doubt, it is *forced* upon him, if it is a real and genuine doubt.

A man who simply denies and contradicts everything, is not a doubter; he is simply an ignorant and conceited fool, who thinks it is something fine and original to set up his own dogmatical contradictions before the thoughtful opinions of wiser men than himself; he has no reason to give *why* he differs, it it is only *he* does not believe. Doubt implies a previous belief, or a knowledge of the fact or person to whom the doubt is applied.

It is no wonder the clergy have such a horror of doubters; for when once a doubt is born in the mind, no effort can exclude it: for a time you may refuse to examine it, but the hidden feeling is so painful, you must make an effort to be rid of it, and the only way to be rid of it is through investigation—and this is what the so-called Christian religion most shrinks from.

It is not only no pleasure to doubt, but it is positive pain to have to doubt either person or thing we once believed in. The feeling of dread we have as to the length doubt may lead us, is a natural one. We know after a doubt or suspicion of the honesty of a confidential servant, or any other person we have fully trusted, becomes confirmed, what a train of duplicities, one after another, is gradually made apparent to us? We look through the past with a feeling almost of shame—shame for our former friend, and shame for the weakness and blindness which have allowed us to be so easily duped; and with a sort of heart-sickness that our trusting faith in another has been so rudely and cruelly dispelled. If great love and affection have accompanied this trust, some men might even say, "I would rather have gone on trusting than have had the pain of knowing myself to have been deceived." Without inquiring here whether such a desire to remain blinded be wise or not, as the first beginning of doubt is involuntary, the only question is, after the doubt has entered the mind, what course is right and best to pursue. There are but two courses, hide the doubt and strive to suppress it, for kill it you cannot; or bring it to the light and prove whether you are right or wrong. In every secular matter we know the latter is the right and just course, but in sacred affairs the clergy tell us the former is the proper course.

If what we believe or disbelieve as to sacred subjects, or our religion, had no influence on our lives or character, their advice might be good; but belief or disbelief in an article of faith is as intimately connected with our life as the belief or disbelief in the truth of a friend; it becomes, then, in this aspect, a secular matter, that is to say, inseparably bound up with our every-day life. In fact, in this as in every other concern of life, there is no broad division between what we call religion and our daily secular affairs, both must be guided by reason, and truth and justice rule them both. What, therefore, influences my every-day life should be a true faith, a

B

fact, an honest person; and should any doubt arise in my mind as to whether the faith, the fact, or the person I hitherto reposed confidence in was not worthy of credit, the only course I am bound to follow is fair, open, and reasonable inquiry.

Should a doubt cross my mind of a subject that could not possibly influence my life, either present or future, I could easily dismiss it; it would neither weigh upon me nor interest me. For instance, I might doubt whether the Gorilla had a *hippocampus minor* in his brain; or, I might doubt whether in the day-time the stars did not wander off into space—neither of these would personally affect me in the least, (though they might affect science). In the same category is the doubt respecting my own existence, whether I believe it or not cannot make the slightest difference, for I shall continue to exist whether I choose to say I believe it or not; but believing or disbelieving an article of faith is very different. Whether I believe that my Creator will punish or reward justly or unjustly: whether I believe that Creator to be a God of wrath, of anger, of jealousy, of vengeance, or of the most perfect justice, love, and happiness, has an incalculable and momentary effect upon my life, not only to-day but from this day to eternity.

How absurd to suppose that God is jealous or angry because we doubt whether there be a God or not. If some little fish in the Thames should say, "Fiddlededee, I know there is no such thing as a Queen of England;" would her Majesty, if made acquainted with the sentiments of the heretical fish, be immediately filled with wrath and jealousy, and swear that when she caught him she would torture him for ever for his disbelief of her dignity and power?

Is God so pitiably *little* as to be angry, because a foolish mortal says he doubts that God rules the world?

Saying we doubt God's existence does us neither harm nor good. The harm lies only in doubting goodness and truth, and worshipping as a God any being who is not perfect in goodness and truth. Believe in truth and you believe in God, whether you own it in words or not; you own it in spirit. He who doubts and hates goodness and truth is the only heretic, and he who worships a vice in the character of his God the only infidel.

Is it not then of vital importance to every man to know whether what we have hitherto been told to believe of God be true of Him or false? The question is so momentous that even if we desired it, we cannot dismiss it as we would a question of no consequence.

Neither is it at all probable that after much pains-taking and labor we have reasoned, and conscientiously sought out a true answer to these questions, that we should be induced to descend to those metaphysical niceties that are of no vital importance ; or even if we did, it would be mere child's play—doing generally neither good nor harm, but if either, good, simply as an exercise to the mind.

Besides the mischief to ourselves of believing a lie, and having stamped on our minds a false impression of our God, by continuing to *appear* to believe what really we do not and cannot believe, we tacitly countenance a falsehood, and help to fetter on others the belief in a falsehood ; and still worse, we suffer a falsehood to grow up in the minds of our children.

To recapitulate. Doubt in itself cannot be sin, for it is involuntary ; and what we have no power either to produce or prevent cannot be a punishable offence.

The only evil of doubt is remaining in doubt. Trying to suppress a doubt is trying to avoid the truth, either because the doubt may prove true, and lead to other doubts : that is, point to other falsehoods ; or, because we are afraid we may ourselves be wrong. In either case, to follow out the doubt is the only right course.

Reason is the only investigator : for that alone enables us to judge between right and wrong—truth and falsehood.

But the clergy say, " Your religion and your Bible are perfectly true, only don't *doubt*—for if you doubt you will perish everlastingly;" but if God were going to put me to the torture of hell this moment (nice sentence this, but still nothing but a *Bible truth)*, if it should so *please* him to torture me for doubting, I could not prevènt myself from doubting; all I could do would be to *say* I did not doubt, but I *should* doubt all the same.

Then the clergy say, " Suppress your doubt—hide it—have faith; and, above all things, don't show your doubts to any one else." Now, if the clergy really believed what they affirm, that our Bible and Articles of religion were both perfectly true, their language would be, " Don't remain in doubt; use the clearest reason you are possessed of, study the reasoning of the deepest thinkers; for the more you reason and the more you study the more true and perfect will you find them." Possibly, indeed, they may use some such language, but they do not honestly mean it to be carried out; for, before the permission is given, they have sought, by every means in their power, to put down and destroy the faculty of reason, by which alone we are able to discriminate. It is like a man using every effort to destroy another's eyesight, and then saying, " open your eye as wide as you like and see for yourself."

Upon the faculty of reason itself the preachers

and teachers of religion have, from the commencement, cast the greatest obloquy, and vilified it in
every way; they would have, and have made us believe,
that this highest attribute of a human being, when
applied to the investigation of the highest interest of
mankind, was no better than a devil's invention.

For this eyesight of the mind, they gave us instead,
"faith"—that is, credulity.   "Don't use your own
eyes, they are bad and weak, see through my eyes,
and have faith"!   What is the meaning of this?

What is the meaning, that from the very dawn of
what we call Christianity to the present day, the
ministers of this religion, from Paul downward, have
constantly and systematically endeavored to keep
the keen eye of reason from looking at and examining
its doctrines and so-called mysteries?

What is the meaning of this?

If we want to find the meaning, we must look to
the *beginning* and *origin* of this religion.

The clergy now but repeat the lesson inculcated by
its first teachers—reiterate the words handed down
to them.   The founders of our creed decried reason
for their own purposes; the clergy of the present
only take up and repeat the well-known cry.

What motive had these men for shunning the light
of reason?

When an honest man has his character aspersed,
does he shrink from investigation: does he not,

instead, court and insist upon the fullest and most open trial? It is the quack, the charlatan, the impostor, and the cheat, who desires to keep in the dark; who kills men's reason by pandering to their credulity, or faith; who tries to awe the vulgar and ignorant by mysteries and miracles, and promises of insight into futurity.

Will God, then, make use of such vile, false, vulgar methods to seduce and wile us into believing a religion, by taking up the method of the common quack and impostor?

The man of truth and science comes to the light, and says, "Open your eyes, use your reason, enlarge it, strengthen it, that you may perceive more clearly that here is *no* imposture, *no* mystery, *no* miracle, but all the work of law—every step of reason an advance to the truth; an advance to a knowledge of the Creator's laws, and through those laws to the Creator. Then we can look up and say, from the mind and from the soul, " THIS is our God?"

It is instructive to notice the church publications of the present day; you see in most of them some such sentiments as these: " Since the church has, unfortunately, no power to stem the torrent of unbelief, or, to keep profane hands from the temple, the fullest investigation is certainly desirable;" which is nothing but making a virtue of necessity, and owning that if they *had* the power of closing the doctrines of the

church from profane reason, they would gladly do
so. Fortunately for us they cannot. Though it is
feared that, owing to the distance of time that has
elapsed from the commencement of the Christian
religion to this time, the very unscrupulous hands
the original Gospels passed through, and the still
more unscrupulous manner in which the Council of
Nice, in forming the *canon* of the New Testament,
voted which books should be considered the Word
of God and which not, it is very *safe* for the clergy
to allow that the fullest investigation is desirable.
For my part, I am *beginning to doubt* the honesty of
those who required the darkening of reason before
they could present their religion to the gaze of the
world.

I wonder whether the clergy think, by granting
that an investigation is desirable, they are granting
their permission to have our creed investigated, or
whether they think any one really waited for their
permission; and, now they say it ought to be investigated, do they help honestly to investigate? No.

It is their religion—the religion they teach, the
religion which they affirm to have been handed down
to them from the Apostles—and would they stir a
step to assist in throwing it open to the fair light of
reason? No.

They say, both in words and in deeds, " We cannot
prevent your searching, for, unfortunately, we have

not the power ; but we will take very good care we do not help you in your search."

One writer says, " Shall we throw open a door to all scepticism and unbelief ? " *

This is but an acknowledgment that if men did penetrate inside, scepticism and disbelief would inevitably follow.

There is no fear of their throwing open any door they can possibly keep shut. They are all gathered inside the church ; they fasten as many bolts and bars as are left upon the worm-eaten doors, and sigh that there are no more remaining to help them to defend their sacred mysteries from the rude gaze of the vulgar herd ; and they set up their clerical and episcopal backs against the doors in the vain hope of keeping out the assembled multitude, who are clamoring for admittance.

---

* I quote from memory ; the sense, if not the words, I have read.

CHAPTER XXVI.

THE TEMPTATION.

I FEAR the quotation may be applied to me, " Fools rush in where angels fear to tread," for attempting to discuss several questions, which have proved "knotty points" to many wiser heads than mine. I fear not to tread anywhere where my feet can carry me, but I would not rush presumptuously to a greater height than my strength will enable me to climb. I would ask the reader's pardon if I have done so, or appear to do so, in this or other chapters.

The sojourn of Jesus in the wilderness was his last preparation, before publicly commencing his office as a teacher of the Jews, and, prospectively, of the whole world.

This retirement of Christ from the world was evidently the result of something occurring at, or shortly after, his receiving the baptism of John.

Those who have followed me thus far, and on whom my arguments have had any weight, will dismiss from their minds a belief in the existence of a being of evil called the devil, or of the possibility of a spirit appearing in a bodily form to bodily sight or bodily hearing.

The baptism of John could not have been christian baptism, or rather, church baptism, in the name of the Father, the Son, and the Holy Ghost, that form of baptism not having been then instituted.

On the subject of John's baptism, Barnes says, "Washing, or ablution, was much in use among the Jews. It was not customary, however, among them to *baptise* those who were converted to the Jewish religion until after the Babylonish captivity. At the time of John, and for some time previous, they had been accustomed to administer a rite of *baptism*, or *washing*, to those who became proselytes to their religion; that is, who were converted from being Gentiles. This was done to signify that they renounced the errors and worship of the Pagans, and as significant of their becoming *pure* by embracing a new religion. John found this service in use; and as he was calling the Jews to a *new dispensation*, to a change in their form of religion, he administered this rite."

It might be thought that John baptising Jewish converts intended *more* than the adoption of a *new dispensation*, or form of worship, namely, a new religion, and a putting away or cleansing from the old.

Jesus, then, by receiving baptism from John, openly professed or entered himself as a disciple or convert of John. Hence the Baptist exclaims "I have need to be baptised of thee, and comest thou to me?"

In this Jesus showed his humility, and it is to be remarked that in his ministry he never separated his converts from the rest of the Jews, or joined them to himself as his followers by baptism. John was, in his preaching, the precursor of Jesus; he began what Christ finished, the overthrow of the Jewish religion, not of Jewish truth, but of Jewish ceremonies and Jewish ignorance and bigotry.

The public acknowledgment of the truths John disseminated, first, perhaps, fully opened to the mind of Jesus, that he was destined to be the great teacher of his people and of all mankind; or the word of St. John might first have fully awakened the mind of Jesus to understand his mission.

The mind is hardly conscious of its own power till it has received confirmation from some other mind. Some man or men must speak to the ear, and say, "Thou art Christ" (or sent), and from God must come the answer in the spirit, "Thou art my beloved son."

As a preparation for his noble work, it was necessary Jesus should spend some time in complete retirement, to examine his own thoughts, try his own strength, determination, and purpose; so he went into the solitary wilderness to live there as John had lived.

In this temptation I consider Jesus as a man. A man of like *passions, feelings, desires*—for, if not, he was not a man in the flesh, and tempted as we are—a *perfect* man, who had every sense perfectly and healthily attuned to receive bodily and mental pleasure.

That the Spirit or Soul was God, I do not question.

It would almost appear from the text, or our interpretation of it, that the temptations were undergone by Jesus, in order to convince the devil that he was the Son of God.

This is somewhat parallel to the story of Job's temptation. It is there recorded that on a set *day* in eternity, there was a grand muster of all the Sons of God, who came to present themselves to their Father and our Father, and that Satan was allowed to mount up to heaven again, and show himself with them. Here, again, is a slight touch of the confusion of ideas, as to whether it is "God tempted," or the "devil tempted," in not exactly defining the devil's place of residence, whether heaven, or hell, or earth; it seems curious that he should be allowed to wander at will between one and the other, first to be the companion of devils, and then of the Sons of God. The story proceeds to relate how God held a conversation with Satan, to which the "foul fiend" answered somewhat flippantly, and because he would not believe that Job was such a perfect man as God declared him to be; He, (God) to prove His opinion correct, and the devil's wrong, said to him, "Behold, he is in thy hand, but save his life;" in fact, inflict any amount of torture upon him, short of taking his life, kill all his children, that is of no consequence, only be convinced that Job is a perfect man.

Are these the words and dealing of God or man? or, if I believed in the devil, I should say, of God or devil?

"Then was Jesus led up of the spirit into the wilderness to be tempted of the devil."

Was it necessary for Jesus to undergo forty days' fasting, in order to give the devil an audience? or was the fasting necessary to prepare him for it?

A man is never tempted by anything for which he has no desire. It is impossible to *tempt* a man, with a thing he cares not for, it is no temptation to him.

To call this interview with the devil a temptation is absurd. It could have been no temptation, no struggle; it must, then, have been undergone simply to satisfy the curiosity of this important and powerful devil, or to assure either the devil or Jesus himself, that in a personal conflict, the latter would conquer.

If God in the flesh met the devil in the flesh in the wilderness, why did they not have a wrestling-match in the flesh together, to see which was the strongest, as it is said Jacob did with an angel?

Mind, if there is any irreverence in this idea, it

arises entirely from putting together Bible words, and alleged Bible facts.

Going out of the way to meet temptation is quite unnecessary; evil has to be conquered in our own hearts daily, we need go into no wilderness to seek it.

I do not impute sin to Jesus in believing the temptations arose in his own mind.

As I have before said, all our natural passions and feelings are good in themselves, and only become sin through over-indulgence. This over-indulgence Jesus resisted, therefore did not sin. He came into the world to judge between good and evil, and, in order to choose the one and reject the other, both must have been presented to his mind; he must have had *knowledge* of both, not through the devil, but through his own mind and senses.

Christ's religion was based on the truths of the Jewish religion, elevated and made clear by his spirit; that spirit also casting out the low, earthly ceremonial worship, with which their ignorance had obscured the truth. We may conclude that the first part of Christ's sojourn in the wilderness was spent in meditating on these truths, and he would foresee what effect they would have on his country and people and the future religions of the world if followed in spirit and truth.

In the knowledge of the truth, the mind rises progressively. In seeking wisdom in fasting and solitude, Jesus followed the example of the Hebrew prophets ; but we do not find after this any record of Jesus fasting ; and also, though John's disciples fasted, Christ did not enjoin it on his apostles.

Perhaps he learnt by this long fast, that bodily weakness was more productive of temptations, than a means of better resisting it; and he learnt here the lesson of moderate enjoyment of all his Father's gifts, which he afterwards pursued in his mode of life.

" And when he had fasted forty days and forty nights he was afterwards an hungered." He was exhausted both mentally and bodily.

By referring to the passages in the Old Testament whereby Jesus conquered the momentary thought of his heart ; or rather, judged by them that to carry those thoughts into action would be unlawful—his train of ideas can almost be followed.

In a more confined sense, we may think that the first temptation was, to use his spiritual power to satisfy his bodily appetite ; or, in a more extended sense, to make it subservient to all his bodily desires, to elevate his position in life, to procure comfort, ease, or luxury, by it. For, had he deliberately yielded to this first thought—and he would only have done so believing it to be right—and had he come to the conclusion that as a rule he might use his power for this purpose, he would, doubtless, have extended it to all the circumstances of his life. The idea was negatived by a remembrance of the text, "Man shall not live by bread alone," &c.

If the reader will look over the 8th chap. Deut., he will perceive how Christ's sojourn in the wilderness naturally awoke in his mind a recollection of the words, and also he will better trace the meaning of them: "And thou shalt remember all the way which the Lord thy God led thee these forty years in the wilderness, to humble thee, and to prove thee, to know what was in thine heart, whether thou wouldst keep his commandments or no. And he humbled thee, and suffered thee to hunger, and fed thee with manna, which thou knewest not, neither did thy fathers know, that he might make thee know that man doth not live by bread only, but by every word that proceedeth out of the mouth of the Lord doth man live."

We may conclude, then, that Jesus decided not to make use either of a miraculous or an extraordinary mental power to obtain bodily comfort, and accepted a condition of comparative poverty, that he might learn in that position to remain humble.

He found it was blessed to be poor, and humble in spirit, that his might be the kingdom of heaven.

There are two other passages in the New Testament, that may be noticed as lessons learnt in this temptation, or rather deep questioning meditation.

s

Speaking of John, he asked, "What went ye out into the wilderness to see: a man clothed in soft raiment? Behold, they who wear soft raiments are in king's houses." That is, among the rich, the lofty, the proud.

Also, when the Jews said, "Our fathers did eat manna in the desert, as it is written, He gave them bread from heaven.", It appears to me Jesus contradicted the assumption that manna came from heaven: "Verily, verily, I say unto you, Moses gave you *not* that bread from heaven." That is, manna ("that bread") did *not* come from heaven; we make it seem to have a different meaning, by laying a stress and peculiar meaning on the word "*that*" instead of "*not*," though the latter is the more simple and obvious reading. Jesus proceeded to teach them that nothing came down from heaven but what was in heaven. Material bread never was in heaven, therefore could not come from thence: "But my father giveth you the true bread from heaven." That is, the Spirit giveth to your spirits that spiritual bread which shall cause your souls to live for ever, and that spiritual bread is every word of God, or the truth.

Turning to the 8th chapter of Deuteronomy, it is there said manna was given the children of Israel to humble them; but to have had " angels' food " showered down for them, could not have humbled them, but, on the contrary, would have made them proud. This idea, indeed, did make them proud, and led them to esteem themselves better and more favored than all other nations and people.

The text also says, manna was a food they knew not, neither did their fathers know; so, being totally ignorant of the food they lived on in the wilderness, they, of course, concluded it was miraculously given, and came from heaven.

The conclusion of the chapter is a warning to the Jews to beware of pride and idolatry, and we may see by it how the mind of Jesus was led to the subject of the second temptation.

These are the last two verses.

" And it shall be, if thou at all forget the Lord thy God, and walk after other gods, and serve them, and worship them, I testify against you this day, that ye shall surely perish. As the nations which the Lord destroyeth before your face, so shall ye perish ; because ye would not be obedient unto the voice of the Lord your God."

Would not Jesus have been thus led in the spirit to the consideration of the holy city, Jerusalem, as it then stood—that beloved Jerusalem, which afterwards he wept over, and spoke those heart-rending words, " O Jerusalem, Jerusalem, thou that killest the prophets and stonest them which are sent unto thee, how often would I have gathered thy children toge- ther, even as a hen gathereth her chickens under her wings, and ye would not! Behold! your house is left unto you desolate."

What, then, should we go out into the wilderness to see? even the soul of Jesus as a reed shaken with the wind. Then he looked towards the temple—that glorious temple, whose pinnacles stood lofty and proud in the sight of all men—that temple of which not one stone should be left upon another, nor of the worship within it, nor one ceremony that should not be 'cast out; and he, who so loved his country, was to lift up his hand to destroy it.

With such thoughts as these, while his heart mourned for his country, and the worship of his fathers, what was the temptation?

We are apt to think that Jesus, though a man in the flesh, was not amenable to physical laws, we imagine if he had thrown himself down, he would not have been killed; but in his body Christ was mortal, he was susceptible of pain, and hunger, and cold; the parts were mortal, therefore the whole was mortal. But to think Jesus would put his life in danger, and then miraculously rescue himself, is childish.

If he was tempted to throw himself from a pin-nacle of the temple, he desired to meet death, and had he really *desired* to die, neither angels nor God would have prevented him from quitting the world, for he said he had power to take up his life or to lay it down.

He was saddened and cast down at the prospect of life before him. He had no right to use his spiritual power for his bodily ease and comfort. He might not rescue his nation; he was to walk among them humbly, and strive to teach them the truth, and they would not hear it: but for all this he should only be hated and despised by those he loved and desired to serve; the cup was too bitter, he desired to put it from him; he would seek death. He was weary of his life, he would seek another world, and yield up his spirit to God, that as an angel or spirit he might be borne to heaven. But the words came to him, " Thou shalt not tempt the Lord thy God." This text is also taken from Deut. chapter vi. 16, and if the meaning be examined, it will be found not at all to express an injunction not to run into danger unnecessarily; such a caution would be very little required, for no man yet hated his own flesh, or wished to injure it, those who run recklessly into danger, are merely stupid and do not see the danger; but it is intended to teach men not to tempt God by murmuring and discontent.

" Thou shalt not tempt the Lord thy God, as ye tempted him at *Massah*."

How, then, did they tempt at Massah?

Ex. xvii. 2—" Wherefore the people did chide with Moses, and said, Give us water that we may drink. And Moses said unto them, Why chide ye

with me ? wherefore do ye *tempt* the Lord ? . . .
And Moses cried unto the Lord saying : what shall
I do unto this people ? They be almost ready to
stone me. . . . And he called the name of the
place Massah."

In another part it is written that at Meribah they
tempted God by murmuring, and said, "Would
God, we had died in the wilderness;" and God
was angry with them, and angry with Moses for their
sake.

From this, Jesus learnt that he was not to shrink
from, or murmur at, any cross his Father might lay
upon him ; henceforth it was " Not as I will but as
Thou wilt," for " Blessed are they that mourn, for
they shall be comforted." From considering the
instructions of Moses in Deuteronomy, Jesus might
have been led to ponder on the power and authority
of the lawgiver, of his complete dominion over the
minds and persons of the Jews.

Moses was a despotic governor over them, against
whose rule there was no question and no appeal; the
voice of Moses was to them the voice of God.

To a person of strong mind, mental usurpation
over others is a great temptation.

Jesus could have assumed as much power as
Moses over his countrymen, not only as a prophet
but as a king—an earthly king, such as they desired,
a mighty conqueror to dazzle their eyes with his

victories. He stood high above all the rest of mankind, saw all the kingdoms of the world and the glory
of them at his feet, if he would but live for the world,
and make worldly dominion his aim in life. If he
would bend the power of his spirit to gain his own
power and glory.

What man with power such as Jesus possessed
would not have enslaved the world with it ?

Buckle says, " There is no instance on record of
a man having power and not abusing it," but Jesus
neither enslaved mind or body ; the church dominion
that has crept into the Christian religion, was
assumed by the Apostles not by Jesus. There is no
need to imagine that Jesus was for the moment
tempted to take authority for a bad purpose ; the
feeling, I imagine, to have been as in " Festus "—

> " Mind must subdue. To conquer is its life.
> Why mad'st Thou not one spirit, like the sun,
> To king the world ? And oh ! might I have been
> That sun mind, how I would have warmed the world
> To love, and worship, and bright life ! "

It is the natural impulse of a strong and good
mind, out of its very goodness and pity, to try and
force and bind people to good ; but it is productive
of no good in the end, it destroys a man's free will,
and prevents him learning for himself that convincing knowledge of good and evil, which he came
into the world to learn ; and also, any person, party,

or church, that thus endeavors to bind a man's conscience, in time comes to stand in the place of God
to that man.   He who leads becomes an idol, and he
who blindly follows, an idolater.

Let no book, no church, no human being be taken
as an infallible guide, or it is an idol.

There is no god but the truth, and that can speak
to the soul of every man that comes into the world;
but it never enslaved, because no grain of truth is
given unless worked for, sought for, striven for; we
work up to it, it will not be brought down to us.

The temptation to assume mental or bodily dominion was the last Jesus had to conquer, his course
was determined; he would inherit the earth by
meekness, not by tyranny; he would not be a mighty
cónqueror, a shedder of blood, a cause of ruin, but
a peacemaker, and a child of God; he would accept
persecution for righteousness' sake, and look for a
better kingdom, the kingdom of heaven; when he
was reviled and persecuted, he would murmur no
more; he would bear all, suffer all, for the love of
God and for the love of man.   Then did the angel
of his spirit rejoice and was exceeding glad, for he
knew that his reward was great in heaven.

What now shall we go out into the wilderness
to see?

A prophet? Yea, I say unto you, and more than
a prophet. For surely this MAN was the Son of God.

Christ's sermon on the Mount may be looked upon, in a great measure, as the fruit of his meditations and great mental struggle in that forty days' sojourn in the wilderness, and is, perhaps, the finest christian record we possess. He opened his mouth and boldly spake the truth.

It is well to mark, and is an answer to those who persist in saying that if we take any of the Bible, we must take the whole of it, truth and error alike, that from the 21st verse of the 5th chapter of Matthew to the end of the chapter, is a contradiction to many passages of the Old Testament, and a greater con · tradiction to its spirit : several of these passages are from the same book of Deuteronomy, from which he had previously quoted to quell the temptation of his spirit. In these quotations, Jesus does not say, God said, or thy Father said, but only "It is written"; this is no assertion of divine inspiration. In the sermon on the Mount, when reference is made to the Old Testament, he said, "It was said by them of old time," the margin more correctly puts "*to* them"; but in either case, this is hardly the manner in which Jesus would have spoken, had the commands been literally the very "words of God," and besides, many of these injunctions spoken to them of old time, Jesus forbids.

In the first part of the sermon, Jesus shows how many precepts are to be understood in a much wider sense than probably either Moses or the Jews supposed.

He forbade swearing in the name of the Lord; this Moses enjoined; and implied that a man sinned not in simply breaking his word, unless he had vowed a vow.

Deut. xxiii. 21, 22—" When thou shalt vow a vow unto the Lord thy God thou shalt not be slack to pay it, for the Lord thy God will surely require it of thee.   But if thou shalt forbear to vow, it shall be no sin in thee."

Jesus said " Ye shall not resist evil," but in Deut. xix. 21 it is written, " And thine eye shall not pity, but life shall go for life, eye for eye, tooth for tooth, hand for hand, foot for foot."

" Ye shall not resist evil *with evil*," would seem to be implied.   Ye shall not take an eye for an eye, blood for blood, life for life, may also be included. Mr. Mills says, seeking to undo an evil by substituting another evil, is "wretched policy."

Here is the beginning of *conviction*.

Christ said, " Love your enemies," but Moses said, in Deut. chapter xxiii. 6, " Thou shalt not seek their peace, nor their prosperity, all thy days for ever;" and again, in chapter vii. 16, " And thou shalt consume all the people which the Lord thy God shall deliver unto thee, thine eye shall have no pity."

All these are no minor commands given by Moses,

in his own name, but all supposed to come from God himself, and are placed equally on the same footing as the commands, " Thou shalt not kill," and " Thou shalt not commit adultery ; " but these last being truths shall stand to the end of the world, but the others, being falsehoods, have vanished away.

All the laws of Moses are introduced by some such words as, " Thus saith the Lord ; " but as Jesus contradicts many, and they are found not to agree either with truth or love—neither in the letter or the spirit, did God speak them.

How, then, shall any man presume to say, we must take the whole Bible, or it must all perish together ? Truth will not die, and falsehood cannot live !

CHAPTER XXVII.

HUMAN SACRIFICE.

"Burnt offerings and sacrifices for sin thou wouldest not, but a body hast thou prepared me."

"Then said I, Lo I come, in the volume of the book it is written of me, to do thy will."

HERE it is said neither burnt offerings nor sacrifices for sin *would God have;* He delighted not in them, He desired them not; was, then, the body prepared *as* a sacrifice for sin?

Was not "the body" the human *life,* not the *death?*

"I will have mercy, and *not* sacrifice."

Was, then, the body God prepared to do His will, a sacrifice?

God said "I will *not* have sacrifice," but we say He sent His Son into the world to *be* a sacrifice.

It is as if a man who had been a thief and robber all his life, beginning to see he was acting wickedly in the sight of God, determined to amend his way, and, as a commencement, commits another great robbery, in order that he may be rich for the remainder of his life, and not require to commit any more small robberies.

This is quite a parallel case in respect to sacrifices.

Human sacrifice God abhors, animal sacrifice He would not have, therefore, to put a stop to both, He offers up his own Son in sacrifice to Himself, to stand in lieu of all minor sacrifices for ever after !

Philological researches lead to the conclusion that Abraham was a sun or fire-worshipper, that being about to offer up his son, according to the Syriac religion, God gave the thought to his mind, why should he take away the life the gods (or God) had given, and think, by it, to propitiate the giver ?

If he was the first man, or even the first of his nation, whose mind perceived a Creator's love, he may, indeed, be styled the friend of God, and also the friend and benefactor of mankind; and well, indeed, might Christ say, " Your father Abraham rejoiced to see my day, he saw it, and was glad."

He saw Jesus in the spirit, that spirit that was in the world before it was embodied in the life of Christ, the spirit of love. It told him that as his Creator was love, and as love gave the life, that great spirit could find no pleasure in blood or death as an offering.

Flesh and blood of a body made of the dust of the earth is no fit offering for a spirit. In *no* case can the fruit of the body be given for the sin of the soul.

And yet we say, that very offering—that very sacrifice—a father slaying his own son, as a human sacrifice, or perhaps even more, a divine sacrifice, God offers up to propitiate His own wrath. But when we turn away with a shudder at the idea of a son offered up to, and by, a father, we are told the sacrifice of Jesus was self-devotion. Christ chose to die for us.

Does this make the sternness of the Father less unmerciful because the son was more heroic and willing to sacrifice himself?

A king would neither be just nor merciful to slay his own son for the benefit of his subjects, if by any other means he could save them, and yet spare his son. Shall we say or think it was impossible to save the world by any other method? Shall we say that, owing to the fall of man in the Garden of Eden, the world, by a knowledge of sin, had got into such an inextricable state of confusion, nothing but the death of *God himself* could save it.

The God of infinite Power, Wisdom, Goodness, has power to pardon through love, not through blood. But if man is not fallen, where is the need of sacrifice? The belief that salvation came to mankind by their brutal murder of Jesus, is, in the grossest and worst sense, a belief in the power of evil to work good, and that God's blessings were given to us through and by sin.

Did man procure redemption by killing the Redeemer?

Jesus said, " To *this* end was I born, and for this cause came I into the world, that I should bear witness unto the truth." And "I lay down my life for the truth." In life bear witness to it, and also, if necessary, by death.

We think we have gained heaven by killing Christ? That crime procured what? Punishment? No; reward!—the reward of heaven.

God is so just he cannot pardon sin, but he gives us heaven through the crime of murder;—so just that eating the forbidden apple in the Garden of Eden caused all men's ruin, but by the infinitely worse crime of shedding innocent blood, man is reinstated in immortality and the joy of heaven!

Shall we say those, and those only, who really killed Jesus will receive punishment, while those who happened to live before and after his time will receive the reward of the murder? We are to receive the wages other men gained for us by crime, while they are to have all the punishment for performing an act which we declare was necessary for our salvation?

I can anticipate an answer to this. It will be said, we did not gain heaven by man's sin, but by Christ's obedience. This is but word shuffling, and leads back to the same ground.

If Jesus came into the world only to be perfectly obedient to all the laws of God, he might have died a natural death, and lived to the end of his natural life; for it is no law of God that a man must submit to be murdered if he can possibly help it. On the contrary, no man has a right to allow himself to be killed if he can prevent it. If a man sees a tree about to fall upon him, and will not move out of the way, he is guilty of suicide. If a man beholding another with an uplifted axe over his head ready to dash his brains out with it, has strength enough to grasp that arm, and ward off the blow, and will not make use of his strength to defend himself, he is a party to the crime of murder; for he quietly allowed a crime to be committed which he might have prevented. The same judgment applies to any person who, through wilful ignorance or laziness suffers himself to be either injured, robbed, or cheated; he becomes, in a measure, an aider and abbettor in the crime. So, if we believe that Jesus had either natural or supernatural power to save himself from crucifixion, and did not use it, such a belief makes us accuse either Jesus Christ or God of being a party to the crime of murder, and Jesus to have committed suicide.

But if it *is* a law of God that without shedding of blood there is no remission of sins, and without shedding the innocent blood of Jesus there could have been no salvation for us, then as those who crucified Christ only obeyed a law of God, that murder was *no* sin, and we gained heaven by *our* own obedience to that law which said, "My son must be slain."

This, then, is our faith.

By Adam's sin, himself and all the rest of mankind after him were debarred from ever again entering that particular spot called the Garden of Eden. Jesus Christ came down from heaven, and men killed him, and so we obtained eternal life !

I suppose, on the principle that two negatives make an affirmative, two crimes obtained one blessing.

By these, we not only procured more than we could possibly have enjoyed in the dull, monotonous Garden of Eden, but the gates of heaven are opened to us.

As I believe in God, and that good worketh good, and evil worketh evil, I say the world must have lost and not gained by the murder of Jesus Christ.

He came to show the world the truths he had heard of his Father; how much more, then, should we have learned,—how much confusion and error have avoided, had not Jesus been cut off before he had barely reached to man's maturity ?

With respect to the narrative told of Abraham, why was it a trial of faith ? If he was faithful, there was no occasion to make trial of his faith. God who can read the heart needs no outward evidence of either good or evil. Our souls lie open before him.

It is those only who cannot discern the invisible, who require visible evidence ; we can judge only by external acts of a man's inward character ; a man makes trial of another's good faith or honesty because

T

he is doubtful of it, and by this means only is he enabled to draw a conclusion, but God need employ no such method.

It is suggested to me that God knew the faith of Abraham, "but he wanted it proved for our benefit."

It is, then, a parallel case to that of Job, who suffered great bodily torture for the benefit of the devil.

So Abraham was to suffer mental anguish for the benefit of mankind.

But God's commands are not child's play, first Do! and then Do not! when His laws, which are universal, and not particular, say, " Thou shalt," or " Thou shalt not," they are eternal and unchangeable.

They are not given and retracted, either out of caprice, or that God thought better of it, and "repented," or for any empty *show*, either to himself, the devil, or ourselves.

Perhaps Abraham was not able to advance his contemporaries sufficiently to make them reject all sacrifice, or, more likely, he himself was not competent to understand fully the light God had sent into his soul. How, indeed, could we expect such an enlightened worship, free from the belief that God's wrath required propitiation, when we have not yet dismissed it ourselves? But the time is not far distant when we shall know that God, who is love, desires *no* sacrifice, but that He desires spiritual worship.

Work is acted prayer; and joy, the true exaltation of the heart in spiritual praise.

Work,—true, earnest work, is not only to ask and desire, but to strive with our bodily and mental strength, for the good that God has set before us. It is the real prayer both of a man's spirit and life.

What do we say to another man, "Don't come begging and whining to me ; go and work."

Those who have not to undergo work for their bodies, let them work for their minds, and they are doing God's work—they bring the spirit of prayer into the life.

We must worship God as Truth, Love, Joy.   This holy and inseparable Trinity.

Approach the idea of body or person to the Deity, and it is not spirit.

We may call this worshipping a *mere* abstract idea, but an abstract idea is the only approach to the comprehension of spirit the mind of man is capable of. Immediately we descend from an abstract idea of God, we give him a body, and worship a body, and defile the spirit.   God and his attributes can be to us on earth nothing but what we call an idea ; but we may take these ideas or attributes, and give them body on earth in our lives—not give them body in the spiritual world, for then we worship in heaven a part of our own human nature.

Such pure worship to a mind not capable of much

abstract thought would appear cold, and, indeed, to some is not possible. As the author of " Creation's Testimony to its God," remarks respecting such pure abstract worship, " Well may we say, like Mary, ' They have taken away my Lord, and I know not where they have laid him.'" But they, like Mary, must learn to look up, to find him in heaven, not on the earth, in the spirit not in the body.

But though we cannot see the Father, nor has any man, we can each of us strive to do the will of the Father; and this is no abstract worship, but the worship of the life. As a father would pardon his son, so have we to ask pardon of our God ; and as a Father of more perfect love and compassion than any earthly father, so will he pardon, love, and direct us.

What has anger, wrath, jealousy, to do with God ?

What has fear and dread to do with Love ?

Anger, wrath, jealousy, are miserable earthly passions, compounded of cowardice, ignorance, and unhappiness, acting and reacting upon one another.

Fear and dread are but reflections of the same—a shrinking from the effects of these passions ; and the greater the power of the wrathful person, the greater the dread. As much, then, as we fear God, so much shall we shrink from him ; but Love is to draw us near him, and give us joy.

Why impute the sin of vengeance to God, and

think he even said, "Vengeance is mine"? What a despicable character is a revengeful man. I see no difference between re-vengeful and vengeful. It is the same passion, only one is the name of it given to man, the other to God; in both it is the feeling of one who treasures up his wrath, till he can, at some moment fully wreak his vengeance. One who "Treasures up wrath against the day of wrath"!

To speak in human language, there is not a thought of vengeance in the mind of God, any more than there is in the heart of a truly Christian man. We are to strive to become perfect by imitating God's perfection. There is, then, no quality in him we may not imitate; but if we should imitate these imputed passions, anger, wrath, jealousy, vengeance, we should become devils, not sons of God.

The fact of the character of a people becoming similar to the character they impute to their God is sarcastically noted by the Rev. R. Taylor, in his "Diegesis." Alluding to our prayer in the litany, "O Lord, spare thy people, and be not angry with us for ever"—he says, "This attribute of being *angry for ever*, is peculiar to the Christian God, and has become, in consequence, peculiarly characteristic of Christians." I hope the reader will appreciate the pungent satire conveyed in this most true sentence.

We are now kept in a sort of middle state, not knowing whether to love or dread him; *both* we cannot do. With our mouths we speak of his love, and, in a measure believe it, but in our hearts we fear and dread his wrath; until that fear of his anger and wrath is cast out, we shall never truly love him, and never truly have joy in our God and Father. And never, by looking at Him as the terrible sacrificer of His Son, shall we view Him in love; and never, by contemplating that dreadful and cruel death of Jesus as a God-appointed means of salvation, shall we see Him in love.

We must look at the life of Christ, that beautiful life, passed in thought, and word, and deed, in perfect truth and love, and which should lead through truth and love to perfect joy.

Many men may, and many have had strength to die for truth or love, but what man has ever yet had strength to live the perfect life of truth and love ?

How little can I now enter into the Church Service; in almost every sentence the idolatrous idea of sacrifice, and the curses of men thrust themselves in, and shut out the love of .God : but how beautiful might be our service of joy and praise on our day of rest from earthly toil; not, then, the task of the day, but one of its pleasures.

CHAPTER XXVIII.

THE EFFECT OF MAGNIFYING EVIL.

I copy the following paragraph from G. H. Lewes's " History of Philosophy," for I think there is in it a germ of a profound truth, and will show a key to some of the misery and wickedness of society :

" A vice sanctioned by the general opinion is merely a vice. The evil terminates in itself. A vice condemned by the general opinion produces a pernicious effect on the whole character. The former is a local malady, the latter, a constitutional taint. When the reputation of an offender is lost, he too often flings the remains of his virtue after it in despair. The Highland gentleman who, a century ago, lived by taking black mail from his neighbors, committed the same crime for which Wild was accompanied to Tyburn by the huzzas of two hundred thousand people. But there can be no doubt that he was a much less depraved man than Wild. The deed for which Mrs. Brownrigg was hanged sinks into nothing when compared with the conduct of the Roman who treated the public to a hundred pair of gladiators. Yet we should probably wrong such a Roman if we supposed that his disposition was as cruel as that of Mrs. Brownrigg. In our country a woman forfeits her place in society by what, in a man, is too commonly considered as an honorable distinction, and at worst, as a venial error. The consequence is notorious. The moral principle of a woman is frequently more impaired by a single lapse from virtue than that of a man by twenty years of intrigue. Classical antiquity would furnish us with instances stronger, if possible, than those to which I have referred."

We may draw from this, that vice has, in itself, no inherent power of vitality; let it alone, and it dies out of itself.

To pronounce vice worse than it is, is productive of more vice.

To call anything, of no vice in itself, sin, is utterly subversive of good.

Good, as part of a good and eternal spirit, is alone undying. There being no spirit or being of evil, sin is but mortal, and a product of our mortal nature. For if sin were produced by an eternal spirit of evil, sin would also be immortal, which it is not. When I say, let sin alone, and it dies out of itself, I mean, neither encourage it nor treat it with scorn and contumely, nor in any way persecute it, for that only makes it stronger.

Goodness cannot be forced into a man, neither can evil be forced out of him.

Encourage the good and the bad will drop off.

I believe this is now the foundation of the present medical treatment of the body, not to attack a complaint with bleeding and medicines, which only weaken the constitution, and render it more liable to disease; but first, if possible, remove any external or local cause of the malady, and then strengthen the body with stimulants and tonics, to enable it to gain strength to grapple with and throw off the disease which is preying upon it.

The soul requires a similar moral treatment, which as yet has never been tried.

Our religious teaching is not to strengthen the good, but to abuse the bad; all we hear from our churches is, sin, wrath, and damnation; these are the three strings continually harped upon, till the heart is sick and weary, and one almost loathes the name of religion.

I heard a sermon preached lately on the text, " I hate him because he doth not prophecy good concerning me, but evil." Ahaz would have had cause to hate Micajah if he had *never* prophesied anything but evil of him, told him he was always wrong, whether he went to the right-hand or to the left. As I, at one time, said, " If all I do, and all I say, and all I think is ' only evil continually,' and every step I take a wicked step,—let all the teachers go to Jericho! and I will go on my own road; it is all one where I go, it seems, except I take the clerical road of semi-asceticism, apart from the world, crucify my body every day, and believe all I am told, neither of which can I do." Here is a maxim in this spirit, "There is no little sin, because there is no little God to sin against;" *ergo*, every sin is a great sin.

Sin has no relation to God, but to the man who sins. If it is a little sin, it will injure the soul of the sinner but slightly; if a great sin, it will injure it materially. The maxim is but saying, that to covet a man's luxuriant carriage is as great a sin as murdering the owner; for, "Thou shalt not covet," and "Thou shalt do no murder," are both commandments, so whichever a man breaks he is equally guilty, and his soul equally polluted. As well say, to cut off your finger will injure your body as much as taking off a limb.

If there are degrees of comparison at all in sin, there are trivial as well as heinous sins.

When the unfortunate man has had the maxim drummed into his ears, and exclaims, "Then, as well be hung for a sheep as a lamb"; the teacher shakes his head, and says, "Oh, fie! It is a doctrine of the devil"! Then his maxim *was* the devil, for it gave birth to the thought. Theologians feel with regard to sin, what was said of Draco: "The smallest offences deserve death"—but I can find no severer punishment for greater crimes. So the church says the most trivial sins deserve eternal damnation; but we can find no more damnable damnation for the most appalling crimes.

I have heard of a funny old lady, supposed to be slightly deranged, who was, however, never so well pleased as when entertaining her friends, and whenever she asked them to partake of her hospitality at dinner or supper, she always concluded with, "But it's all filthy—it's all filthy"! Now, whenever I hear St. Paul's words, "All our righteousness is as filthy rags," I think of this old lady. We must do all the good we possibly can, and then say, "But it's all filthy—it's all filthy." It seems to me this is no great encouragement to ourselves, or *les autres*.

Some people also calls themselves the chief of sinners, but, at the same time, think that by so saying they are really the chief of saints. Such sentences can proceed but from one of two motives, hypocrisy, or a keen sense of humiliation almost amounting to despair. In the latter sense, every one who has striven for a high, ideal perfection in anything, will, at some periods, utter such a sigh in words; but such a feeling, for a continuance, will produce complete enervation and depression, and if it become habitual the man lays down his arms; he has no life or energy to strive more.

But this is the thought the church would have us

feel habitually and constantly. Yet it is a feeling
that lowers, not raises; producing either hypocrisy
or despair.

Fancy a young student in art, working under a
master of great power. The more talent the young
artist possesses the more will he be conscious of his
defects—everything he designs appears like a miserable, deformed caricature, in comparison with the work
of his master—everything he tries to color but a
wretched daub; every touch of the brush, a streak of
paint, and nothing more.

What will the master do with such a student? If
he understands men as well as art, even if the first
sketches are daubs and caricatures, and he cannot
see a trace of genius in them, if he sees the earnest
and intense desire, and that most valuable of all
qualities, perseverance; if he is wise, he will know
there is genius behind, and will work itself through:
and if he have these qualities he *will* work, if not in
his studio, it may be in the studio of his rival.

What will he do then? Will he encourage or
condemn?

I do not say defects should never be pointed out
or corrected, but I do say that with every one, whatever their object in life, encouragement of the good
is more potent, and more useful, than blame of the
evil. I do not think fear of danger, or even of death,
has more than a momentary effect in checking vice;

immediately it is familiar to our mind it ceases to become a check, and not only is no check, but inevitable danger produces the wildest levity and disorder.

Look at London at the time of the plague; in every house where the plague was not, there was feasting and license. Look at the prisons of Paris at the time of the Revolution, when, at all hours of the day, some of the men and women who were carousing together, were taken as victims of the guillotine, the prisoners were wild with gaiety and licentiousness.

Do you think those unfortunates deserved perdition more, because they were laughing and talking, singing, dancing, and sinning, to the last moment of their lives ?

I do not. Their crimes were the fruit of the madness of despair.

The behaviour of some of the people of London at the time of the plague, which we are apt to consider with horror, was wise in their generation. Physically speaking, gaiety and forgetfulness were the best medicines they could take.

Some time ago, here in Taranaki, when the war was dragging its slow length along, with all the anxiety of war, and but little of its excitement, when the people were all huddled together in the wretched little town, weeks and weeks of pouring rain, and a leaden sky, fever and diphtheria among the people, the hearts of fathers and mothers sore for the loss of their little ones, others trembling for their own lives, or the lives of those dear to them, some people gave parties; the clergy frowned, the other folk said it was *tempting* Providence even to talk of gaieties; every body ought to repent, and, as the Vicar of Wakefield said, the advice was, "My children, go and be miserable!" But to have helped these poor people to shake off their fear and depression, would have been far more christian, and also far more wordly-wise. If they could have had something to amuse them, to take off their attention from themselves and their losses, and anxious anticipations, fewer would have been seized by fever; if they had had even the most foolish and ridiculous mountebank to make them laugh heartily once a day, fewer would have died. Besides death by disease, what was the consequence? There were no innocent amusements, so men drowned their uneasiness in drinking. Natural feeling *will* work out somewhere, if not in innocent pleasure, then in vicious excitement.

And whose fault is it?

Our church-religious-crushing-process is thus producing vice to the present day.

Where love and joy, and encouragement are spoken once, death and perdition are spoken a hundred times: and the clergy say, "You do not like religion. You want to throw it off because it exposes your vices. You hate it because it does not prophecy good concerning you, but evil"!

But if it is so hateful to have nothing but evil pointed at you, is it the way to bring us to love religion ?

No one likes to be constantly scolded and blamed, and told he is an abominable outcast.

Is it the privilege of the clergy, always to bruise and probe this one spot, because they know it is raw and sore ? Out upon such ignorance and cruelty ! If men could hear a sermon but once in a few months spoken by some man of genius, endowed with a large heart, full of love, which would speak to them of the great amount of real goodness and truth, and kindness and charity in the heart of every man living ; that perfection is *not* above their reach, that some day man *will* be perfect, and that he is even now on the road to it—how would the hearts of the men of the congregation be illuminated, and their souls be uplifted ; and as they left the house of the God of Love, with the joy of their hearts beaming on their countenances, how would the desire arise to be worthy of the preacher's words and good thoughts respecting them !—and how would they hasten to reach the goal of perfection he showed them !

But an orthodox minister cannot preach this, for he does not believe it. He believes in nothing but

the utter depravity of man. An orthodox churchman is the most thorough sceptic on the face of the
earth, the greatest disbeliever in the power of goodness and love; he believes that evil, and hate, and
fear, are more powerful in the human heart, and are
its prime movers.

It is frightful scepticism, withering to their own
souls, and causing the depravity of despair in the
minds of their brethren. They have not only caused
sins to appear greater than they are, and so *made*
them bigger; but they have called good evil.

Every earthly pleasure has been called sin, till
it has become sin. Everything like pleasure and
enjoyment has been thrust out from the company of
the good, so the *world* have taken it all to themselves, and got drunk upon it, and become diseased
upon it; and the good have become starved and thin,
bloodless, and joyless. In everything earthly there
is more or less of sin, for we have not yet reached
perfection. In pleasure there is some sin, but there
is just as much, or more, in the avoidance of pleasure.
The man who tries to become perfect by separation
from the world and the pleasures of the world, not
only injures himself but all society. He makes
himself, whether he allows it himself or not, a hater
of mankind and a despiser of their joys. And if he
really has good in his heart, he deprives mankind
of its good influence, and as much as he abstracts

himself from his fellowmen, their haunts, pursuits, and pleasures, so much does society sink and become more degraded; and in their pleasures especially, is this good influence of rectitude more necessary and more desirable.

Those people who take such infinite care of their souls, afraid of receiving a taint of sin, are like those poor, wretched, shivering hypochondriacs, who spend their time in nothing but trying to avoid anything unwholesome or deleterious to their constitutions; afraid of this, that, and the other, for fear it should disagree with their stomachs or their livers, or their chests, and in the end, become so delicate and sickly they are afraid to let the breath of heaven blow upon them.

It is the same with the religious hypochondriac; in the end he becomes so weak and sickly he is not fit for the atmosphere of the world in which he was born to live. Let us go to our balls and parties, concerts and dinners, operas or races, anything not absolutely vicious in *itself*, and if they give us any pleasure, let us be pleased, and not poison it by calling it sin. Yet let us not forget to carry with us wherever we go, the talisman of truth and love.

Speak not falsehoods of ourselves or of our neighbors. Let us utter no uncharitable, malicious, or spiteful words of our brothers and sisters, and let us not wrong one another by impure thoughts.

υ

If we do this, we do *better* than if we had stayed at home, conquered no evil in ourselves, and given no good example to our neighbors.

A few such, walking in society—call it fast society, or what not—who could enter into its pleasures, and joy in its joy, still preserving the upright attitude of rectitude and truth, would be the reformation and saving of society.

We cannot get good, or pleasure, unadulterated and pure, and separate from evil; but it is better to let many trivial sins pass unnoticed, rather than with unholy, scorching finger, shrivel and burn up one little grain of good, or joy, by pointing at it as sin.

The flesh must not lust against the spirit, but neither the spirit against the flesh; nor one fight against and try to overcome the other, but both, while on earth, work in harmony together.

I am not confounding the two, calling good evil, or evil good; evil is always evil, and it can never while it lives produce good, but the way to kill it is not to avoid it. "To know a thing you must also know what it is *not*." Our lesson is to learn what is truth, and to know it we must learn what it is *not;* and till that is learnt evil will not die.

Neither is it the way to purify and elevate society to abase it, and all that is called good separate itself from it. The signs of the times are curious—the needle of truth is oscillating widely, yet seems to point to the rising again of the depressed, abased, and degraded.

Those we have cast down and trampled in the mud and mire of the streets, and looked upon with scorn and loathing, are coming forward; they are now riding gaily in our parks, jostling the high-born in the resorts of fashion; and proud mothers and proud daughters are bewildered at the phantom they see rising, which they thought they had trampled down. Trodden down, indeed, but not killed. Poor creatures! let them rise—in God's name let them rise, and come out of darkness, and degradation, and ruin. For, are they not our sisters?

I see not evil in it, but good, much good—good to the vicious, and good, also, to the so-called virtuous. I mean not to imply that both are unequally unchaste—they have one sin, and we *all* have some other. Which is the worst, let God judge.

Why should women be so hard and uncharitable to women? Many appear to consider that by treating these unfortunates with the greater scorn, and passing them by on the other side, they lay a higher claim to be thought virtuous and honorable themselves.

It is not generally found, with regard to other vices, that those which a man most loudly inveighs against, he is always most innocent of.

CHAPTER XXIX.

THE JEWS.

I MUST return to a subject I touched upon in the beginning of the book, relative to the ultimate earthly dominion of the Jews; for I find I am combating a world-renowned faith, "believed in alike by Jew and Gentile. . . . Sir Moses Montefiore and Dr. Cumming"—that, as a "climax to the world's history, the chosen people shall all be gathered together at the holy city."

The paper I quote from is *Macmillan's Magazine*, of April, 1863:

"Who can tell how soon they (the children of Israel) may be gathered, in the most simple and natural way, from all corners of the earth, whither the Lord has driven them, and brought to Jerusalem, 'upon horses and in chariots, and in litters, and upon mules, and upon swift beasts.' Or, as Dr. Cumming insists, the original word, *Kurkaroth*, should be translated 'upon chariots revolving with the swiftness of the clouds,' which may, probably, odd as the coincidence sounds, indicate the new-planned Syrian railways."

Very odd indeed, I should say.

Dr. Cumming is a wonderful man; *that's* the way to make out prophecies—first translate a word to make it fit into the place you want, and *insist* upon it, then discover a wonderful coincidence.

I will try if I cannot read a more conclusive interpretation *to the very letter*.

"*Some on mules*," decidedly that must be the "old clo" men on donkeys.

"*Upon horses*," flashy young Jew gents, plentiful in gold chains, mounted on their "bits of blood."

"*In chariots*," well-to-do respectable Jews in their *own* carriages.

"*In litters*,"—let me see—what does that mean? I can think of nothing but invalid ladies in sedan chairs. And last of all, the great body of the wealthy Jews, coming in the newly-planned Syrian railways, alias "*swift beasts*."

It puzzles me to understand what *upon* chariots means, or how *chariots* can be made to revolve; it seems an odd sort of locomotion.

Now I have it. Upon coming in sight of the Holy City, the Jews inside the newly-planned Syrian railways will get into such a state of excitement, they will clamber "upon" top of the carriages, and wave their hats and pocket-handkerchiefs, so that the train will present the appearance of a revolving cloud: most likely, also, such will be the excitement of the children of Israel, some of them will tumble off and get hurt, so these, literally, will have to be carried in " on litters ! "

Now I challenge the great Dr. Cumming himself to interpret a prophecy more *plainly* or more *literally* than this ; really I have done it so well I am almost inclined to believe it myself.

On the other hand, it seems to me that such a climax would be the ruin of the Jews. As a separate nation, at the present day, they could not exist.

They are neither producers nor artificers, they are only barterers and traffickers.

They are circulators of wealth, not makers of wealth. They may be great, or as D'Israeli says, the greatest musicians, artists, historians, *literati*, or politicians, but none of these are producers of wealth; and the great and peculiar talent of the Jews is the merchandizing talent, from the smallest to the widest extent.

They act as middle men between producer and consumer, and without both, and living amongst both, they would be nothing.

They do not appear, from the least to the greatest, to have any agricultural tastes or talents ; they care not patiently to extract from the earth the raw material, by which labor only do we procure any real increase of wealth. Neither are any of them, as far as I know, great manufacturers or mechanical geniuses ; they care not to turn their attention to converting the raw material into articles of commerce; but when the raw article is collected, and this converted into manufactured goods, the merchant steps in, and distributes these over the world.

To make a great nation, you must have a due proportion of all three classes.

It is not owing to outward circumstances that the Jews have been forced into one line of business; for years, especially in England, every road has been open to them, but they have never chosen any other.

Whatever may have been their skill and love for any other employments in former days, at the present they do not appear to evince any desire to return to them.

Their skill and love is to trade in gold.

No isolated nation of merchants alone could exist. Their business depends on living in the midst of producers and consumers, and constantly watching, with the eye of a hawk (or a Jew's eye) the fluctuations of the market, and, by acute calculation, anticipating the exact moment when the consumer will require such and such goods, and where he can find the cheapest producer to supply that want.

What would the Rothschilds and Montefiores do, "settled down" in Jerusalem? And even they would do better than the poorer and smaller traffickers, because a great part of the business of the former can be carried on (I suppose) by correspondence;

but what would become of the innumerable pawn-brokers, money-lenders, bill-brokers ? &c., &c. The Jews themselves are much too prudent to require the services of either. How would the English Jews, French Jews, German Jews, Spanish Jews, all speaking different languages, and having imbibed different national peculiarities, care to live together again as one nation ?

By-the-bye I never heard of a Scotch Jew or an Irish Jew, I suppose because the first are too prudent and latter too poor, to enable a Jew to fatten upon them.

If Jerusalem was open to the Jews to settle in to-morrow would they go there ? Would they leave their lucrative employments in their several countries, for a residence in a nation of their own countrymen, where none of their businesses would bring them any gain ?

But if they are so anxious to go to Jerusalem, why don't they go ? I should fancy Baron Rothschild would find no difficulty in purchasing it for a suit-able " consideration." There was a talk of some such plan some years ago ; why was it not carried out ? Did not the Jews find the spirit move them to move ?—or did the contemplated purchaser come to the conclusion that it would be a very bad invest-ment for his money ?

The Jews being no agriculturists, are no colonists.

They never set foot in a colony, till it has sufficiently advanced to require and support traffic; where there is wealth to be *found* they will go, but where it has to be *made* they will not go.

Here is shown the Jews' peculiar talent:

It "could not but be noticed in going from class to class of these very sharp boys (in a Jewish school), that their chief sharpness seemed to be in figures. They did everything else very well; but when they came to arithmetic, they took to it like ducks to the water. In lengthy and involved mental calculation, the acuteness of these young Israelites was something preternatural; you felt that they were capable of spoiling the Egyptians to any extent, not necessarily by any dishonesty, but simply by the force of natural genius."

They have now found that place in the world for which this "natural genius" best befits them. But of what use would be this talent if they were amongst no Egyptians to spoil?—of what use their "astonishing faculty for amassing and retaining wealth," if they lived in a nation apart, amongst those whose chief desire was also to amass and retain wealth, but without producing it?

I believe it was no religious, or rather bigotted, feeling, which caused men to dislike Jews; it proceeded more from the notion that they gained or drew off wealth from the people amongst whom they resided, but produced none themselves. I do not mean that they arrived at such a conclusion from any knowledge of political economy, which shows they are unproductive laborers; but they observed, that though the Jews neither grew crops, nor manufactured goods, they somehow contrived to get rich at their expense.

The more ignorant the people the more the thought would present itself that these cunning strangers in some way preyed on the vitals of the community, and that they were cheated and despoiled by the Jews.

This need not be the case. The class to which they especially belong are necessary to the health and well-being of a community. They are not the food that sustains the body; nor the blood which is elaborated from the food, but they are the force which circulates that blood to the most remote extremities of the body, so, though not absolutely the cause of the nourishment of the body, they, by a circulation of this nourishment, strengthen the hands of those who procure the food.

The Jews as a nation are clever and acute in the extreme; prudent and calculating, orderly and moral, and submit quietly to either kind or cruel discipline. It is possible, if they retired from the different kingdoms to live by themselves as a nation, circumstances would compel them to become producers and manufacturers; but it would be following uncongenial pursuits quite contrary to their natural bent and inclination; and what a man does without zeal or pleasure, and out of his natural line, he never does well—they would find, in a short time, they would have to import goods, and could export nothing in exchange which other nations would care to take; and if they could not find their legitimate food they would devour one another.

In their business transactions Jacob is their prototype—a man's need, improvidence, and exhaustion, is their opportunity to gain a birthright or livelihood. But it is better that Esau should find Jacob there with his mess of potage than that he should die of hunger. And it is good for such scatter-brain impulsive youths as Esau to pay dear for their imprudence; perhaps it may teach them prudence. Also, as Jacob ran great risk in expecting payment from such an unthrifty person as Esau, he had every right to charge him a heavy per centage in consideration of the risk he ran; but if Jacob had not met his brother at the proper moment to offer his food, he would have missed the birthright, and most likely some one else would have fleeced Esau, and he would have been no better off.

The Jews led a nomadic life until Joseph, by a successful transaction in corn, was enabled to introduce them into Egypt; here they flourished, till the nation amongst whom they sojourned got jealous and uneasy at their increasing wealth and greatness, then they wandered into the wilderness, very possibly because forced to depart out of Egypt. They then desired the cultivated lands and wealth gained by other nations; and partly by cunning, and partly by the strong arm, they succeeded in conquering these nations, and most unjustifiably, in the name of God, seized upon possessions and property which they had neither paid for nor worked for; but having no power of cohesion as a nation, they were, after awhile, ousted from their ill-gotten gains and lands, and became dispersed among all nations, to follow the vocation for which their peculiar genius best fitted them. Though outwardly persecuted, they supplied a want to these several nations; so, though they hated them, they found they could not do without them. Being wise, they bent their heads to the storm, and it passed over them; being clever, and possessed of marvellous energy and force of character, in time they rose to become great, and rich, and powerful.

It is not to be denied that formerly the Jews appear to have been an agricultural nation, at least, they were so for a while. For some time after the death of Moses, they must have been too much occupied in fighting to attend to the cultivation of the soil. From the Egyptians, the Hebrews learnt the art of husbandry, and Moses, in his wisdom, made laws to support and encourage agriculture.

. All nomadic people look upon agricultural pursuits as contemptible, and only fit for slaves. Flocks and herds kept on nomadic (or wandering) principles, do not tend to draw a nation together, but to scatter. Unless fed by food produced by cultivation, when flocks and herds increase, the owners must divide, one to the right, and the other to the left, as did Abraham and Lot.

When the Jews became a nation, by unrighteously seizing the wealth for which other men had digged and ploughed, they were held together only by some strong minds, who exercised a religious despotism over them. Their prophets appear to have been their real rulers, and their kings were under their control.

The reign of Solomon was the culminating point of the Jewish national glory, wealth, and religious enthusiasm.

It would appear, even, that not until the time of David did the Jews gain possession of the upper city. This fort on Mount Zion they wrested from the Jebusites, and after its reduction it became the royal city. " Solomon, on the submission of the Edomites and surrounding tribes, diverted the current of eastern trade through his dominions."

Jerusalem was, then, the centre of the wealthiest and most civilized part of the world ; now it is surrounded by poor and semi-barbarous countries.

Solomon's wealth was gained, partly by commerce, and partly by slaves. "But of the children of Israel did Solomon make no bondmen, but they were men of war, and his servants, and his princes, and his captains, and rulers of his chariots, and his horsemen." The Hebrews, doubtless, considering that men of war and court hangers-on were more honorable than tillers of the soil, an opinion very prevalent to the present day.

Emerson writes, "In the early history of Asia and Africa, nomadism and agriculture are the two antagonistic facts. But the nomads were the terror of all those whom the soil or the advantages of a market had induced to build towns." So, the Hebrew writer makes the first murderer, Cain, a tiller of the soil, that being thought a degrading employment, but Abel, a keeper of sheep. So, also, the slave's offering of the fruits of the ground was not supposed to be a fit propitiary offering to the Creator, but it must be one of the flock, a bloody sacrifice : so, also, the first *slaver* of the earth, and murderer, builded a city.

But those who dig, and plough, and sow, and reap the fruits of the earth are not slaves, but the only really independent men, for the producer can, in a rough way, live without either manufacturer or merchant, but the manufacturer cannot live without the agriculturist, nor the merchant without both; and manufacturers, merchants, court, army, alike depend on the labors of the agriculturist for their subsistence.

Solomon, at the latter end of his reign, appears to have rebelled against the power of the prophets. He was a man of superior learning to the rest of his contemporaries, so that his wisdom was looked upon as something miraculous. He had more extended communication with other nations, and was led, perhaps by his enlightenment, to question their authority. Doubtless, also, his vices turned away his heart from God, though questioning the authority of the prophets, and turning from God by vice, are by no means synonymous.

With the death of Solomon, the last vigorous hand that held the Jews together was unclosed, the strong grasp relaxed, the cord that bound them in one was unloosed; the first shake separated them, and they dropped to pieces.

Even at the time of Solomon's death, their tributaries were ripe for revolt, and complained to his successor of his galling bondage, and, when not listened to, they broke away from his yoke.

Many men of great force, subsequent to this period, endeavored to cement them together, with more or less temporary success.

What do the children of Israel wait for now? Is it not for their earthly Messiah, a mighty man of wisdom and strength, like this Solomon, only more Godlike, who shall bring all the kings of the earth, and the kingdoms of the world to pay tribute and homage to them!

They do not want to *buy* Jerusalem, it must be *given* to them, or in some way be miraculously placed in their hands. They cannot make themselves a great nation, for they do not know the way; they have not worked up to it—they have not yet practised the first step—they have not yet learnt, nor have we ourselves, that a great nation cannot be made by conquest, by slaves, by vice, or by gold.

How rooted is the idea that God works by evil instead of good. These wars and plunderings of the Hebrews are excused in them, as they were a " peculiar people"—the peculiarity being, that they were desired by God to propagate His religion by crimes which He condemned. We think the Jews had the noblest and purest knowledge of God, while all other nations were miserable idolators; and to extirpate this crime of idolatry, God allowed, or even more, made use of the crime of murder. We say it would have been *impossible* for monotheism to have held its ground if the idolatrous nations surrounding the Hebrews had not been slain.

We say, God's ways are not our ways. They are not our ways, because they are infinitely juster and holier than our ways. God does not contradict himself by commanding us not to commit a sin, then show that he works by that sin. These are man's ways.

We now acknowledge this as the very antithesis of good government: "This balancing of evil with evil, instead of combining good with good, is wretched policy"—but thus, by balancing evil with evil, we say God educated and governed the world.

, No, these are *not* God's ways, but man's ways; and God lets us work out our own ways till we find out our mistakes for ourselves, and then begin to work the right way. It is not that God's way and God's justice has changed since the ancient days, but that we have changed and learnt to see more clearly and justly.

Monotheism was not advanced by wars and bloodshed, but because it was the truth; and it would have stood, if not a drop of blood had been shed to uphold it.

The Jews, in truth, are a wonderful people; they now not only stand between man and man—producer and consumer—throughout the world, but they remain to this day between us and God!

The man Jesus, a Jew, we worship as a God.

The Old and New Testament, the writings of Jews, we also worship.

The church built on this Jewish foundation, we also worship.

What greater triumph can the Jews desire?

w

These men, these Jews, whom we thought poor, and mean, and contemptible—made them bow and cringe to us,—yet these men were our masters, and we their slaves ; we ground their bodies to the dust, but they enslaved our souls !

What dominion can the Jews desire greater than this ?

Every civilized nation bows to the name of a Jew, as God !

Every child is taught to worship that Jew !

Every savage we endeavor to civilize is taught to worship that Jew ?

Truly, that meek man, Jesus, inherits the whole earth ! And yet these foolish Jews see not how much more magnificent is this dominion of the soul, than if Jesus had been to them the greatest earthly king, or the mightiest, most overwhelming conqueror.

We have no cause to hate, still less to despise these men, though we have every right to guard against them. They can do us no mischief, if we do not suffer them to lead us blindfold.

That they have enslaved our souls these many years is more our fault than theirs ; we insisted on being blindfolded, we refused to examine, we refused to question and search for ourselves, we voluntarily signed the deed of infallibility and inspiration, and by doing so mortgaged to them our beautiful, free estate of the soul.

But it is time to break their yoke from off our necks, it is time to recover our free birthright. Let us pay off the mortgage and redeem our rightful property, for through the riches they handed over to us, we have become rich.

Let us give them back the riches of charity we learnt from Jesus, the riches of love given us by Jesus, and let us take back what, not Jesus, but the Jews, apostles, and prophets, deprived us of,—our liberty of soul; and though we have not observed it, we have been thus gradually paying them back, and as we are beginning to show them christian charity and christian love,—not treating them with scorn and contempt—lo, insensibly, has our liberty flowed back to us. Yes, brother Jew—for brother you are in Jesus, though you own it not—and with that acknowledgment in spirit and in truth, of brother in Jesus and joint sons of God, is your dominion of the soul gone.

CHAPTER XXX.

JOY. IMAGINATION. SUPERSTITION.

It is a great text with churchmen : " Out of the mouths of babes and sucklings Thou has perfected praise," and that if we desire to win heaven we must become as little children.

Have they ever given themselves thoughtfully to discover *how* young children give praise to God, or what is the one marked difference between themselves and young children ? They tell you of child-like *faith*, child-like *obedience*, child-like *reverence :* but I will ask any one, who has children of his own, or in a school, or in any other way has had the care of children, whether, naturally, a child has an atom of either of these qualities ; whether, on the contrary, these dispositions have not slowly to be instilled into them, by unceasing care and watchfulness, patience, and an infinite amount of good temper, if you can command such a valuable requisite.

Children, then, have to learn these qualities from adults, not adults from children ; in this, they are to become like men, not men like children.

Now, let us inquire into their " pure, unquestioning faith ;" which means, in other words, that a child believes everything you tell it. If so, they believe because they have not sufficient reason to question. As is their measure of ignorance, so is their measure of pure church faith; but as soon as they begin to reason they begin to question. But I very much doubt a child's being so believing; they are credulous, if you like.

My servant told my little girl there were witches still in England, and for some time I could not disabuse her mind of such folly; but when I told her the earth moved round the sun, and not the sun round the earth, she replied obstinately, and I must own, somewhat rudely, " I am sure it does'nt " !

That such a feeling (that is, disbelief of facts, and credulity of the marvellous) is common to all ignorant people is well known, and will not redound much to the credit of the church interpretation of faith.

It seems to me the peculiar and *only* difference between men and children is their joyousness.

They praise God continually by their unconscious thankfulness for the blessing of life.

Has any man, I wonder, such a real appreciation of LIFE, as truly to say from his heart, " I thank God for my creation " ? Does he not, rather, say, with a sigh, " Would God I had never been born " !

This is not a right feeling; it is ungratefulness to God, who brought us into the world, and gave us life that we might be happy.

Children, why are you all so miserable?

Does it tend to make you happier to tell you it is because you are abominable, degraded, sinful creatures?

Does it make a little child, that has tumbled down and hurt itself, leave off crying by giving it a slap or a shake, saying, "You naughty little thing, to go and tumble down and make all your clothes dirty"! But this is the sort of discipline we poor grown people usually get, to make us of a more cheerful countenance. That sin is partly a cause of our unhappiness is undoubted, but unhappiness is a much more prolific cause of sin. It is, again, action and reaction; increase the one, and you increase the other. Lighten the burden of sorrow, and you lighten the burden of sin.

To ascribe the joyousness of children to their superior innocence, is a mistake.

To ascribe it to their amenity from pain or sorrow, is also, I think, a mistake; they have, I believe, as much as they can bear. There are as many cries as laughs in a child's day.

What we love in children, what touches our heart, is not their freedom from sin, but their freedom from care.

Those who are able to note the dispositions of children will find that even from infancy they sin.

The period of childish innocence is inappreciable;

immediately they quit the state of a mere animal they evince passion. A child commits sin, as much as his faculties are capable of committing, indeed, in proportion, they commit more sin; for no good motive or principle having had time to grow up in their minds, they are at the mercy of every gust of passion, which only the external authority of parent or teacher keeps in check; and children, particularly men children, are frightfully cruel.

But I maintain it is no more a proof of superior virtue or innocence in children, because their thoughts are not impure, or they do not commit the same sins as adults, than it is superior virtue in a deaf and dumb man, that he, with his lips, does not utter curses and oaths.

Purity is not lost through knowledge. A father or mother of fifty years of age may be as pure in mind and body as a child. If purity is only possible in childlike ignorance, it is worthless; if it breaks under the first step of knowledge, it is as vain and useless as a thread of spun glass to bridge Niagara.

Whence, then, this joyful light in the eyes of a child, and the happy tone in their little voices?

It is because they have not yet had dinned into their ears, that everything they look at with pleasure is sin; that everything they hear with pleasure is sin; that every happy, thoughtless word they speak is sin; that even what is pleasant to them to eat and drink is sin; that smiles, laughter, merriment, fun is sin.

But there *is* sin mingled with it all. Let any one pass a day with half-a-dozen healthy children, however young, but past the first utterly helpless days of infancy, and let him see if there is not sin amongst them, and let him see how much childlike obedience and childlike reverence he will procure from them, unless, indeed, he chooses to make use of fear, and then you have sent away joy. And woe unto them who thus offend little ones.

If you take away joy, by substituting fear for love, you bring in misery, and multiply sin a hundred-fold.

Here is a picture of a workhouse school on a *gala-day* :

"The first time I made acquaintance with the children of C——— Workhouse School, I went with some friends to see them receive presents of toys, sugar-plums, &c., collected for distribution among them by some kind-hearted ladies. We began with the nursery, where the babies and children under three years old are kept. It was a cheerless sight enough, though the room was large and airy, and clean as whitewash could make it; and the babies, there were about twenty altogether, showed no signs of ill-usage or neglect. Most of them were healthy and well-fed, and all scrupulously neat and tidy. But it was the unnatural stillness of the little things that affected me painfully. All remained perfectly grave and noiseless, even when the basket of toys was brought in and placed in the midst of the circle. There was no jumping up, no shouting, no eager demand for some particular noisy or gaudy plaything. They held out their tiny hands, and took them when they were bid, and then relapsed into quiet dulness again, equally regardless of the ladies' simulated expressions of delight and surprise, made for their imitation, or the good clergyman's exhortation to them to 'be good children, and deserve all the pretty things the kind ladies gave them.' The children were standing quiet and silent before the yet untouched tea and plum-cake, listening to a long discourse from one of the clergymen, interspersed with anecdotes of sweet children, who, unfortunately, all died while still of very tender years, which it might, perhaps, have been better to defer till after the good things were disposed of."

Here is plenty of most *unchildlike* obedience and reverence, but what do we miss in the picture? that which makes the child—*Joyousness.*

And what is the fruit of this life, devoid of pleasure, and in its place, obedience and reverence inculcated by fear? It is told in a sentence: " In one metropolitan union, inquiries being made concerning eighty girls, who had left the workhouse, and gone to service, it was found that *every one* was on the streets " !

I have not quoted this for the sake of children, for I believe now the system for them has been greatly altered. But I do so because our church religion is carried on in this very workhouse system. Separation from the world, and obedience and reverence, inculcated by fear : and the effect on men is the same as on children, producing misery and vice.

Everything that is delightful and pleasant to the senses they have damned ; and, as if that were not enough, we must have the load of our supposed first parents' sin put upon our shoulders ; nevertheless, we must say, " Thank you," very humbly—be very quiet, orderly and good, and try to deserve all the blessings our prison-house affords. Poor children ! no wonder you look unhappy and depressed, and your souls are heavy and bowed down.

I wish I could fill the soul of every man with the joy I see in the bright flowers, the glorious sunshine, and the happy looks and voices of children.

There would be little sin left, if our hearts were full of joy and love. We ought to be as happy as children ; nay, I am convinced we might be. As we grow up and our minds are enlarged, we have a greater capacity for enjoyment, and a wider range of pleasures, yet we do not enjoy them.

We are even afraid of the word " pleasure," as if the very word was sin. We may have what is called happiness, which is something very holy, and calm, and *quiet*, and *orderly*, and divested of everything like free, care-less, thought-less, true enjoyment, we must never for an instant forget that we are s—i—n—ful creatures, with the load of Adam's, our own, and no knowing how many other people's sins upon our immortal souls.

. We have, it is true, more mental care and pain to bear than children; but we are not allowed to take what is God's own compensation for our harder struggle, as great an increase of bodily and mental pleasure and enjoyment, so to effectually prevent our having any pleasure in it, we are surrounded with the galling restraint of fear.

We fear pain, we fear poverty, we fear old age, we fear death, we fear hell, and last, and worst of all, we FEAR GOD! And our inward wretchedness writes itself on our careworn anxious brows. We *fear* God! Thereby putting Him in the same list with all we dislike, shrink from, and strive to avoid.

Besides, the freedom from care, which produces childlike joy, there is another attitude of a child's mind, which is little appreciated or noticed, but one we might well study to copy.

. A child lives in the present, and is happy in the present; but men forget that the present moment is the only one in which they really *live*.

Yet the life that is *with* them they never care for, or ever condescend to look at.

They gaze on the past with a reproachful look, as if it had deprived them of something they could never see again, and then to the future with dread, lest it should take away what is still left them.

They hardly ever say to themselves, "In this moment only *I am*—in this moment only *I live*—and in this moment, therefore, will I try and be happy, and take with thankfulness or joy all the good God apportions to the moment. You cannot lay it by, any more than you can the moment, and think to receive it again at some future time with interest. Joy put aside will never again offer itself; but if you had swallowed the morsel of nourishment when it was offered, it would have strengthened you to seek for more. By refusing it, you have weakened and stunted your growth.

"Let the dead past bury its dead." Never let your thoughts "cling to the mouldering past," or your *present* joy will moulder away to ruin with it. Never look at the past, but to gain experience from it, as a stepping-stone to mount to higher joy. *Believe* in *life*, not only in another world, but also in this. Never dread to meet your life, even though its future comes to you with gray hairs and a wrinkled brow. As there is joy now, believe there shall be joy then.

It is but for a little while that a child lives in the present. As soon as thought awakes, and his eyes begin to look on life, he lives out of the present, and feeds on hope. Hope is good, but it should not carry us out of the present, for it has then no balance to steady itself by, and degenerates into imagination.

Hope, to be good and real, must be fit to last through life, and have its foundation in the present, as is the *now*, so shall be the *then*; but the language of imagination is, as is the *now*, so shall *not* be the *then*. I say hope *degenerates* into imagination, because imagination applied to the life is deadly.

Imagination cannot last; about the middle of a man's life it withers away, and he feels desolate and forsaken. He has fed himself with the sweet food of imagination, lived on day-dreams, then, when it gradually dawns upon him that none of these bright pictures can ever be realized, and because he has chosen to live in a world of his own fancy, he thinks the world God made for him to live in—the real world—has no joy in it.

I write this because I have passed through it, and know how bitter is the awaking.

I lived in day-dreams; thought the life I imagined was brighter than God's life, so when real life was forced upon me, I found it dull and wretched, and was disappointed and discontented; wrote miserable poetry, as I suppose every one does who is intensely miserable or in love, and who feels a necessity for expression, as a relief. At the end of a long dismal piece, which I should be very sorry to inflict upon the reader. I endeavored to accept my supposed destiny—" For," I wrote,

—Disappointment is the doom of man
The end of every hope and every plan !

I carried these lines in my mind as a motto for a long time—tried to become callous, to fear nothing, and care for nothing, but to take all, good or bad, with a sort of all-in-the-day's-work feeling.

But no one who has any feeling at all can exist long in this stagnant state of mind ; he will either sink in despair or rise again to hope.

By thus for a time cutting myself off from hope or fear, I also cured myself of the disease of imagination. I expected nothing, so not only was I never disappointed, but I also found that real good came to me, when and where least expected.

Then, came again the aspiration for happiness. I wrote—

Why is earth so fair ?
Why all things so glad ?
Why all nature free from care,
While man alone is sad ?
*   *   *   *
*   *   *   *
The joy to earth thou dost impart,
To man, kind nature, give ;
Oh, lift his drooping head and heart,
And bid him smile and live !

For myself, my wish has been realized, I now no longer expect the happiness or goodness of an angel, or perfect spirit, while still in a mortal and imperfect state, neither do I believe that all earthly hopes and plans are doomed to disappointment; but whatever a man works for, that he has. In this there is no luck, no chance, no variableness, no possibility of being baulked or disappointed. It does not follow that a man always gains what he intends or desires to gain at the commencement of his work; for we work almost blindly, and till we are half-way through our work, or, perhaps, not until we have reached the end of it, do we clearly see what we have been working for; but it is a law as immutable as every other law of force, that work gains what it was truly aimed at, and the gains are in proportion to the strength employed.

It is not "Hope told a flattering tale," but Imagination. Hope is true. Imagination it is that speaks falsely. The poetry of youth is, "When I am a man;" the poetry of age is, "When I was a boy," writes some one. But it is not poetry, for that to *be* poetry, must be real and true, and neither the look the boy takes into the future is true, nor is the look the man takes back into the past true, both are distorted and false pictures.

And what a contradiction it is. Up to a certain period we look forward for happiness—never find it—then look back, and fancy we *have* had it. Can you be said to have been happy, when at the time you were not conscious of it; and if you have never lived in the present moment, you have never been conscious of it, therefore, never happy.

Yet, because we have not yet perfect happiness, we need not throw aside the few grains we have, say they are a sin and a snare, and endeavor, instead of taking these, to seek those that are at present completely out of our reach; we must be educated gradually in joy, as well as in every other perfection.

I must again guard against misapprehension, lest I should be thought to mean that we can have no spiritual pleasures.

Let imagination try to look at the joy we may have when perfect—in this we will never be disappointed; but let it not spoil the enjoyment the present moment affords. We cannot force ourselves on to perfection any quicker by suicide of the body; and suicide comprehends something more than depriving ourselves of life, as murder comprehends something more than killing our neighbor.

The mischief of imagination is, that it shoots ahead of the line of life, too fast and too far, and when reality will not follow where fancy has led, we are offended at life; and disappointment drops us as many degrees below the line of life, as fancy had raised us above. But the line of life ought to be a gradual rise from childhood to our last sleep—to rise from that spot whence we laid down to begin another and brighter day; then sleep, then wake again, and yet again and again.

(Ah! I am inveighing against imagination, yet where is it now leading me?)

Now, this feverish imagination, that doubles back upon itself, what is it but superstition?

It is the natural rebound of the ball which the young force of joy has thrown so far. It is shown in the belief that what has gone before is the best, the only good, the only beautiful.

The pagan doctrine of reminiscence, and the Hebrew one of innocent happiness in the Garden of Eden, are both the results of this rebound.

It has been said that science is daily more clearly disclosing to us that our beginning was low and mean, that perfection has to be reached, not that it has gone before, and we are fallen from it. But though science is preaching this truth to us daily, in so loud a voice that none can shut their ears to it, yet we refuse to listen, because our own feelings, Hebrew prophets, and Greek philosophers, all agree that the instinctive feeling in man is, that he is a fallen creature.

May not the enigma, or seeming contradiction, be reconciled in the manner I have indicated, as being the effect of a diseased imagination, producing superstition.

x

I copy the Greek idea from G. H. Lewes's "History of Philosophy." Plato says:

"Now this mode of apprehension is neither more nor less than the recollection of those things which the soul formerly saw when it journeyed along with the gods."

All our recollections of truth are performed in the same way. It is as if in our youth we had listened to some mighty orator, whose printed speech we are reading in old age. That printed page, how poor and faint a copy of that thrilling eloquence! how greatly do we miss the speaker's piercing, vibrating tone, his flashing eye, his flashing face. And yet that printed page in some dim way recalls those tones, recalls that face, and stirs us somewhat as we then were stirred. Long years and many associations have somewhat effaced the impression he made, but the words serve faintly to recall it. Thus it is with our immortal souls. They have sojourned in that celestial region where the voice of truth rings clearly, where the aspect of truth is unveiled, undimmed.

They are now sojourning in this fleeting, flowing river of life, stung with resistless longings for the skies, and solaced only by the reminiscence of that former state, which these fleeting, broken, incoherent images of ideas awaken in them.

Aristotle disputes Plato's ideal theory: "He too

was aware that reminiscence was indispensable, but reminiscence of previous *experience*, not of an anterior state of existence in the world of ideas."

The Hebrew idea of Eden is the picture of the life of a child, a retrospection of that life, filled up by the rebound of imagination, which results in superstition.

An unconscious infant knows not evil, therefore man originally knew it not. A child knows no shame, therefore Adam and Eve were naked and were not ashamed.

An infant has not to toil for his daily food, nature provides it. Therefore man had not in the beginning to eat bread in the sweat of his brow, nature gave him fruits.

An infant knows nothing of danger, that wild beasts will devour and thorns prick. So, in Eden, wild beasts did not devour, and there were no thorns.

A child knows nothing of death. Therefore Adam and Eve were not to die.

A lady remarked to me that the study of Eden always appeared to her like a story told to children; well it might, for it is drawn from the life of a child, which superstition supposes to be the only happy state on earth.

Every man at some time of his life feels vaguely in his mind the doctrine of reminiscence. Does this proceed from the fall of man on earth in Eden, where none of us have ever been ? for if we had, there would have been a Garden of Eden still, as a place of trial for future children of earth ; or, from having before lived in a higher state of existence in another world, or is merely memory of the days past of our own present short life ?

We are inclined to think that before we were men we were something better and nobler than we are at present. Nearly every one at some imaginative period of his life—at about the turning-point, when imagination is beginning to think and feel sad, and look back to the time when it did not think—such a feeling is called forth by whatever is beautiful or lovely with which his soul has the greatest affinity :

> Often, when sounds of music filled my ears,
> Almost to tears have I been moved, so soft
> The melody would steal into my heart,
> And make it ache with very loneliness.
> Yet, it was soothing, too, and comforting;
> The strains I seemed to know, I must have heard
> Them once before.   'Twas something long forgot
> Brought back to recollection, and the tones
> Had meaning strange, and seemed to speak to me :
> But now my ears were dull, and could not hear ;
> My heart was dull, and could not understand.
> I listened—trying to unseal my ears,
> Then, like the mem'ry of a dream at morn,
> I caught a dim and momentary view
> Of some far distant land, where once I'd been,
> Methought, and heard those wondrous strains before.

Whether we embody our ideas in words or not,

some such feeling of dim recollection is, I think, common to all—to all, at least, who have at some moment of their lives a glimpse of the soul through the mind.

If we accept the Hebrew idea, that we are fallen because one pair fell on earth, then this world is but a state of punishment, and, as a punishment, we are living here under curses, yet for sins committed in this state of punishment for former sins, we have still the punishment of hell; then for sins committed in hell, we ought to have a second hell, &c.

But this life is not a state of punishment, but of work and trial.

The story of the Garden of Eden and Adam and Eve's fall will not satisfy the mind for its instinctive feeling of what we suppose to be reminiscence. Plato's idea comes nearer the truth, confirmed by our own instinctive and involuntary feelings.

There is, undoubtedly, at some moments, a feeling that seems to unite us to a higher existence.

But is it reminiscence or anticipation?

A look back, or a look forward?

It is an intense and exquisite pleasure, like the lightning flash, gone almost before you can look at it. You see a beautiful face, or a lovely statue, or you love, you walk out into the clear bright sunshine on an early spring morning, you hear music; for an instant they are familiar to you, they greet you, you *know* them, and you think it is "something long forgot brought back to recollection." Yet not the thing itself, but the soul or spirit of the thing, the holy joy. It speaks you know not what. But is it recollection ? Is it not rather affinity ? A chord struck by some unknown hand, that vibrates in our souls.

" We know there is a God, by affinity with our own souls." And is not this joy the response of the God-like spirit within us ?

It is the touch of God to make us look upwards. Life is progress. Recollection draws the soul back, anticipation urges it forward.

Reminiscence and memory is regret.

Anticipation and hope is joy.

Science and the Hebrew legend agree in this, that the dawn of man's existence upon earth was like the first few days of the life of an infant, innocent only in knowing nothing, and little, if at all, above the life of an animal : but immediately the consciousness of existence was perceptible to the mind, the desire to know came with it.

Science and the Greek philosophy agree in this, that we are indissolubly united to a higher nature, and a more glorious being, and occasionally a divine light reveals this to our mental vision.

All these are truths, the falsehood lies in the assertion that the desire to know, was sinful—that in seeking to gratify this insatiable desire, which God has planted in our hearts, to draw them up to heaven, and above animalism, called down upon us His wrath and curses.

There is falsehood also in the Greek superstition that heaven is behind us instead of before us. That at some past time we did sojourn with the gods, instead of at some future period we shall be sons of God.

And what has caused that other phase of superstition, which seems to be turning half the civilized world crazy at the present day? Is it not from the confusion bred in our minds by the belief in an evil spirit, the devil, being abroad in the world, though ordinarily invisible to us; and from the Bible telling us that spirits, both good and bad, have been visible to bodily sight and hearing? So we have arrived at a belief in the possibility and even probability of their appearing, and talking to us again. This age shows the working out to its climax, of a falsehood which the world has so long credited.

If any one can thoroughly and reasonably convince himself of the impossibility of the existence of the devil, and is fully sensible that spirit cannot have bodily organs visible or hearable to our bodily organs, will he afterwards believe in ghosts, spirit-rapping, or mediums?

But this is more credulity than superstition, which

latter I take to be inordinate fondness and veneration for the past.

The dislike we have towards theories of development either from animals, or even the low beginning of savages, is it not from the idea that instead of being something lower before we were men we were something greater ?   It is like when, in the beautiful story of " Undine," she promises to tell Margaret of her parents, the latter is eager and longing to know the secret ; she fancies, from her own beauty and elegance, they must be prince and princess at least ; but when the poor old fisherman and his wife are introduced to her, she is aghast, she raves, she weeps, —it is utterly impossible ; *those* people could never have been her parents !

Now we, from having seen these hints of beauty and inexpressible joy so far above us, think they are the effect of memory—the recollection of a region of truth, love, and joy, we once inhabited ; and then to be told our existence dates from an animal life, nigh unto the very beasts of the field, is a dreadful shock to our feelings.   We are offended ; we won't have it.

We have been brought nearer to the first cause or fact of existence, which Greek, Hebrew, and all other philosophers looked eagerly for.   We looked up amongst the angels, and lo ! it is down among the brutes.

We *may* occasionally have a touch of memory, but it is of a lower, not a higher life.

We acknowledge we came from the " dust of the earth." We believe it to be true, though we have never seen a man made from the dust of the earth; but we know we are of it and return to it.

Why should it be thought a degradation that that dust of the earth should have travelled up through ages and ages in the bodies of animals till it reached our bodies. It is dust purified, refined by many processes.

There seem to be as many facts to disprove as to prove an animal bodily development; but there is everything to prove and nothing to disprove a mental development; we see that, however slow the progress in the world, in nations, and in individuals. If there has been so much time, care, labor (humanly speaking) taken to develop the body, the mere shell, surely the same might have been taken for the mind.

Let us divest ourselves of reverence for the past; it is a foolish and ignorant superstition.

We know nothing of the feelings of our first infant days, we as yet know nothing of the world's infant days; and because we know nothing, we fancy they were the best and happiest. Every step gained in knowledge, ought to be a step gained in happiness, if we do not suffer imagination, like " vaulting ambition" to "o'erleap itself," and leave us afterwards, exhausted, disappointed and looking back.

We think the bud more beautiful than the flower. The child more lovely and happy than the man. God's beginnings better than his endings!

So we thought that despotism would be the best form of government, provided only the perfect despot would be found; but Mr. Mill proves it would be the very worst for any but children, or savages, who are children in mental growth, showing the first-fruits of unchecked passions.

The government to which men are gradually working is republicanism, or freedom; but if seized too soon, before society is prepared, like the effect of youthful imagination, it recoils upon itself, and produces confusion, disorder, and ruin.

We must be educated for happiness, as well as for every other good. Many people fancy they only require a lot of money to make them happy, but nothing can be a greater mistake. If a man had millions, he could receive no more joy or pleasure from it than his own capacity for joy would allow.

Let an ignorant man, one little above an animal, whose only pleasure is the public-house, obtain riches, will any amount of wealth make him happier than he was before? To be condemned to live in a palace, with everything beautiful and costly around him, beautiful music, pictures, statues, books, delicate food, rare wines, what would he care? what pleasure would they give him?

When we read of such sudden transformations of condition in a fairy tale, we unconsciously fit the man to his altered circumstances, but nature does not so, and through this it is that reality disappoints imagination.

That a man, on a sudden, may have given him magnificent palaces, gilt coaches, if he cares to drive in them, or a woman, glass slippers, &c., if she likes to wear them, is nothing fairy-like or impossible; but that he or she should be as suddenly transformed to be enabled to appreciate them, is the fairy impossibility.

A man such as I have pictured, could only have pleasure a little higher than the brutes. The luxury of beauty and grace, the repose of all harmony, purity order, cleanliness, with which wealth could surround him, would be only to him an irksome restraint, he would long for what he considered his *liberty*, that is, liberty to make his dwelling and surroundings as filthy, coarse, and brutal as his own nature; and the only use he would make of his wealth, would be to indulge to the full his animal propensities, and so become more wretched than he was before.

This is but the lowest picture; but it is true from the highest to the lowest gradation. As is the capacity for joy, so far only can *any* good gift yield pleasure and happiness. Where wealth ministers to vice, because it does not know where to look for pleasure it produces only more misery. But of this also men have to be *convinced*, in learning what is joy by knowing what it is not.

To what has our boasted wisdom led us hitherto? It has pasted over everything this motto, "*vanita vanitatas*"—"starred it" in such large letters that almost as soon as a child can say its alphabet it is forced to read it. But it is bitter wisdom; yes, I tasted it, and it was very bitter—so bitter that I would have none of it. It has been put to my lips many times, but, if I can help it, I will never drink it.

Can we not find a better motto for the world and all things it, than that of the disappointed, discontented *roué*, Solomon, who greedily clutched at every good or pleasure within his reach, whether his or another's, then pronounced it all "vanity and vexation of spirit." If he had tasted *true* wisdom and goodness, it would not have left such a bitter taste in his mouth.

There are two classes of silly children in the world. Those who creep about as if they had been whipped, and remain in constant expectation of being whipped again; and when flowers or sugar-plums are offered them, with a smile, instead of the rod, with a frown, hang down their heads and will not look, and will not eat, for fear of getting an extra whipping for so doing; or if they do receive them, partake as solemnly and listlessly as the joyless workhouse inmates, before spoken of. These are foolish children.

There are those, again, who seize and devour all the cakes and sweetmeats they can get hold of, then complain that the cakes are *nasty*, because they have made themselves sick with them, and blame every body but themselves because they are sick. These are very foolish children.

Have either of them found true wisdom ? Have they not rather found what it is not ?

Let us no more be foolish children, or unhappy children, but free and joyous children.

See the rod changed into bright green leaves and glorious blossoms ! Let us crown our heads with them, and play with them, and smell their sweet fragrance. Let us joy like children, not come reeling drunkenly along like Bacchus and his beastly crew.

Oh, mankind awake ! Shake off this nightmare *Devil*, which has been pressing on your hearts. Drink *this* wine of joy. Pass round *this* loving cup. You shall taste it as you have never tasted it before. There is no bitterness, no "vanity of vanities" at the bottom of it, but *life*. Drink it ; and your souls shall leap up with joy and strength to work the work that brings you on to heaven, and your hearts shall say, "I thank God for *Life* !"

How beautiful the world has been growing to me while I have been writing. No more the world of chaos, sin, punishment, devils, but only men working to know, struggling to be happy, mounting step by step nearer to God—but working for themselves, struggling for themselves, so that when knowledge is gained, and joy found, and we are perfect, we shall yet be free !

I place my belief in our Father's dealings with his children by the side of the orthodox faith, as stated in Dr. M'Caul's essay, "Ideology and Subscription":

"*Man, conscious of inherent weakness, longs for union with God.*"

Is man conscious of inherent weakness ? Is he not conscious, rather, of inherent strength, latent strength, grasping for something above, but, half-blind, seizing hold of many wrong, before finding one right pulley to raise himself upwards.

"Oh, I feel like a seed in the cold earth quickening at heart, and pining for the day," is the feeling of the soul. "*In the incarnation, God and man become one*" !

No, that will not satisfy. Any one who has the intense desire for expansion, for upwardness, will involuntarily feel that this is *falling*. Instead of man, by work, by strength, led on by unspoken longings, mounting to God and heaven, God is degraded and brought down to earth. Not all

mankind slowly approaching nearer to God, but God
stoops and enters one man. Here, again, instead of
work, there is a gift; not only God's degradation, but
man's degradation : a gift can never make us rise.*

* God degrading himself to the level of our understanding is the
ground or argument upon which the christian "plan of salvation"
is built, as shown by Archbishop Tillotson ; and his arguments are
copied by most of the defenders of Christianity to the present day.
I copy some of them from the Rev. R. Taylor's " Diegesis," with
his comments upon them.

" Secondly, I consider, in the next place, that in several revelations
which God hath made of himself to mankind, He hath, with great
condescension, accommodated Himself to the condition and capacity,
and other circumstances, of the persons and people to whom they
were made. For the religion and laws which God gave them (*i. e.*,
the Jewish nation) were far from being the best, [indeed !] God
gave them *statutes that were not good*, that is, very imperfect, in
comparison with what he could and would have given them, had
they been capable of them."

" This might have been fair-play, provided God Himself was *not
able* to enlarge or improve their capacity." (The Rev. R. Taylor's
remark is just, and besides, the very way to prevent them from
enlarging and improving their capacity was to bind them down to
an imperfect religion and *statutes that were not good*.)

" But in history and fact, this is certain, that some notions, and
those very gross and erroneous, did almost universally prevail ; and
though some of these were much more tolerable than others, yet
God seems to have had great consideration of some very weak and
gross apprehensions of mankind concerning religion. And, as, in
some of the laws given by Moses, God was pleased particularly to
consider the hardness of the heart of that people, so he seems likewise to have very much suited the dispensation of the Gospel, and
the method of our salvation, by the incarnation and sufferings of
His Son, to the common prejudices of mankind."

" Good God ! could a bishop, in stronger significancy, discover his
heartfelt hatred of Christianity ? He held Christians to be more

" *Man feels himself exposed to a strange fascination which attracts him towards evil, and draws him away from God.*"

Is there any fascination in evil for itself ?   Do we

hard-hearted than Jews themselves, and so God suited his religion to their hard-heartedness."

" The world was much given to admire mysteries, most of which were either very odd and fantastical, or very lewd and impure, or very inhuman and cruel.   But the great mystery of the incarnation of the Son of God was such a mystery as did obscure and swallow up all other mysteries.   Since the world had such an admiration for mysteries, *that* was a mystery indeed—a mystery beyond all dispute, and beyond all comparison."

"Oh, spirit of Voltaire ! Was ever sarcasm on earth more sarcastic ! Was it, in plainer language, that an Archbishop of Canterbury could have told us that the Christian religion was the oddest, the lewdest, and the bloodiest, that ever was upon earth, ' beyond all dispute, and beyond all comparison.' "

I need not copy any more.   It seems to me that churchmen neither consider nor care what vileness they heap upon the character of their God, so long as they can prop up the belief in their idol, the Bible.

For God's sake, men, see the infamy you have heaped upon Him.

In one text, in St. Paul, He appears like a very Moloch, *making* us believe a lie that we may be damned ; and in this he appears cringing and crawling before us, making a religion to pander to our vices and ignorances, that he may save us.

He makes His only Son to be tortured and to die, because Christians, the wretches, liked *blood !*

Men had "gross and erroneous " notions, so God, " out of consideration " for our gross and erroneous notions, kindly made a religion for us, that was gross and erroneous !

Men were hard of heart, so God was "pleased particularly to consider " this, so, to feed and encourage our vile cruelty, He vouchsafed the world the bloody spectacle of His Son's suffering not follow evil because we *think* there is good in it? we cannot help fancying there is some hidden sweetness and pleasure in it; we are anxious to taste it—to know it. It is the intense desire of happiness, ignorantly pursued—the many wrong steps taken before the right one is found.

Do we really love evil knowing it to be evil? I think not.

It is well known that those books which display wickedness in its naked deformity do little or no mischief, but only those which throw over sin a gloss of beauty which does not belong to it. Over some vices the gloss of fortitude, endurance, and courage; on others, of elegance, refinement, and love. This outside varnish it is that fascinates us—not the sin; and we are unable to perceive that it does not

and death—faugh! it makes me sick. Does the "scheme of salvation" come from God or men-devils?

When a wise man is the companion of a foolish one, what should he do? sink his intellect and conversation to the drivelling of the fool, or endeavor to improve the capacity of his companion, by striving to advance it to his level?—any one can answer which is best, which is wisest, which is right. So, then, judge of God: never seek to bring Him down to the dust, either in body or spirit, but know that He seeks to raise us up to Him, in wisdom, goodness, and immortality.

The very admission that our system of religion is suited to our imperfect capacity, and is a condescension to it, is a tacit acknowledgment that what God took the trouble to give us by a peculiar revelation or inspiration, we cannot help seeing is now really below our natural uninspired reason!

Y

emanate from it, or is connected with it. If there is
anything that gains our admiration in the character
of a vicious man it proceeds from some virtue he
possesses in spite of his crimes ; or, if a fictitious
character, the virtue exists only in the imagination
of the author, and, very possible, in real life would
not be compatible with the vices he draws.

"*In Christ he meets, baffles, and overcomes, the
personal agent of all temptation.*"

In Christ's doctrine of love we may certainly conquer evil, and so be saved many false steps, but to
talk of the "personal agent of all temptation," is
nonsense. A man's desires are his own tempters,
and ignorance leads him astray to satisfy those
desires.

"*Man feels himself a slave to nature, over which a
sure instinct tells him that he was destined to rule.*"

We do not, I think, feel ourselves quite slaves to
nature ; but we have not yet the dominion over it,
which a sure instinct tells us we *are*, not *were*, destined to obtain.

"*In Christ he exercises that dominion, making all
physical forces subservient to his will.*"

What, in the name of common sense, has Christ
to do with our having dominion over "physical
forces" ?

Scientific knowledge alone, by acquaintance with
physical laws, will give us dominion over nature,

making physical forces subservient to our will; by this knowledge, which year by year we work out for ourselves, we gradually raise ourselves from being slaves of nature, to making the powers of nature our servants.

"*Man fears disease, affliction, and bereavement. In Christ all sorrows become medicinal, and conduce to the perfection of renewed nature.*"

Here is the material and spiritual jumble again.

Disease is bodily pain, affliction—and bereavement, mental pain; but all three are classed together, as medicinal and conducive to perfection. If disease be so, we had better leave off calling in the doctor, and submit to be made perfect by medicinal disease! It may be "medicinal," but the less physic we take the better for our constitutions.

To say that man naturally fears and dislikes both bodily and mental pain, is a tacit acknowledgment that he naturally fears and dislikes what is evil, both for body and mind, and that his natural desire is for good. Christian resignation may make us receive ills if irremediable, without murmuring—that is tempting Providence; but I very much doubt whether disease or affliction generally improves the temper or disposition. If a person keeps a good temper when suffering pain (a fit of the gout, for instance), or escapes being fretful under misfortune, it is more the result of his good disposition previously, which he preserves in spite of bodily or mental ailment, than the cause of it. We often say we must make allowances for much irascibility of temper, because he or she who shows it "is such an invalid"—or "the temper has been soured by so many misfortunes." There is another fact to be considered, you hear sometimes of a person spoken of as having become quite amiable since his or her illness; but it must be remembered that a disease is often many years secretly brooding in the constitution—and that stealthy working of the poison may cause excessive irritability, which the visible breaking out of the disease may really allay. Health and happiness are much more conducive to the perfection of our nature, than any sorrow. Joy and love are the best medicines.

"*Man has two great foes—Sin, and Death, the penalty of sin.*"

I have endeavored to contradict the idea that death is the penalty of sin, Neither sin nor death are our foes. Death always was our friend, both before and after Christ, and sin is but another name for experience.

"*Christ crushes sin, and expels it from his dominions.*"

Can either the writer or the reader explain, in plain words, the plain meaning of this sentence? How does Christ crush sin? and, what is intended by his dominions? earth or heaven? Sin is not yet crushed or yet expelled from the earth, from mankind generally, or even from the hearts of the "select little flock," and sin never was in heaven. When men have worked out of sin, they will emerge from it, and the teaching of Jesus has helped us forward to that end.

. "*Moved by the Spirit of God, the mind of man from age to age has uttered aspirations, more or less imperfectly comprehended, for a Saviour, a righteous Lord, a manifestation of God, in a loving human person.*"

Yes, every age has had its idol!

The first light of thoughtful reason in a man's mind led him to look up; he saw the step above him, thought he saw God, and so worshipped it; he mounted that step, then worshipped the step again above him, and again arose. Idolatry is no sin to the mind not capable of greater enlightenment.

And is the desire for the increased "manifestation of God" no longer craved for by man's soul? If so, our souls are dead indeed. But if there is still this unutterable longing, shall not its aspirations be answered? But I sincerely trust that not again will man ever look for a manifestation of God in *any* human person.

We now worship Jesus—a man. We have yet to learn to worship God, as Love; and further, God, as Joy.

Now, reader, what think you, if you have read my words thus far ? Which will you choose ?

Truth, Love, Joy—which looks upwards and on-wards—or, the story of the Garden of Eden, whose fruits are curses and fear, which looks backwards and downwards ?

You can not have both, for they are contraries. If one is truth the other is falsehood. They are the opposite ends of the poles—leading two different ways.

Which way will you steer your vessel ?

CHAPTER XXXI.

CONCLUSION.

Do we not desire a universal religion? How shall we obtain it till we acknowledge a universal God?— not in words only, but in deed. And how can we recognize a universal God if not in a universal inspiration, or truths of God, as free, wide, and open as the air we breathe and the light we see?

We shall never behold it in a partial or individual inspiration; for, what is partiality to one nation or one person, but another name for injustice?

We know if a father gave all his riches to one son and left the others to starve, he would be both unjust and cruel, yet we say our heavenly Father gave his spiritual riches but to one nation.

It appears somewhat a puzzle to many what is to become of savages, or those we call pagans, who never heard of Jesus. Some say they will be saved, others, that as they know not Jesus and the "scheme" of salvation, and have not been baptized, they shall be damned; and if we really believe the doctrines of both Protestant and Roman Catholic churches, such surely must be their fate. What shall we say, God is unjust, or the doctrine is a falsehood? I prefer saying the latter. Can God be just, and yet act with the greatest *injustice* to more than the half of mankind?

St. Paul endeavors thus to reconcile justice and injustice: " For as many as have sinned without law shall perish without law"—which would seem to imply they should all be condemned or " perish," without having a word to say for themselves—"And as many as have sinned in the law shall be judged by the law"—so these shall have the benefit of a trial. But he goes on to say, " For when the Gentiles, which have not the law, do by nature the things contained in the law; these, having not the law, are a law unto themselves; which show the work of the law written in their hearts."

Which is best, to have the law written in the heart or on tables of stone? And how was it the Gentiles did " by nature," or natural reason what the Jews required or had an outward supernatural revelation to instruct them in? Or, how can we have the audacity to say a man who has the law *only* written in his heart, and obeys it by his natural reason, has " not the law," and that God never spoke to him as he did to the Jews?

I say the man who had the law of God written in his heart, and shown to him through his mind had the true spiritual inspiration; and the man who believed he had the law written by the finger of God on pieces of stone, had the false inspiration!

St. Paul says, "The law worketh wrath, for where no law is, there is no transgression."

If so, then better without law, for according to this rule, those who "had not the law," never transgressed, so instead of perishing without law, they ought all to go to heaven without law.

One would think the devil made the law, as it only "worketh wrath." It appears to be only a contrivance intended to catch men, that God, or the devil (?) might send them to perdition by it: the sole use and beauty of it being that they, the sinners, or he who should be the punisher, might have the satisfaction of knowing that they, the sinners, had been punished lawfully.

The only way to escape this dreadful law, we think, is to creep behind Jesus Christ.

Here is an extract from a little book on "Sacramental Meditations," published by the Religious Tract Society, speaking of the joys of heaven: "How insufficient to entertain or delight us! yea, the presence of God himself, the all-comprehending, the incomprehensible Jehovah, how insupportable and terrifying would it be, if thou wert absent! *It is thy presence, blessed Jesus, that makes heaven so suitable and sweet!* "

This is our feeling towards God our Father. The

Jehovah of the Jews, the dreadful, the wrathful, the vengeful giver of the law, on the mountain that shook and trembled. Is the picture so very different to that of the Greek Jupiter, the Thunderer, holding the lightning in his hand ?

And now, although Jesus showed us the love of the Father, we do not give this belief in love to God himself, but solely to the man Jesus. Instead of yielding the loving worship of our hearts to the great God, we give it to the man who was " sent " as a Christ, to teach us that love. God is still to our hearts the God of wrath, the punisher, the sender into hell, and this, we suppose, constitutes His justice : but Jesus is our God of love, who defends us from the consuming wrath of our Father, and who entreats for us " with groanings that cannot be uttered," and this, we suppose, constitutes the mercy of God, constantly pleading that His attribute of justice shall be rendered nugatory : in short, it is the idea that in heaven, justice and mercy, or truth and love—for justice and mercy are but God's application of truth and love to all created things —that these two are " antagonistic," one to the other.

What is the great foundation and corner stone of this supposed justice, which " somehow," by some scheme, God has got over. "He is so just, He cannot pardon " ! This seems to be the *summum bonum* of our idea of His justice ! But if it was really unjust for God to pardon, why did He lend Himself to the scheme of salvation, in order to accomplish it ?

We have been straining at this miserable gnat for centuries, and swallowing I don't know how many hump-backed camels. God is so just he cannot pardon offences against himself, but he can be unjust to the whole world, by showing partiality, by loving Jacob and hating Esau, without a cause (and no cause is attempted to be shown). He can tell falsehoods, by saying one thing and meaning another; desiring Abraham to kill his son, when he never intended him to do so ; He said " cursing" when he meant "blessing." He says we are to obey the laws and do no murder, but, by disobedience and murder he allows us to gain heaven. He said, thou shalt not take eye for eye, tooth for tooth, but took the life of him who said it for our lives. He cannot pardon us, but he turned out the criminals of heaven, and suffered them to tempt and ruin mankind.

Where is justice ?

Ye blind guides ! where is justice ?—or what is justice ? Do you know ?

You know—every one of you, in your hearts—that to forgive another any offences against yourself is *not* injustice. You know you are told to forgive until " seventy times seven "—you know you pray,

" Forgive us our debts as we forgive our debtors."
Then, with the same breath, you say, for God to forgive us without *blood* and *murder*, called " sacrifice,"
is contrary to justice!!

   How can we love God with the horror of such
a false doctrine hiding Him from us ? We do
not love him—we dread him ; and we cannot do
both.

   We know if a man said he loved and feared, or
dreaded the truth, he would be talking nonsense, he
could not do both ; if he really loved the truth, he
would not fear it; and if he dreaded the truth, he
could not really love it. But our litany makes us
pray to God, who is Truth, to enable us to love and
dread Him. We cannot do both, and we do not do
both. We dread God, and shrink from Him, and
hate Him, *because* we dread Him. But we love the
man Jesus, because we think he hides us from this
terrible God, from whom we shrink.

   Is it not shameful, and unkind, and ungrateful to
think thus of our Father ? Give back the glory that
is due to Him—the glory of love. It is idolatry to
give it to any man who has ever lived upon this
earth ; and that man who said, " Hear oh Israel !
the Lord thy God is one God "!—and who said,
" Love the Lord thy God with all thy heart, and with
all thy soul, and with all thy strength"—would be
the very first to tell you it is idolatry.

The worship of Love, which is the only true worship, belongs only to the one God—the universal Father of all mankind.

How shall we go to the Mahommedans, and say, " God only spoke to the Jews, he never spoke to the Turks ; your prophet is an impostor " ! The Turks might say, and rightly, " If your God never spoke to us, he is not our God ; we will believe in the God who has spoken to us, and we know and feel that he has spoken to us in our Koran, and we will believe in him." They do right to hold fast the truths their God, who is also our God, has spoken to them by Mahomet, but he, no more than Moses, or any other man, is infallible, or has perceived all truth.

Theoretically there are only two hindrances to a universal religion : the acknowledgment of a universal participation of insight into infallible truth (some more, some less), and the acknowledgment of all earthly teachers as fallible. Practically there are many hindrances, for all nations are not more capable of comprehending a pure spiritual religion, than all people are fitted for perfect republicanism. They have not worked up to it ; but for all civilized nations to acknowledge such a principle of universal religion would be as beneficial as the acknowledgment of the principle in a perfect government, that all men have a right to freedom.

If we wish for a universal religion, we must examine all religions, search all scriptures, all words of truth, for one sees what another does not see.

The laws of God are not written on paper, or miraculous stones tumbled out of heaven, or thrown up from the bowels of a volcanic mountain, but on the rocks, the sea, the earth, over the visible creation of the whole world, and on the soul of every man who ever existed. Let us examine and seek to find *here* God's almighty and eternal laws, not of wrath, or working wrath, but perfect good, and blessing. God gave not these laws as punishers. It is only *un*just human laws that punish (such, for instance, as laws against smuggling). Neither are they to be put aside as inoperative by the coming of Jesus. Truth or justice is not to be " got over " by any " scheme." In this sense, that of abstracting from the strictest justice by mercy, there is no pardon—for such a pardon would be *in*justice, as much as it would be unjust of Queen Victoria to exercise the prerogative of mercy in pardoning and letting loose up on society every convicted felon; for, remember, a sentence passed upon a criminal is not for punishment, in the sense of inflicting evil for evil, pain for pain, eye for eye, (which would be the punishment of hell, God inflicting evil for evil !) but for the protection of the innocent and for reformation, that the offender may again be brought to obey the laws. Of God's just laws—merciful *because* just—not one jot or one tittle of these shall ever pass away till all be *fulfilled*, that is, obeyed. No blind and idolatrous faith will gain us heaven till we know and have obeyed ALL God's laws. For if God shows and gives us earthly things to know and to obey, and we have yet neither wisdom nor power to do either; how shall he give us heavenly things to know and obey?

We have to travel up to perfection in time, before we can reach the goal or summit of it in eternity.

Is the ignorant savage as fit even as we are for heaven? He is no more fit than the man of mere animal instincts to live in a palace. Neither can the savage be eternally punished, for that would be unjust; and equally unjust to give him the same reward as those who have toiled for goodness. Here I contradict the lesson given in the parable of the laborers in the vineyard. It is perfectly true that God can do as he wills with his own; but it is impossible for God to be unjust.

Also, such a mode of hiring laborers, giving those who toiled all day only the same wages as those who worked one hour, could not be repeated. If the owner of a vineyard or a farm professed to act in this manner, he would get none to work for him till the ninth hour, unless, indeed, the laborers were slaves, and compelled to work. So, if God gave it as his law, that he would reward his children alike if they worked all their lives, or only two or three days, just at the end of their lives; men if they really believed this would *not* work till then. But they are told, in reply, it is *uncertain* whether, for these two or three days, God will give us heaven or not, besides, we may be taken away at any moment before we have time even to work that short period; in fact, the great inducement given to make us work, is the *uncertainty* of salvation—God's will is *uncertain*, it may please Him to take us before we have time to repent. How horror-struck are people when a man dies while in the act of perpetrating some crime, we think God has seized hold of that very moment to bring him to perdition; whatever his former life may have been, from the fact of his *very* last act being a crime, he is sure to be damned. We must be good, for life is uncertain; we may die in the night, and have omitted before sleeping to say our prayers, and it is quite *uncertain* how God will, therefore, receive us. But God does not look to one crime; whether that crime be committed in the last hour of life or in the beginning, it is an equal stain to the soul. God looks to the general health or disease of the soul, not to any particular or isolated act of sin.

If we are not *certain* of God's strict justice, the very foundation of our souls is shaken. We must "work out our own salvation," NOT in fear and trembling, but in joyful love and trust in God's truth, believing that that truth will, in perfect justice, give to every man according to his works.

Where in nature could we find a parallel to such a leap as we expect to take after death? at once, without bridge or due gradation, from the lowest to the highest, from next to an animal to next to God!

In everything we can look at, in everything we can think of, progress upward is so slow, it is impossible to observe it; you can no more perceive it than you can see a blade of grass growing, or watch the oak tree growing, and these are quick in their growth in comparison with mental progress.

But if the soul of the barbarian is as well prepared for heaven as our souls, why do we seek wisdom?

If ignorance *is* bliss, why toil we for knowledge?

Let us bring up our children in brutal ignorance.

Let us be consistent, and say at once whether it is good or evil. If it be good, it is taking us to heaven, if it be evil, it is degrading us below the earth.

Is knowledge only for personal convenience, to gain us agreeable food, fine clothes, large houses, handsome furniture, swift travelling, or even temporary pleasure to the mind and senses? or are they not all, besides being pleasant in themselves, but a means to an end, that end, the increased capacity of the mind for joy.

z

What of those who are content to wait, folding their hands together, and saying they shall know bye and bye ?

Yes, they will know—when they have learnt.

Do we think what *Life* has not taught us, *Death* will ?

Do we think light will come to our spirits, like a flood, in death, and show us all things ?   Then why do we toil in life ? and why is the desire given us to know, if, in a short time, we shall know all things, if only we are good ?

Sleep is the image of death : what does sleep teach us ?   " The night cometh, in which no man can work."   There is much work to be done, and how little has been done.   Does it require a fresh pair of hands every day to build a house ?   What advantage would it be to the master of some manufactory carried on by complicated machinery, to have to take new, raw hands into his premises every day, to carry on his work ?   Why should God take fresh souls every life, to work his work ?   But we want to fly off to the palace of the master, after doing one life's work.

I think we have many lives on earth before us, and but a few, in comparison, behind us.

Is it a weary thought ?   Then let us take from life, at the same time, its gall and bitterness, and we may not find it so weary.   Remember that our

Father is indeed "Parent of Good," and the almighty life-giver to nought but good. Be satisfied with God, be satisfied with His laws, be satisfied to work His good will. Remember, also, that as He is both good and almighty, He is not the creator, permitter, or sufferer of life to any devil or immortal evil.

How can we, in this short life, work this great work, the good will of the Almighty? Have we more lives than one? That there is an intermediate state between the life on earth, and full blessedness in heaven, is a dim notion floating in the minds of most men.

The Roman Catholics have embodied it in their doctrine of purgatory. Fortunately, we Protestants have not chained up this half-formed notion to a set doctrine, and padlocked it with curses, but we have some vague idea that when Jesus said to the thief on the cross, "to-day shalt thou be with me in paradise," he did not mean heaven, but some lower state: for if good and bad souls are, immediately after death, sent, one to heaven and the other to hell, why afterwards call a judgment day? Here, again, is the mere show and mockery of justice—reward or punish first, then try, and either acquit or condemn afterwards. But if every man is condemned or acquitted upon leaving, or rather before leaving the body, then the dead, small and great, have no need to be called up again to stand before God to be judged ; they have been judged already.

When St. Paul speaks of a seventh heaven, he implies different degrees, and the possibility of progress in eternity. Jesus also the same, when he says, " In my Father's house are many mansions."

So, between the highest heaven and our earthly state there is an intermediate state ; and such an idea bears its confirmation in our inmost feelings. Our church imagines it a kind of second-rate heaven—we talk of the " place of happy departed spirits." The Romanists suppose it a sort of second-rate hell (taking hell to mean the perfection of misery, if such a contradiction in terms can be allowed).

What means our belief in, and desire for, the " resurrection of the body " ? but that body cannot live the life of spirit.

What means our desire to meet again friend to friend, and the feeling of uniting again only as spirit to spirit does not satisfy, and is cold ? We feel as if flesh to flesh we had not severed yet, and could not yet part. And do not some friends and lovers *know* each other from the first day they meet ?

How can there be a higher or a lower heaven ?

I wish the reader would pause and consider whether, as God is eternal, unchangeable, and perfect, heaven must not be the same ? Heaven is not the abode of God in the same sense as a house is the abode of a man, or the earth his dwelling-place, so that he can only occupy as much space in it as his body for the moment requires. God fills eternity; there is no part, then, changeable or less than perfect, but degrees of comparison imply changeability and something less than perfection.

How can we progress or advance in heaven? We only mount up to good by overcoming evil. If, then, from earth we were transported to some paradise, and in paradise there was no evil to overcome, we advance no higher than the step we left on earth. Neither will the minor torture of purgatory advance us to good, but, on the contrary, make us recede from it, there being no goodness to advance to.

To increase in perfection we must have evil to recede from, and good to advance to; and such a state of being can only be present in time. Where, then, but on earth shall we be able to overcome evil, which is ignorance, and so rise step by step from the less perfect to the perfect?

It might be asked why, if such be our progressive destiny, had we not one long life, till our final elevation was reached, instead of many short lives? I answer because we have not perfect strength, any more than we have perfect knowledge or goodness. How could we sustain our present life if it did not alternate in day and night? We must gain strength of soul to live eternity—we could not bear it yet. We look up to the sky and think we see myriads and myriads of stars, when, in fact, what we behold, is only the countless reflection and refraction of a much smaller number multiplied by the atmosphere, as we may reflect a candle in a dozen mirrors.

Why not men's souls but the repetition of former souls, as our bodies are the repetition of former bodies ? but each man sets his own mark upon his soul ; over his body he has little or no control, to make it grow or not grow, to gain a limb or a hair even, but the growth of the mind and soul is under his own care, it is his own work either to shrink, wither, and collapse it—let the rank weeds of the body overgrow and completely hide the beautiful flower of the soul—or he may enlarge and expand it, without limit as to its possibility or power of expansion. So we might think that mind or soul would not, after death, be separated or diffused like the body. We all think our souls are our own, we seem to possess more right and claim to them than to our bodies.

Another answer to the question, why we have not one but many bodies, may be found in one of Æsop's fables—"The Moon and its Mother." A young moon said, "mother, why don't you make me a little coat, which shall fit me quite tight?" "How can I, child," said the mother, "make a coat to fit one who is first a new moon, and then a full moon, and then, again, neither one nor the other ? "

Some say they do not expect, after death, to be transported into heaven exactly, the peculiar abode of God, but only to another and better one than this we are now in; in fact we are tired of this one, the cry is:—there is nothing *new* in it, "nothing new under the sun"; here, again, we echo Solomon; but could he have been suddenly transported from a day in his life to a day in ours, and beheld the discoveries of modern science, I think he would have said there were a great many "new" things since that time. It is true, in one sense, that there is nothing new under the sun; all that has to be discovered is, and always has been in the world, but when found, it is new to us. It is also curious after any great new light of thought has been opened to the world, we find hints of it scattered up and down in the earth, which we had passed by before a hundred times without notice; and these things will always remain a secret till the peculiarly constituted mind arises which has to reveal this light to the world. There may be nothing new under the sun, but the sun shining upon an object hitherto shadowed in darkness, is presented new to our eyes: and the world, when we next wake in it, will be "new" in this sense.

What know we yet? Place in your hand a little pebble, a leaf, a drop of water, a seed of corn, look at them, and ask yourself what you know of them.

Different sciences have told you something relating to all of them, but how much more remains to be told? Why desire more when these you know not? Each of the small objects contains millions and millions of atoms, and every atom has a word to tell us. Yet this world which God made for us, we think in one short life we have seen enough of it; we wish ourselves well out of it, we have lived in it quite long enough, it is a miserable place, and the next time we wake up it will all be burnt!

Fortunately, God values his own works more highly than we do, and he never destroys them.

We talk of purifying the world by fire. What is there impure in it? It is as God made it.

But fire is not a purifier, it is a separator merely, a destroyer of life. What fire leaves in the hand is only the most material and earthy part, dust; the more æthereal it drives off into the air.

What advantage would it be to begin the new world on the black and desolate cinders of the old?

Yet we do not mean that exactly, it is to be a sort of *spiritual* fire to burn up *material elements*.

We think when we rise in this other world, then all knowledge is to be *given* to us. It is the same old story, in paradise we are to have no work. What we want God to do for us principally is to save us *trouble*. To save us the *trouble* of working to goodness, by being goodness for us—to save us the *trouble* of working to wisdom, by giving it to us for nothing. But no, neither nature, nor nature's God, ever indulges·our laziness.

It will put before us the same leaf, stone, water, seed, and say, " Child, learn this lesson first, before I show you another."

Will a master set a boy to solve the first two or three simple problems in the first book of Euclid, then skip the rest, and try the seventh book ? The boy could not understand them ; they would be unintelligible hieroglyphics to him, for every successive problem comprehends and involves the one preceding it.

It is only by knowledge we are able to appreciate knowledge. How much should we value wisdom, if it was given to us intuitively—inhaled, as we draw the air into our lungs ? How often do we think of the clear, transparent atmosphere that works the machinery of our bodies ? We consider any little foolish miracle more wonderful, more exemplitive of God's glory, than this calm, unobtrusive, all-pervading, life-sustaining element. So would wisdom be lightly esteemed, if bestowed without labor on our part. By labor we set our mark upon a thing and make it ours.

We are always lusting for gifts. What gain will that man *give* me ? What pleasure will that woman *give* me ? In short, will any person or thing *give* me anything more than my own faculties justly entitle me to gain or enjoy? No. If they fill your hands ever so full, it will not nourish nor satisfy; you will go back more empty and weary than you came.

Let us go heartily to work. I see not why, in this work, religion and science should be divorced, as some now say it must. Why should not science perceive that it is approaching to the knowledge of God through His laws? And why should religion be left behind in childish ignorance, as a sort of superior human instinct, good in itself, but in no way connected with science?

Nor do I find there is a beginning of a separation, but, on the contrary, the commencement of union.

Periodical and other works, some time ago, all, except those especially devoted to religious topics, seemed to be ashamed to speak of God—to own Him, appeared methodistical and hypocritical; now, you hardly take up one without finding His name spoken of in a free, manly, yet reverent manner. Religion no longer belongs to a certain set, or a particular party. The present discussions are not carried on by different sects, by paltry High and Low Church— but by the world. Nations converse with nations on the subject—England, France, Germany, read one another's books, and compare one another's arguments. In which field are we most likely to find the universal truth : in the narrow, sectarian one, or in the free, open, and unprejudiced one ?

A friend once tried to make me believe I was religious, at a time when the words *religion* and *duty* were sickening to me. I would not allow that I was; she said, " Why, then, do you love truth ? Is it not from a religious feeling"? " No," I said, " not in the least ; only because I think falsehood mean and cowardly."

I suspect some feeling such as that which prompted my answer, must have influenced many writers in so rigidly, and even contemptuously, excluding religion from their writings; for the hypocritical or ignorant, begging, whining, grovelling before God, which many thought to be the very essence of religion, was nauseating. (My friend, your religion was none of these.)

Let us take men of science and philosophers as our true prophets, priests, and teachers ; for which are most likely to teach the truth—those who own they know but little, but are devoting their lives to discover more ?—or those who remain idle, assuming they know " all things necessary for salvation," and in reality know the least ?

This text has become such a cant phrase, we do not fully appreciate its audacious magnitude : " All things necessary for salvation"! We do not yet know " all things necessary" for this day of our mortal life, but we think we know "all things necessary" for immortality! We hardly know the A B C of the world we live in, but imagine when we die, if we believe in Jesus, we are sufficiently capable and prepared to understand all the wisdom of heaven. But knowledge of the physical laws no more comprehends "all things necessary for salvation" than does the knowledge of the moral laws alone. We have to learn to be obedient to both; for this reason religion and science should be united, not again antagonistic, but one aiding the other.

Why do we instinctively dread ghosts, even though the spirit of a dearly beloved friend?

Is it not because the mind is not prepared to see spirit?

For the same reason, though we may love God, we shrink from beholding Him; we feel we are not ready.

What is the dread of death, but the fear that when separated from the body, we shall be forced to behold the Great Spirit? and it is a consolation to think of meeting Jesus after death, seeing God only through him, not this utterable spirit, but one who has been a man like ourselves, and is still in heaven, as we suppose, in a glorified *body*.

Thus our very reason and instinct prove to ourselves that we are not prepared for eternal spiritual life.

As the brain dies with the body, why should not all connection or consciousness of soul be also removed and darkened, till the mind in the brain joins again body and soul, in the same manner, though more completely, as consciousness is for the time veiled, as mind and body nightly sleep ?

This would account for forgetfulness of past lives.

When a man is rendered insensible by a slight concussion of the brain, he usually not only quite forgets the cause of his insensibility, and has, on recovery, no knowledge of the accident that has occurred to him, but he also loses memory of the few seconds previous to the concussion. A similar state to that produced by concussion of the brain, I should imagine to be the one at death, that is, total suspension of all feeling, apprehension, or consciousness. Even from day to day what do we recollect of the feelings of the soul or mind ? after a night's sleep very little trace of previous thought is left. We remember the little trivial acts and affairs of the body, but unless some unwonted event has stamped a peculiar impression on the soul, very little of our mental life can be recalled. Our life from year to year makes a gradual alteration in the soul's aspect, but very little or none of this can be noted day by day ; and this is all we could remember from life to life, our bodily existence was nothing, and has vanished. Besides, if there is truth in what I am putting forward, we are but in the life of childhood, in comparison with the lives before us; memory is weak in children, particularly memory of thoughts. Does a child ever remember what it *thought* yesterday? Mental knowledge of the past and the future increases in manhood.

We need not fear to meet God. He is very merciful, He will not affright us with spirit, either in the body or out of the body, till we have strength and power, *will* and *desire* to see and know it.

If we attempt to analyze our idea of God, to our minds, He is but an immense lonely desolation.

He is companionless, there is none His fellow, for there is but *One God*.

He is unchangeable, passionless, always has been, always will be the *One Great Alone*.

Always the same, from eternity to eternity, the *Changeless*.

If we will consider a little, it is this awfully removed, far-off, eternally receding from us, that is appalling; and yet, though so far away, He is upon the hand that holds this book, and over us all, and above us, and in us, at all times, and in all places.

To keep our souls healthy, sane, trustful, before this awfully sublime eternal presence, we must know and feel that this spirit is love. Add to the picture but the very faintest idea of wrath, and the sight would be insupportable to the living human soul.

It is almost impossible for us to conceive that this one spirit is self-sufficing for infinitely intense joy.

We have hardly yet learnt to think of God as Love, still less do we understand that God is Joy. In Himself and in all His works, for ever and ever, bright, glorious joy. Our hearts have scarcely even uttered the prayer, " God give us joy." We seem to think we have no right to it, it would be presumption to expect it, all we can ask our Father is that He will not make us miserable for ever !

The difficulty of believing God alone, and yet inexpressibly joyful, may have led the minds of men to imagine a companion for God in a Son, the man Jesus, and also that this man should be as a shield between us and God.

We need not fear, we shall never see God till the sight of the soul is strong enough to look upon Him, to behold Him, not in terror, not in dread, but in exquisite love and joy.

Another supposed necessity of man's nature is, for having a God who can compassionate our sufferings, and this may have assisted in the formation of the idea of this fabulous monster of a deity, half God, half man, " We have not a God who cannot be touched by a feeling of our infirmities," expresses this want of the heart, that our God should feel for us, sympathize with us, be pained with our pain. The feeling in reality proceeds from the greatest selfishness, and is, therefore, one which God would never gratify; we are not satisfied that our fellow-mortals should be "touched by a feeling of our infirmities," that is, feel grief at our pain and trouble; but we want God to feel pain for us. This is impossible for the perfect joy of the eternal God cannot feel pain, or His joy would not be perfect, and compassion and pity are but shades of pain. It must follow, then, if God does not and cannot feel compassion and pity for us, our lives are not to be compassionated and pitied; there is no occasion for God to bemoan for us, so neither we for ourselves. Let us have done with this discontented, unmanly weeping, and whining, and moaning for ourselves. There is no need for God to pity us, He knows the secret of our lives, and knows it is not so lamentable as we suppose.

St. Paul accounts for the reason why Jesus is touched with a feeling of our infirmities, because "He was tempted in all points like as we are, yet without sin." This is a contradiction, as I have endeavored to show in the chapter on "Temptation," Jesus could not have been tempted as we are: that is, tempted to the commission of sin, without having that sinful temptation or desire in himself, if without sin he could not have been tempted as we are, nor have felt as we feel, nor have been touched with the feeling of infirmity, which is weakness. A person might as well say, " I know the feeling of burning, for I once thrust my hand into the fire, but having previously dipped it into some chemical mixture, I was not burnt." Most certainly we should say such a man could not be touched by the feeling of being burnt.

. What a pleasant picture of heaven we have drawn to be sure ! From the time of the "fall of man" to the day of the last judgment, God must have been constantly miserable at our unhappy fate; that is to say, if he really is a merciful God.

When Jesus, the Son of God, or God himself, or both together—which is it ? or a man, a God, or both together—which is it ?—when this anomalous being was upon earth, suffering daily, and, at the time of his cruel death, when we suppose all the torture and misery and punishment for sin, were poured upon his head, what misery there must have been in heaven ! Now, Jesus is making groanings for us that cannot be uttered ; surely, then, the other inhabitants of heaven cannot be very happy and joyful. In short, all heaven, and God, must have been in tribulation for this foolish, unhappy little world of ours ! If the devil wished to work God a mischief, surely he has well succeeded ! Then, in the Revelations, the souls of the saints are seen gathered together under the altar (what an exceedingly unpleasant idea), and crying out—these vindictive,

A A

implacable, and blood-thirsty souls!—" How long, oh Lord, holy and true, wilt thou not avenge the blood of thy saints"? So also in the parable of the importunate widow; the elect are represented as crying night and day for vengeance.

Last of all, the heavens are to become the scene of God's vengeance! and thousands on thousands, and millions on millions are to be thrust down to hell to gnash their teeth in hopeless, endless agony. Then, all these blessed saints, and martyrs, angels, and cherubims, having seen accomplished what they so long cried for, will sing for ever, " Oh be joyful"! basking for ever in the eternal sunshine of heaven, while below them remain for ever the abode of the damned, where, perhaps, these blessed saints have sisters, brothers, fathers, mothers, wives, husbands; yes, even their own children, enduring pain and agony for ever, "And the smoke of their torment ascendeth for ever and ever"!

My God! how long shall these lies be believed in Thy name?

How long shall we blaspheme the goodness and love of God, by believing such horrors?

Who but men with the hearts of devils could have imagined anything so cruel and atrocious? ·

Oh reader, whoever you are, man, woman, or child, *do* not continue to believe this, it *cannot* be true, it *is* not true. It creates in me a sort of frenzy when

I think of it; when I think that God should be so dishonored, and the souls of men should be suffering under such a fearful belief, and that some clergymen are so cruel-minded, they would, if they could, prevent relief from coming to you; I believe, even, some would be sorry and disappointed at finding there was no hell : it seems uncharitable to say so, but it only follows the rule, a cruel religion makes a cruel heart.

It is wonderful to me that the inward and irresistable conviction of a man's own soul does not lead him to feel and say at once, " I know this cannot be true." It is so palpably opposed to everything good in ourselves, opposed to kindness, opposed to love, opposed to philanthropy, opposed to every virtue which we desire and seek to increase in, and by which we come nearer to God ; it must, then, be opposite to the nature of that God we, by these virtues, draw nearer to ; if, then, opposed to our best and noblest feelings, and to the nature of God, how can it be true?

May this foul blot of hell, devils, torture, be soon obliterated from our picture of God's ever-glorious, ever-joyful eternity.

In this hell we have imagined we might indeed call for God's compassion and pity, because then enduring pain to no end or purpose. Here we have no need of His compassion, for He knows that our trivial pains and griefs (and we all make more of them than there is any occasion for) are but the laborious steps by which we surmount our ignorance, and God also knows that His thoughts, His justice, never planned, never devised, never willed such a horrible fate for the souls He caused to be born into the world.

It is also, remember, just as cruel a falsehood to think that God is at this time torturing the former dwellers in heaven, whom we call devils, or that the good angels are witnessing the tribulation and anguish of their former companions ; and if men on earth love one another, surely angels would have a greater love for each other, so grief for their own loss, and their former loved companions' woe would be greater.

It has just occurred to me, while writing the foregoing sentence, that the devil is a person we have the privilege of hating, we may *exercise* our hatred upon him, no one ever pities or compassionates the poor devil for the pain he is suffering, or the unhappy devils generally ; they hate us, we suppose, and they are suffering a *just* punishment, so it is not expected, it might even be wrong, in fact, it is quite ridiculous to imagine we could feel any sort of *christian* charity for them. I wonder whether this is the sort of phlegmatic feeling one would be blessed with in heaven, supposing our friends, relations, and children were in hell—God forbid !

So it would seem to be; for witness Abraham, the friend of God, looking down calmly on the torture of Dives, (whether taken literally or typically, the spirit is the same) the latter rich man crying out to Abraham for a drop of water to cool his parched tongue, there is first the cruel mockery of calling him " son," then Abraham argues on the justice of God, because Dives in his lifetime received good things, and Lazarus evil things, " now he is comforted, and thou art tormented; " whether the argument convinced Dives or not, it was quite sufficient to convince Abraham himself, and Lazarus comfortably reclining on his bosom. How could they feel pity or compassion for one so *justly* punished ? no, *they* could not feel pity, these blessed spirits, but the poor suffering wretch in hell could feel pity. " Oh father Abraham," he said, " send to my brothers, to save them, if possible, from feeling what I feel." This poor wretch had a fellow feeling for those who *might* suffer as he suffered, but Abraham could feel no pity for one who was then suffering before his eyes; and in heaven, the abode of the God of perfect love, they were not allowed by that God to show mercy and pity, or to give the one drop of water to alleviate the torture !

The man who said " before Abraham was, I am," represents him in his final blessedness in heaven, in a more odious light than ever he appears in his lifetime; then he was kindly, generous, hospitable, one who knew love to God and love to man.

How could Jesus, if he had, as we suppose, come down from heaven, have displayed us such a revolting picture of it; how could he, whom we think the very mirror of God's love and mercy, have shown that in heaven, God would not allow the exercise of love and mercy?

How could the man who said God would reward any one, even for giving a cup of cold water to a thirsty child, say that the same God forbad in heaven the giving of a drop of cold water to a man suffering agony?

If such be heaven, may I *never* go there!

If such be the feeling of the blessed saints, may I *never* be one of them!

Why even we, stony-hearted and selfish as we are, could not bear to look upon such agony, endured by any man, and but for a few days; and what disgust and hatred should we have for the brutal tormentor: and shall we say that such a one as this is our Father? shall we worship such a God? I will not. No God of Jewish invention shall be my God, neither God Jehovah nor God Jesus, for one is half fiend, the other half man. I will worship one who is altogether God, and altogether perfect—as perfect an idea of God, at least, as a greatly advanced, though still imperfect age, can conceive of God, more perfect than any Jew could ever imagine, more perfect than the founders of the christian religion could imagine.

. Why, should we be bound down to the Hebrew notions respecting the beginning and ending of man ?

The *origin* of the human race is a subject that belongs solely to science to discover ; the *end*, purely to speculation—neither involve any moral truths. We are now aware that the Hebrews were totally ignorant of science, neither was their genius in the least speculative.

. "It may serve to bring into relief, the fact that the Bible does not pretend to teach the sciences; if we remark, that the word *astronomy* does not occur in the Bible, while that of *astrology*, as we have seen, is found in some of its pages. In truth, the Hebrew race were not a speculative, still less a scientific people."—*People's Dictionary of the Bible.*

Yet, knowing this, we still allow them to bind us down to their traditional idea of man's commencement, and to their idea of a future state.

Their legend of the origin of the human race will, each successive year, more clearly be proved incorrect ; their ideas, also, of another world, were most puerile and circumscribed.

" ' The heaven and the earth ' constituted the universe of the writer." The former was " conceived to be a ' paved work of sapphire stone' (Exod. xxiv. 10), as a bright solid firmament expanding on all sides above the earth (Gen. i. 6 ; Dan. xii. 3), dividing the waters into two portions—one above and one beneath itself; which firmament, at least at a later period, was thought to extend upwards into several vaulted canopies, so as to form heaven on heavens even to to the number at least of three (Amos ix. 6 ; 2 Cor. xii. 2). . . . The stars were distinct solid bodies, called forth every night by the Almighty, who, sitting upon the circle of the heavens, and stretching them out as a curtain and as a tent to dwell in, brought out the numerous host of heaven, and called them all by name, innumerable though they were (Is. xl. 22—26 ; Ps. civ. 2 ; Gen. xv. 5). Some idea seems to have prevailed that the stars were living beings, sons of God, which may have been the germ of the heavenly host in the sense of a celestial hierarchy (Job i. 6, xxv. 5, xxxviii. 7 ; Is. xlv. 12) ; hence, a divine court ; Jehovah sitting on his throne, and all the host of heaven standing on his right hand and on his left (2 Chron. xviii. 18), and the Almighty is, therefore, termed Jehovah of hosts."—*People's Dictionary of the Bible.*

Their notion of our future blessedness after death, represented heaven as a place of social enjoyment, in which were gathered together the patriarchs, the prophets, "and an innumerable company of just men made perfect." In reference to this opinion Jesus represented Lazarus in Abraham's bosom;

that is, reclining next to him at table, as John leant on Jesus' bosom at supper, this being considered the place of honor next to the master of the feast. Agreeable, also, to this view of the joy of heaven, Jesus said he would drink no more of the fruit of the vine with his disciples till he should drink it new with them at a heavenly feast.

Supposing Jesus had no further insight into futurity than that expressed in the current ideas of the Jews who were his contemporaries, or even that he purposely left it to the increased enlightenment of men's minds to work out more spiritual ideas for themselves, it serves to prove how little we can depend on what we have styled " revealed religion " for what we have also called "*religious* truths," as if any truths could be *ir*religious, or any truth less than perfect good. It serves also to show not only how incorrect was the Jews' information on scientific subjects, and on the origin of the human race, but that their ideas respecting the constitution of the heavens, the nature of the Great Spirit of heaven, and our future destination after death, were equally incorrect. We are almost startled on thus looking back on St. Paul's idea of a third heaven, and on what Jesus and his Apostles taught on these subjects, to find how insensibly but widely we have advanced : and what we considered " great religious truths "—which, had they been so, would have remained unchanged and unchangeable—have been year by year as shifting as a sand bank.

. Our superior enlightenment, wider basis of scientific knowledge, clearer appreciation of the beauty and loveliness of God, must lead us to a higher and nobler speculative view of the end for which this great God has destined us, and how He is leading us to that end.

I was reading aloud a child's story.

A poor man, who thought himself a " miserable slave," because he had to work hard under a master from Monday morning till Saturday night, for the support of himself and his family, was sitting alone grumbling at his hard fate, when a fairy in the shape of a little man, dressed all in green, appeared close beside him ; after some conversation together, the latter said :

" Why you see, Tom, you must have money. Now it seems to me that there are but four ways of getting money—there's Stealing."

" Which wont suit *me*," interrupted Tom.

" Very good, then there's Borrowing."

" Which I don't want to do."

" And there's Begging."

" No, thank you," said Tom, stoutly.

" And there's giving money's worth for the money, that is to say—Work, Labor."

" Your words are as good as a sermon," said Tom. *

* " Tales of Orris," by Miss Engelow.

It is a very good sermon, and nature is preaching it every day, but the lesson it teaches we do not understand. We know if a man has not the goods of this world on which to support life, the only legitimate, the only honorable and manly way to attain them is to work for them, but we think the only legitimate, proper, and *religious* way of gaining heaven, the soul's life, is to borrow and beg it of Jesus Christ !

"Beg and pray, pray and beg," is the standard motto of the church, "but never expect anything for your work."

What is every lesson of the world of nature intended to teach us, but a spiritual truth ? Nature is our only key to the knowledge of God. What is the lesson of work given us for, but to teach us an unchangeable truth—that God will have us work for the life of our bodies, for the life of our minds, and for the life of our souls ?

I feel more sure that this is the lesson we have to learn, from the very arguments adduced to hinder people from inquiring into these "hidden mysteries."

"The wisdom of man is foolishness with God," it is said, *ergo*, we ought to be content to remain in foolish ignorance, that we may be acceptable to Him.

"Of what use is it to inquire" ? they say, "rest quiet but a few short years, and it will be all the same to you whether you know or whether you do not know." "*What good* can you do by trying to upset our faith"? "*What good* has Bishop Colenso or any other done by trying to show falsehood in our Bible"? "Who can show us anything better than has been shown in the Bible"?

What feeling is it that dictates these questions, but the very rooted and grounded belief that no human work of the mind in this, its noblest and most glorious work, can ever meet with the reward and just payment that it receives in every other employment in which it engages.

Manual labor receives food and raiment.

Mental labor, besides food and clothing, gains ease and beauty; makes the elements of the world its servants, and unveils wonder after wonder. But those who seek to find out God, and the hidden mysteries of the soul, and legitimately work for it with the best strength of the mind God has given them, men dare to say to them, "Hold! you must not work in that direction; it is improper to pry into *God's secrets*— you must only look on at a distance, and be *amazed* and *fear*, and crouch down on your knees, and lift up your hands, and cry and *beg*. If you work ever so hard, you will never gain a ray more wisdom than was revealed (or given) to the prophets and apostles"!

No; a few more years, and death will *not* give us what life has not worked for.

· He is the slave who begs, and borrows, and takes gifts; he is the free man who works honestly and cheerfully for his master, and joyfully receives his just wages.

I do not say we should *not* pray to God. If a man was starving and refrained from asking a loaf of bread from a friend, who would gladly supply his necessities, he would only show a foolish pride; and we are in want of many things, and God is rich in them all—he delights to give—but he gives no more than we can use and will work with. A man who continued indolently to subsist on his friend's charity would be contemptible; so, if we remain all our lives content to "pray and have faith" (that is, *borrow* other men's thoughts), we are contemptible beggars.

Let us no longer borrow the fruits of the labor of other men's minds respecting God. Nor let us beg God for the life of our souls. Let us stand up as free servants of our beloved Master; and know that he is not only our Master, but our loving Father, and we all his beloved children.

Let us break the two chains that held us on either side, at the beginning and the ending. Between the scientific and the speculative knowledge that remains? This, which Jesus declared to be " *all* the law and the prophets":—" Thou shalt love the Lord thy God, with all thy heart and with all thy soul, and with all thy strength, and thy neighbor [which is every human being] as thyself."

There are three processes whereby the mind learns to see God—Affinity, Analogy, Reasoning.

The knowledge of God given by affinity is produced and increased by obeying the moral law of God: These precepts are, in their first germ, the intuitive perception of the soul, and constitute the resemblance between man's soul and the Spirit of its Creator.

The more, therefore, we act in obedience to this law of the soul, called conscience, the more we increase the soul's likeness to God, and so are we the better able, in the absence of other means of knowledge, to comprehend the Maker, by greater affinity to Him. By affinity we learn God's attribute, Truth, for truth comprehends all.

By analogy alone do we arrive at a glimpse of the nature of the Great Spirit. It is said that analogy is useless, because it can *prove* nothing, nor can we prove anything respecting the nature of God, we cannot even prove the existence of a God, we can only judge of it by analogy, seeking God in His outward works, by unwearied diligence and watchfulness.

The third process of the mind unites the two former. It is true reasoning applied to the things that are made. It is the mental power of comparison tested by truth.

What is the power of reasoning but the power of

correct comparison ? All logical rules are included in this one. " Two things that are equal to one and the same thing are equal to one another." You take two things, and compare them with a third, if they both bear an exact likeness to the third, you argue they must both agree or be like one another.

Knowledge of God by affinity is gained by leading a truly good life, and arrives at a very just but not entire or complete knowledge, and is the only knowledge of God practicable in the infant age of the world.

Knowledge of God by analogy is arrived at by science. Every fresh discovery of the physical laws adds to our means of comprehending the Maker of the works and the laws.

By true, that is logical, reasoning, can we advance from affinity and analogy to a step further and higher in what is called intellectual speculative knowledge of the unknown nature of God.

Properly speaking, it ought not to be speculative, but purely, severely, and correctly deduced and calculated by logic. It must be thoroughly and truthfully wrought out, figure by figure, not guessed at or " hit upon " by speculation.

Speculation may be true, or may be false, but real logical deductions *must* be true, because every sharp instrument of criticism it uses is a known truth, if not, the reasoning is not logical.

It also follows that no man can thus reasoningly arrive at a true knowledge of God, who has not the love of moral truth in his own soul, as well as the scientific apprehension of truth in the works of God.

If the base or sides of our sought-for triangle are incorrect, the whole calculation from them is incorrect.

The first two processes of the mind are almost inseparable. Morality is the foundation, sure, certain, unchangeable as the eternal God.

Sir James Mackintosh says, " Let all the books of false religion (why false ?) be opened, and it will be found that their moral system is, in all its grand features, the same. Such as the rule was at the first dawn of history, such it continues to the present day."

These books, called false, showing a true morality, prove themselves at least to be true on the ground of morality. Apply to this Aristotle's saying, "Men differ, but men also agree; they differ as to what is fleeting, but agree as to what is eternal. Difference is the region of opinion. Agreement is the region of truth."

Now you have the whole world open before you, that you may see on what men differ, and on what men, the whole of mankind, agree. They differ as to man's beginning, they differ as to man's ending, they differ as to the nature and attributes of God, they differ as to our relations with God, and as to a future life : these things, therefore, belong to the region of opinion, and are fleeting—they are, and always have been fleeting, they have insensibly changed as much from the time of Jesus to our time, as they did from the time of Moses to that of Jesus. But men of all nations, all people, all religions, ancient or modern, agree in the truths of morality ; morality, therefore, is the only sure and eternal basis of truth.

Some men there are, however, who, instead of seeking religion in this universal truth, prefer to look at it in the " miracle-mystery, the resurrection-mystery, and the nostril-mystery."

A universal instinctive moral law, breathing God's image into our souls, I consider to be the sure foundation of our knowledge of God.

But what is the use of a foundation, unless we build upon it ?

Archimedes said, give him only a fulcrum and he could raise the world. But what would be the good of a fulcrum if he did not use it ? Of what use is this fulcrum of morality, if we do not raise ourselves thereby ?

To accomplish this we must have a lever, and the force or motive power to raise the weight or resistanc at the other end of the lever.

Morality is our fulcrum, science our lever, reasoning our motive power.

B B

The fulcrum is perfectly useless alone. Morality cannot be of any service without some portion of knowledge and some slight effort of reasoning. It is shown in that apparently simple sentence, "Thou shalt love thy neighbor as thyself."

Sir James Mackintosh goes on to say, " The facts which lead to the formation of moral rules are as accessible, and must be as obvious to the simplest barbarian as to the most enlightened philosopher. The motive which leads him to consider them is the most powerful that can be imagined, it is the care of his own existence."

But how much science is required for the proper and due care of our existence, I have endeavored to show in Chapter XXII., and how much enlightenment is requisite for true self-love. It is therefore vain to say the ignorant man or the savage understands this as well as the philosopher; it is untrue both in theory and in practice.

Also, to make this true self-love, or morality, work up to the knowledge of God, gradual steps of analogy and reasoning are requisite, the love of self teaching the love of man, the love of man teaching the love of God. This knowledge of God re-acting again downwards to increased love to man, and truer love to self.

The same writer proceeds, " The case of the physical and speculative sciences is directly opposite."

How so ? when the first helps to keep the body in health and extend his powers, the latter to expand, ennoble, and, by so doing, give joy and freedom to the mind ; physical and so-called speculative sciences only continue what morality began.   But Sir James says the motives which induce us to explore these things are comparatively weak, being " curiosity, or at most, a desire to multiply the conveniences and ornaments of life."   Morality, then, is supposed to be more valuable, because it is learnt in the desire to gratify our animal desire for food, &c., for this can be the only feeling of the barbarian; and science and speculation or philosophy are supposed to be of less value, because they minister to the beauty and ornament of life.   But immediately the savage advances to the civilized man, the softening and salutary effect of beauty and grace are desired, and help to raise him above the brute.   Yet we think simple obedience to the moral law is enough to take us to heaven.   I am not now speaking of the church creed on the subject, which adds faith in the *blood* of Jesus, but the conviction of thinking men, that to believe in God, and lead a good life are all-sufficient. I do not believe it, though the idea of men requiring a knowledge of science and philosophy in order to enter heaven, may be met with a shout of laughter. I think they do so require.

Firstly.   If we really believed this doctrine, that

obedience without knowledge is sufficient for salvation, there is a stop to all advancement, the world would immediately come to a dead-lock ; but, fortunately, men's " curiosity " or desire to know, has prevented this catastrophe. Now, a doctrine which, if believed in, and followed, would produce destruction to the work of the world, cannot be a true doctrine, it must therefore be a falsehood ; and a curiosity or desire for knowledge, which, in the teeth of this false creed, and in spite of men's laziness and desire to leave off working, has sufficed to keep the world going, and has given us all the wonders of science to beautify and give pleasure and joy to our lives, is right, and everlastingly right, and necessary for our salvation, for salvation is gained by it, because we work God's eternal work by it, and, thanks be to God, that no men's theology has been able to keep the head of science under water, though it has pressed upon it and stamped upon it with all its wicked might; and why ? Through ignorance.

Secondly. As I have before said, knowledge given us without labor we should not value ; the idea of getting it all, bye-and-bye, for nothing, makes us even now look upon it with something like contempt.

Thirdly and lastly. We do not know *how* to be obedient without knowledge. Morality, science, reasoning, cannot be separated, but together must educate the perfect man. The laughableness of this idea arises from the fact of the impossibility of our being able, in one short life, to gain this knowledge.

It comes to this, then : if it is unnecessary to know, it has been unnecessary from the very first creation of man ; the world ought, then, if men followed this supposed dictate of God, to have remained where it was, and never advanced one step.

Who will say " yes " to this ?

Or, if to know is necessary for every man, then we must have many lives to learn to know in.

Who will say " yes " to this ?

People allow that it is necessary for the world, and the men of the world, to advance, from age to age, and that they, and it, have done so; but what use is our advancement to those who are dead and gone before us, unless they participate in it ? or if a state of perfection is to be reached on earth, called a millennium, of what use is it to us unless we partake of it ?

A millennium is either a positive good or a positive evil. If a positive good, we who, in this our day, are giving our work to advance it, desire to partake of it as much as those who may happen to be in the world at that time. But if the good who have been buried have gone to heaven, then keeping the good who lived in the age of the millennium, a still longer time on earth is a positive evil ; or even if not risen to heaven, still keeping them on earth for a thousand years would be an evil—they had better been transported to heaven at once.

Men and women, what is it I am writing to you? I cannot tell. Is it the greatest nonsense or the greatest wisdom? I cannot tell. Is it a new word that has never yet been spoken, or is it some old word that has been thrown aside long ago?* I cannot tell.

* That which I have written is not, I find, an entirely new idea. There is the doctrine of metempsychosis taught by Pythagoras, *and in that doctrine, I believe, lies the germ of the future religion of the world.* What were the particular theories of Pythagoras on the subject, beyond its being a belief in the transmigration of souls, I know not, therefore cannot tell whether the opinions I have arrived at, at all coincide with his.

"The Diegesis" of the Rev. R. Taylor, from which I before quoted, says of Pythagoras, after he had "broached the notion of the existence and the immortality of souls, it was but a second, and a necessary step, to find employment for them; and that of their eternal migration from one body to another, after every effort that imagination can make, will be found at last as consistent with reason as that of their existence at all, *and that in which the mind, after all its plunges into the vast unknown, must ultimately acquiesce.*

"The metempsychosis overthrows the doctrine of the everlasting torments of hell-fire, and, on that account, is less congenial to *christian* dispositions."

"As much as this doctrine is now scouted, it was held, not only by almost all the great men of antiquity, but a late very ingenious writer, philosopher, and Christian apologist, avowed his belief in it, namely, the late Soames Jenyns."—*Higgins' Celtic Druids.*

"It is not, indeed, rational; but what metaphysical speculation of any sort is so? Had it been more frightful, it would have been more orthodox."

I have endeavored to show my ideas as being something more than a mere metaphysical speculation; but as the *only* rational, *only* logical, *only* just conclusion we *can* arrive at. How true

I ask myself these questions daily. It is the last thought in my mind as I lie down to rest; it sleeps

appears at every turn, the maxim, that to be convinced of a truth, we must first be convinced of what it is not ?

Accompanying, on either hand, the doctrine of the immortality of the soul has been on one side the belief in hell and demons, and and on the other, the escape from these by the imputed righteousness of God ; both being the offspring of the idea that one life in the body was all that was granted us to prepare the soul for eternity, and the feeling *of the impossibility*, in such a short period, of the soul becoming fit for such an eternity. The soul must, then, either be everlastingly punished for sins it felt it could not be entirely purified of, or God, by his righteousness, must do for the soul what the soul could not possibly do for itself.

It was necessary, then, that both these beliefs should be worked out to their natural termination, and prove themselves either true or false before men (in the latter case), would accept the one plain, straight course before them, that the soul without wrath, damnation and devils on one side, or weak and vicious gift of imputed merit on the other, must, in several lives, work for the gradual growth and development of all his moral and intellectual faculties, till he reached perfection.

The doctrine of hell-fire, and the doctrine of imputed merit are tottering on both sides of us. The doctrine of the immortality of the soul stands fast and sure as a rock. What can we have ?

We know we are not entirely good or entirely bad. If there is no hell for the partly bad, and no " make-weight " of imputed good for the partly good, what is there for us but other lives in which to conquer evil by overcoming it, and increasing our goodness by honestly working for it !

This can only be accomplished in a world of time. The doctrine of eternal damnation and of imputed merit (which is in reality nothing but a falsehood, that is, imputing to us what we have not got ; saying we are good when we are not good), are both untenable and mischievous. If we will not, therefore, receive the doctrine of the soul's development through many lives, we must return to the belief in annihilation.

in my mind during the night, and wakes with it again in the morning. I am bewildered. I like not to encourage myself in the thought that I have a new truth to give to the world. I am ashamed even to write it; it seems such a monstrous vanity—yet I know I am not vain. I go over the same ground every day, and try to find my answer. I know I have never read in any book what I have written in these last chapters. I reconsider my arguments, but can see no flaw in them (but I suppose I could not, see them even if there were any), every fresh trial brings me, more convinced, back to the same ground. I had not a thought of what I have written in this chapter when I commenced to write. It has developed itself under my pen. The thoughts do not seem to be mine; they are so new to me. I can scarcely believe my own conclusions.

But why should the great God have intrusted this beautiful truth to me? I am not good—I am not even truthful, though I desire to be so. I have told and do tell many falsehoods; I do not visit the poor, or watch by the sick, or teach children at a Sunday-school; and I have no desire to do either of these three. But I respect those who can do these dreadful offices.

The contemplation of the things I have been writing about has made me more patient and more truthful. And when I think of the weight of hell and devil, sin and wrath, I have lifted off my soul, I feel that if not a leaf of one copy of my book is cut, I have a reward that compensates for all my labor ; but how much sweeter if I can do the same for others, as I have done for myself. If I can make the children leave off crying when they go to bed, as they have hitherto done, though ready to drop off their chairs with weariness, and their eyelids drooping with sleep. They need not fear the dark any more, or shudder with that nameless dread which is the misery of childhood's life.

I have tried to avoid writing what is contained in this chapter, thinking it only fancy. Where the parenthesis occurs, " (I am inveighing against imagination, and where is it now leading me ?) " I put down my pen, and would not write any more for some time. I said to myself, " Imagination is trying to run away with me, but I will not let it, I will keep a tight grasp of the reins, sit firm and square in my saddle, look well before I leap, not let my head grow dizzy, not rush too hastily, nor yet be afraid of the leap." When I began writing again, I went away from the subject : I tried to avoid it, but I came up to it again. I must leap over, I cannot help myself, and I will take the chance of a cracked skull or broken bones. I wonder whether the earth is as hard as it used to be ; I am inclined to think not, or else a Son of earth lived and died in vain. He tried to soften it, and as no true work is in vain, I think it must be softened, so I do not think it will break my bones. Or shall I fall and say like young Arthur :

-    Oh me ! my uncle's spirit is in these stones.

Heaven will not take my soul, it is not near heaven yet. I shall sleep quietly through the night, and wake in the morning nearer heaven than I was the day before. Will England take my bones ? I don't think it matters to me or anyone else whether England, or who, which, or what takes that handful of dust and lime.

Children, are you as cruel as you used to be ? It seems to me I could forgive anyone who would cheat, rob, or even try to kill me ; when the first mistake of anger was over, I think I could say, "Poor man, you only thought to gain some pleasure or gratification to your feelings and passions by it, but you are mistaken ; you have committed a foolish error, you have not learnt your lesson, you will only have to go back and learn it, you have gained nothing, and if I can learn my lesson, you have taken nothing from me."

To forgive is very easy, unless we are in fear and dread of injury, but if our would-be enemy *cannot* injure us, we may forgive him, and not only forgive, but be sorry for him, for he has injured himself, not us. But this is all nonsense, I must go back and try and talk sense again.

No, religion and science must not be divorced; they must be united in a holy bond, or no new thought of philosophy will be born into the world.

If we want to understand God's government with the world, we must look to political economy and the social sciences, and wherever you can place your finger on a proposition which you can say for *certainty* is a rule of good government, by and through that law it is that God does, and always has, ruled the world; because, in that sure axiom, you have arrived at a sure truth, and that is a ray of God. If it *is* a truth of good government, so God governs. If God does not so govern, it is *not* a truth of good government.

So I say that God's mode of governing the world will be better learned by studying the sciences relating to good government, than by studying the Old Testament.

The Jews thought a great nation could be made by gold, by slaves, by conquest, so they imagined God allowed them crimes to procure these means of making a great nation. Their ideas of good government were faulty, for the object of good government is to make a great, free, and good nation, and as their ideas of good government, and of what constituted a great, free, and good nation were wrong, they arrived at a wrong idea of God's government and nature. Their conclusion was wrong, because their scientific premises were wrong.

By this we can estimate the incalculable advantages we have derived from science and philosophy working on a basis of religion or morality. This knowledge has reacted downward and thrown an increased light on morality, which is truth.

Political economy would be nothing without a sure basis of justice, which is the application of truth; and truth cannot be thus justly applied without the light of science. Thus, then, the folly of talking about obedience being sufficient without knowledge, morality, without science; for one cannot proceed a step to application without the aid of knowledge.

The Jews, beyond all other nations, kept to the sure foundation of morality; they had very little science, but they applied that little correctly from having this true foundation; but where their science was false, they strayed into falsehood, corrupting thereby their moral rules, and they supposed that God did the same.

Other ancient nations had more science, but their foundation was not sure, their fulcrum was unsteady, it was so weak they could not raise anything with it; when they tried with their strong levers and great strength to raise the weight, the fulcrum crumbled underneath it.

What is the great aim of social sciences? Mr. Mill declares it to be, "The mental and moral culture of all mankind, which alone would fit them for personal freedom, and give them a just distribution of the fruits of labor." If this is, in truth, the object of a perfect government, I unhesitatingly say, it is the object of God's government, both in this world and in the perfect government of heaven. But if not God's motto, J. S. Mill has not found the motto of good government, and he, or some one else, will have to search till they do find it, and not only to find it, but to act it before they see or enter the perfect government.

We gain nothing by taking away a particle, a grain, a hair's breadth from justice.

Mercy will not stand between us and justice, it would do us harm, not good. Mercy is not a nobler attribute than justice, even though Portia may say so.

I was wrong in saying that mercy was the application of love to mankind, as justice is of truth. A lover does not feel mercy for his beloved, a mother does not feel mercy towards her children. Mercy is the preventive of anger or cruelty, not of justice, for when mercy prevents justice, it vitiates it.

But perfect love knows neither anger nor cruelty.

I know of no word that defines perfectly the application of love, as justice does of truth.

The word love is sufficient of itself: God's justice and love towards us; for perfect love is perfect justice, and perfect justice is perfect love. This justice is not the justice of a judge, but the justice of a giver of perfect laws, who, like nature, will not suffer one to be infringed without its inevitable penalty.

It is only the *un*just judge who suffers the importunity of the widow to gain her point. If what she desired was right to be granted, a *just* judge would have given it without importunity ; but if *not* right for her to have, *no* importunity would gain it.

Neither, I thank God, do we stand in the relation of criminals before Him, but of dearly loved, though ignorant children.

There has a great and unanimous cry arisen from those who have read Bishop Colenso's volumes* and other works on the same subject, that the writers have taken away the stay on which men rested, and given them nothing in return. Have I done so ? Have I given nothing for what I seek to remove ?

I have earnestly sought to give something better, but I am too near my own thought to know whether or not it is better.

Remember once more, dear reader, how Jesus told you to judge of false Christs, and false prophets, and false doctrines :—" By their fruits ye shall know them."

---

* I think critics have been rather severe on Bishop Colenso, simply, because he could not go further than he did ; he could not construct as well as pull down. His book is spoken of as a mere

book of sums; but I think it is that very simplicity, which made its use—he gave the best talent he had to search for the truth.

These errors in calculation may have appeared of greater moment to him than to the general reader—as a florist may think a flower imperfect from having some little flaw, which the amateur admirer would pass by without notice.

These errors are of moment, though not of great moment; if a man declares he has eaten three pigeons when he has only eaten two, we cannot be sure of his truthfulness, and it is as well to be aware of his error, for every falsehood is mischievous, though it may be so small as to be unnoticable; but when this small falsehood helps to support a greater, it must be removed.

If Bishop Colenso and others have done nothing else they have carted away a quantity of rubbish, and made the ground clear for the new builders.

Colenso is also censured for offering a prayer to Ram, for the reader's consolation; he, doubtless, offered them what had afforded consolation to himself. Ram is the same as God, if we attach the same meaning to it. The Great Spirit is not called in heaven by the word " God," any more than he is called *Dieu*, or *Dio*, or *Gott*, or *Eloi*, or *Ram*. " Ram " is as good a word as " Gott," if it conveys the same spiritual significance to our mind. If the prayer to Ram is a good prayer, let us pray it ; in praying to the Spirit by the name of " Ram," it may seem to us like addressing a stranger ; but so would " Dieu " or Eloi" be to those who did not speak French or Hebrew.

One of the answers to Dr. Colenso's book, written by the Rev. F. Moeran, Professor of Moral Philosophy, has been sent me to read since I concluded my book. I add a few words respecting it in this note.

The usual word-bugbears are put forward in the beginning, to prevent people from questioning and making free use of their own free reason, such as " Its only legitimate consequence is Atheism" —" It savours suspiciously of Deism"—this shows " Dangerous indications of that culminating Rationalism," &c.

The Professor exhorts men, however, not to be in the least alarmed, or even astonished ; he assures them "we" knew and prophecied before what should happen : " That unhappy publication ' Essays and Reviews,' was really no sudden meteor of lurid light, bursting upon our unprepared eyes—filling us with amazement at its unexpected appearance, and of vague fears of its consequences. . . . It was the natural result of the existing condition of thought among a certain class of men. We know of the wood which yielded the bow, of the tendon which formed the string, of the hand which adjusted the arrow. For *we* know whence this state of things originated, how it was strengthened, and what were its aims."

Why could you not say plainly, Mr. Professor, that you (or *we*) know very well that Mr. Jowett's and Mr. Baden Powell's bows and arrows came from the devil * and you hope—no, not hope, only, fully believe—that both the gentlemen and their weapons will go back again there very soon. For their wicked thoughts lead directly to "downright atheism," and atheism to anti-christianism, and anti-christianism to hell. What can be a plainer or more natural sequence?

But, says the writer, though the only legitimate consequence is atheism, "It is a fortunate matter that the same incapacity for sound thinking which prompts men to regard difficulties in the light of objections to revelation, saves them from perceiving and adopting the only proper result of their own arguments."

They *would* become atheists, and the natural sequence *would* follow, only, *fortunately*, they not being "sound thinkers," like the Professor, do not arrive at the "proper result of their own argument."

Poor Mr. Moeran, I pity him, if *he* should be betrayed into taking a first wrong step, into what dreadful abyss would his capacity for "sound thinking" lead him !

I would not advise any one to become a "sound thinker."

This is a specimen of the Professor's "sound thinking," and logical reasoning, which, reading further on in the book, I find he takes upon trust from the Bishop of Durham, and he in like manner from Origen :

"For, if we deny the Bible to be God's work, on account of its *difficulties*, we must, *for the same reason*, deny the world to be His work also."

---

* A tacit but undesigned compliment, by the way, to the arguments of the Essayists having superior force, power, and *fire*; though the production is styled "an unhappy publication," and by some one else, "an otherwise contemptible book."

I call this anything but sound thinking or sound argument.

The *difficulties*, in the two cases are not similar, do not proceed from the same cause, and need not, therefore, result in the same conclusion.

The difficulties urged against believing the Bible to be the work of God, lie in its being inconsistent with nature and natural laws and contradictory to itself, and the closer we examine the greater these difficulties become. I hardly understand what difficulties in the world the Professor alludes to; there are practical difficulties presented to every man in the world—such as sickness and poverty; or there are the difficulties of not comprehending all the laws of nature; but no one has any difficulty in believing the world to be the work of God, because it is inconsistent with nature or contradictory to her own laws; but so far otherwise, the closer and more microscopic our scientific investigation of the world, the more beautiful the harmony, and perfect the consistency of these laws appear.

If I was taken before a tumble-down wooden house, and desired to believe that, formerly, that very house which I saw, had been a stone house built by a celebrated mason, and was "expressly told," that the stone was miraculously converted into wood by that mason. I should have a *difficulty* in believing the assertion. But if I came to a high stone wall, solidly and perfectly put together, I should have a *difficulty* in jumping over it; but that would not make me deny that the wall was a stone wall, and built by a mason.

Or to put the argument syllogistically:

I find a *difficulty* in believing this house to have been formerly built of stone, and changed into wood by the mason who built it.

I find a *difficulty* in jumping over a high stone wall, because I am not strong enough.

Therefore, as there is a *difficulty* in both cases, a learned Professor tells me I must inevitably be led to deny that either are built of stone or by a mason.

Mr. Moeran declares the difficulties of the Bible are only "natural *improbabilities*," because he can "satisfactorily account for them on religious grounds;" by which he means miracles, proving by this, in requiring miracles, that they are natural *impossibilities*. This he even subsequently allows.

Relative to Dr. Colenso's difficulty of believing the possibility

C C

of the whole immense population of Israel, as large as that of London keeping their first passover in a single day, Mr. Moeran says, " These difficulties are strongly put. There is a circumstance in the history which fairly abates the force of some of these. Yet there is no occasion to dwell upon such mitigations, because the whole argument is vitiated by an enormous oversight, which proves, that however keenly Dr. Colenso has examined those portions of the account which contain the difficulties, he has wholly negatived those other parts which supply the answer. This oversight is the absolute exclusion of all Divine agency, as the cause of these results, and therefore, as the solution of these difficulties "

Of course; as I before said, cry out " A miracle! a miracle!" whenever you want one, and every difficulty is salved over.

Again, the Professor writes, " But to infer thence, that what is impossible for the one set of two millions, must be equally impossible for the other, is the unequivocal rationalism of insisting that none but human agencies can be admitted."

Observe, in the first quotation, miracles are styled, "divine agency" while works produced by God's natural laws are only " human agencies."

In these assertions lie the whole force of the question now at issue.

The rest of Mr. Moeran's book is filled up by disputing whether Bishop Colenso is right or wrong in holding his bishopric, or whether his particular calculations are right or wrong; but these comparatively trivial matters have nothing whatever to do with the great question at issue, which is, Is God's nature, and are His dealings with mankind *revealed* in the sudden, claptrap, conjuring quackery of miracles, making known His laws to mankind by contradicting them ; or, in His natural laws, unchangeable and eternal, because eternally perfect, and not to be improved or made more beneficial to mankind by having a bit clipped off here, or a bit altered there, or an extra bit patched on anywhere where most wanted? *This* is the question we have to decide.

I should imagine that Professor Moeran had studied moral philosophy more in the school of metaphysics than of logic, two very different schools, though by most people supposed to be one ; and the most misty metaphysician is generally supposed to be the most learned logician.

In page 54 is a most delightful specimen of the *sacredness* of supposed truth being *guarded* by metaphysical subtilty.

" But the objector *is bound* to prove its falsehood, otherwise he only raises an objection. but does not substantiate it (right), hence it is plain how much more is required from the assailant of divine truth than from its defenders. The former is bound to disprove every conceivable expedient of reconciliation, the latter only to suggest any one of them. Proof of the truth of any is not incumbent on the one, proof of the falsehood of all is obligatory on the other. *But disproof of any probable hypothesis can only be effected by disproving it as a fact.* This the objector against the Bible cannot, unless he arrogate omniscience, attempt, and, unless he be omniscient, effect."

Mr. Moeran declares the objector *is bound* to prove what he affirms to be a falsehood, but by a process he well knows to be utterly impossible, both in this and every other subject.

Falsehood in everything would thus indeed be well guarded.

CHAPTER XXXII.

MORE LAST WORDS.

I AM sorry to end, yet I am very tired of writing. I put down my pen, close my book, half glad, half sorry it is finished.

Now, I send it on its way. It will have to take many journeys before its destination is reached. It will reach it, I hope, in safety—the words safely into some printing-office, and the thoughts safely into the hearts of my readers.

And I expect to be paid, too. Half-a-year's good honest, hard continuous labor, in writing, reading, and thinking, besides the previous preparation of the life, deserves its proper wages.

Gifts I hate, but payment is an acknowledgment of so much worth; and as much as is the market value of my work, so much wages I shall have.

I see a hint thrown out here and there by the church party, that the anti-church party write for " pay." I suppose the one party receives payment for their books as well as the other. Bishops and learned divines, I believe, are usually thought to like money as well as others, and why should they not ?

Though to be paid may be a pleasant thing to look forward to after your work is done, I do not believe that with either party the desire for "pay" enters as a *motive* for writing.

My intense and earnest desire has been to give Joy through Truth and Love. If I succeed, I have the most glorious reward any man can have.

If any amount of praise or money come to me, I shall be pleased, in fact, very much pleased, but if not, I can do without it.

Now, I have six long months to wait before I can hear what "the world" will say to this poor little book of mine, or whether "the world" will say anything to it. For though I contemplate publishing in Melbourne, of course, I look to the centre of the civilized world for my final verdict.

. I feel inclined sometimes, reader, to beseech you not to laugh at me or abuse me, and, at others, to tell you, I don't care a straw whether you do or not. But there is a touch of shabby beggarliness about the first, and of impertinent defiance about the second, which I neither admire or feel—so I will do neither.

I am not afraid of the public; I know it is generally a good-natured public, to what it knows to be an honest effort. I am more afraid of myself and my own inability to do what I wish to do.

Neither do I believe that men hate truth—I believe

they love it ; and it is this very jealous love of truth that makes it excessively dangerous to try and pull away from them anything they suppose to be truth. When anything new is brought them, they suspect it, and will not receive it till they have found out what it is made of, and sometimes the poor body who brings it gets so pinched and probed, thumped and pummelled, that it dies after it. But I suppose it can't be helped—I suppose it is " all right."

If any silly people think to frighten me by making great, long, ugly, shocking faces at me, I shall take the liberty of laughing at them.

I am going to try and wait patiently, and meet all that comes to me with a cheerful countenance and a joyful heart. I know I shall be wise in this, if I am foolish in everything else.

I send my song, which I have sung while writing.

If a poet will put some new verses to the music, it will be better, and then some composer put some better music, it will be better still ; then it will be like the Irishman's knife, the same knife, only with a new handle and a new blade.

So works nature and nature's God, quietly and insensibly. One half of the old knife is taken away, leaving the other half in our pocket, till it has become old and familiar to us ; then is taken away the other half, and it is done so quietly and gradually, we feel as if it was still the same old knife.

And what remains of the original material? Nothing.
There is only the old love for it, and the old use for
it; and what makes it useful? but the same old
metal, and it is "true as steel."

Now I call that very neatly carved out of an old
knife.

Reader, good-bye, I do not say "God bless you,"
for God *has* blessed you.

SONG.

Let us praise our great Cre - a - tor: Praise Him

now with heart and voice, Casting fear and casting sorrow From the

heart, let all re - joice. For the God who made us bless'd us; On His

love we still re - ly, For Thy thoughts, my God, my Father,

Never change and ne - ver die.

Let Thy holy spirit lead us ;
And in life Thy truth reveal.
Let Thy love surround us ever ;
And in love our sorrows heal.
Joy in heart and soul inspiring
Man's true praise to God above,
Hope in time and hope eternal,
Rest in Truth, and Joy and Love.

Printed by CLARSON, SHALLARD, & Co., Melbourne and Sydney.

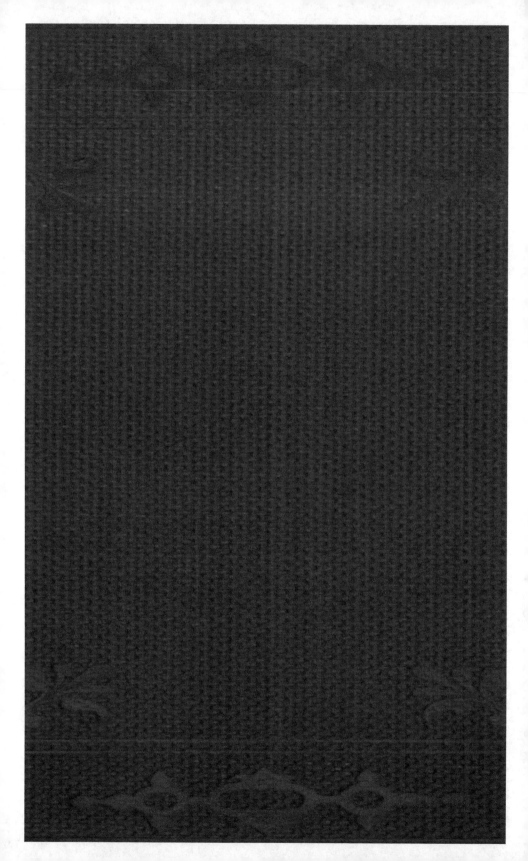

Check Out More Titles From HardPress Classics Series In this collection we are offering thousands of classic and hard to find books. This series spans a vast array of subjects – so you are bound to find something of interest to enjoy reading and learning about.

Subjects:
Architecture
Art
Biography & Autobiography
Body, Mind &Spirit
Children & Young Adult
Dramas
Education
Fiction
History
Language Arts & Disciplines
Law
Literary Collections
Music
Poetry
Psychology
Science
...and many more.

Visit us at www.hardpress.net